EACH IN HER OWN WAY

EACH IN HER OWN WAY

Five Women Leaders of the Developing World

Marion Fennelly Levy

with an introduction by
Sue Ellen M. Charlton

Lynne Rienner Publishers   ◆   Boulder & London

Front cover photographs for paperback edition, from top: By John Isaac, United Nations photo # 153311; by Piers Cavendish, courtesy of Save the Children; courtesy of Ray Witlin of the Ford Foundation; by Bernard Wolff, courtesy of the United Nations Fund for Population Activities.

Published in the United States of America in 1988 by
Lynne Rienner Publishers, Inc.
948 North Street, Boulder, Colorado 80302

and in the United Kingdom by
Lynne Rienner Publishers, Inc.
3 Henrietta Street, Covent Garden, London WC2E 8LU

Library of Congress Cataloging-in-Publication Data

Levy, Marion Fennelly.
    Each in her own way: five women leaders of the developing world /
by Marion Fennelly Levy.

        p.   cm.
    Bibliography: p.
    Contents: Hasina Khan—women and community development in Bangladesh — Elvina Mutua—small business enterprises for women in Mombasa, Kenya — Reyna de Miralda—organizing peasant women in Honduras — Elizabeth O'Kelly—technology for women and the corn mill societies of Cameroon — Aziza Hussein—family planning and family law in Egypt.
    ISBN 1-55587-093-7   ISBN 1-55587-094-5 (pbk.)
    1. Women social reformers—Developing countries—Biography.
2. Women in rural development—Developing countries. I. Title.
HQ1870.9.L48 1988
305.4′2′091724—dc19   87-26844
                                                                          CIP

British Library Cataloguing in Publication Data

A Cataloguing in Publication record for this book is available from the British Library.

Printed and bound in the United States of America

The paper used in this publication meets the requirements of the American National Standard for Permanence of Paper for Printed Library Materials Z39.48-1984.

To the five women whose lives inspired this work,

and to the countless others whose stories may never be told

CONTENTS

PREFACE

Much of what women do in this world—the labors that keep families and communities functioning—is not reflected in the gross national product of any country, is not a factor in economic planning, and is rarely part of recorded history. In much of the developing world, these omissions are particularly incongruous when one considers that women are major participants in agriculture and food processing; the United Nations estimates that they probably do more than half the world's work. Yet, because the economic and social support that women provide society is not part of the cash economy, it is often invisible. The "invisible woman," then, has been an international phenomenon, and nowhere more so than in the most conservative and traditional societies. As family well-being, if not survival, increasingly depends on women, it is more important than ever that women's labors be recognized and upgraded. The long-term food crisis in Africa brings home this point most vividly inasmuch as women farmers are estimated to be responsible for 60 to 80 percent of Africa's agricultural labor; yet they most often lack the means or skills to increase their production.[1] It has been said that the future of that continent lies in the hands of the African farmer and her husband.

But change, welcome or not, is sweeping over the world, brought on by national independence movements and the end of colonialism; by the revolution in technology; by the enormous expansion of communications; by international economic forces and urbanization; by both the rapid growth in population and modern methods of fertility control; by the impact of Western ideas and values, and the reactive upsurge of nationalism and religious fundamentalism; and by the growing awareness among women all over the world of their more rightful role in society.

For women who have benefited from increased education and greater job opportunities, the changes have generally been welcome. But those who do not share in those advantages can see their traditional role and status, both in the family and in the community, being undermined. As men go off to the towns and cities for paid employment, often learning new skills, women are being left behind—figuratively as well as literally. One need only think of the growing number of households headed by women to understand women's new responsibilities and, all too often, their new burdens.[2] Where the traditional extended family has broken down and the state is unable, or unwilling, to provide the support services that the families customarily had shouldered, women are worse off than ever.

The United Nations Decade for Women that ended in 1985 generated an important body of information and testimony about the true condition of women worldwide. The three women's conferences during the Decade amply demonstrated that a revolution of international magnitude is occurring, centered on women's aspirations and accomplishments; they also dramatized to governments the fact that economic and social development will not be achieved without the active and skilled participation of women. These are changes that are working toward women's greater equity in many societies.

At the first UN women's conference, held in Mexico City in 1975, an attempt was made to present a unified expression of women's needs. Ten years later, at the final conference in Nairobi, a greater acknowledgment of the divisions caused by cultural, economic, and political forces was apparent. The recognition of diversity did not negate the consensus that women are particularly handicapped by poverty, malnutrition, ill health, illiteracy, isolation, and lack of access to resources. Most of the world's women, particularly rural women, have a common catalog of needs: access to income-producing activities; training and education; health services for themselves and their families; family planning; improved legal rights, particularly those related to family law; access to such resources as credit; participation in community decision-making and the political process; and, for rural women, improved technology for agriculture, food processing, and water and fuel collection. In particular, the aim of the "Forward-Looking Strategies" that grew out of the Decade for Women was to propose how governments, private agencies, and women themselves might respond to those needs.

Prodded by the activism generated by the Decade, many governments made substantive efforts to upgrade women's status. Previous development efforts that counted on a "filtering down" of national economic development to the poor have generally been repudiated, though not totally abandoned. As the poor have been more accurately identified as disproportionately composed of women, development efforts have been changing course. The question increasingly being posed is how to reach the village level and find out what women really need.

Programs for women have tended to center on their traditional roles as mothers and housewives: Home economics rather than income generation has been the subject. As Mayra Buvinic points out, welfare-oriented strategies based on women's customary roles prevail throughout the developing world. "With the exception of family planning programs, they are politically safe. [They] do not address the issues of women's poverty and their lack of access to economic opportunities and resources." On the contrary, they perpetuate the exclusion of women from mainstream development programs.[3]

Nongovernmental organizations (NGOs) working in development have had the opportunity to be more flexible than governments in responding to women's real needs. Although international NGOs tend to carry with them a Western set of values, the best have taken great care to work within the cultural context of particular communities. A positive effect of their presence in development programs in Third World countries has been, I believe, to expand the options available for women. Agencies such as UNICEF, the Overseas Education Fund, and the Save the Children Federation have emphasized the role of women in family and community welfare and in development activities. They have been at the forefront of programs operating at the village level. A critical difference brought about by NGO initiatives has been the provision of funds and resources to women's programs that are not provided by governments.

Of course, such initiatives represent only a small portion of international development efforts, but they often constitute the most creative and experimental part. A government's strong commitment to raising the status of women is a crucial element of these efforts if it includes women's increased participation in the political process. For the five women whose stories are told in this book, NGOs have played a pivotal role at moments of critical decision, both in their personal lives and with respect to their work.

Women's groups and organizations have been a principal vehicle for advancing the cause of women, as this book demonstrates. In some countries, such structures have long existed; for instance, women's saving societies, work groups, and social-welfare clubs flourish in Cameroon. By contrast, women's groups at the village level do not form part of the tradition in either Bangladesh or Egypt, where such groups are of recent origin. In such a setting, governments or NGOs trying to mobilize women have had a more difficult time. For many women, including the five leaders described in this book, women's groups or associations have provided an essential platform of support and an opening to a larger world.

My purpose in writing this book is to record the work and spirit of five extraordinary women leaders who have made significant contributions to the lives of women in Third World countries. It has been sobering to realize that their work might not have been recorded or remembered were it not for these stories. I also hope to give a face and a voice to issues that confront many rural women in the developing world; indeed, the fields of expertise and endeavor of these five leaders quite accurately outline the issues that are of primary concern to most rural women. Elvina Mutua of Kenya concentrates on farm women's small-business enterprises; Hasina Khan of Bangladesh works in non-formal education and integrated rural development; Aziza Hussein of Egypt is at the forefront of both the family-planning movement and the effort to win greater protection for women under the law; Elizabeth O'Kelly, an ex-British colonial officer, pioneered in efforts to provide technology appropriate to women's work and started the successful Corn Mill Societies of Cameroon; and Reyna de Miralda of Honduras helped to form a national organization of peasant women, thereby bringing them into the political process for the first time. Elizabeth O'Kelly, Elvina Mutua, and Aziza Hussein had worked in behalf of women in the early 1950s, before women's activism became as common as it is today; hence they are continuing a long tradition within their own countries of working for the advancement of women. Although their programs concentrate on particular aspects of women's lives within a specific cultural setting, the problems they address transcend national boundaries. And as these problems are the daily concern of most rural women, it can be said that the goals of the Nairobi conference are being brought to life.

It was hard to choose five particular women to write about. My own experience as women's program coordinator for Save the Children from 1975 to 1981 took me to many developing countries and gave me the opportunity to work with women of great leadership ability and accomplishment. I consulted dozens of people I knew in the field of international development to identify other outstanding women, keeping in mind the geographical and cultural diversity that I wished to encompass. The women whose stories appear in this book were named again and again as being in the vanguard of the most promising changes. They have managed to initiate extraordinary programs in large part because they are themselves extraordinary. Each has taken personal risks in her own society in order to accomplish her goals. The cultures within which each has worked call for behavior very different from that of women in the Western world, and all five women have had to endure the suspicion or disapproval of important people in their lives. They come from widely divergent backgrounds, from the most privileged to the least, and from sharply different cultures; but each of the women was sufficiently stirred by the injustices that she saw and lived through to devote her life to programs that might help to redress the balance between men and women. Their motives have ranged from the pragmatic to the idealistic, from "there's a job to be done and let's do it" to a burning sense of injustice. Whatever the divergent reasons that drove them to take uncommon courses, they share a determination to help women improve their lives.

Like all of us, of course, they are products of their individual societies and began their careers with a set of beliefs, prejudices, and expectations not too different from those of their peers. In their early days, they all seemed to accept the traditional view of women's role, within the context of their own cultures, and only later recognized how sharply limited their choices had been.

I had met three of the women before I even thought of writing this book. I knew Aziza Hussein when she was the delegate from the United Arab Republic to the UN Status of Women Commission and when we were both connected with the International Planned Parenthood Federation. I made the acquaintance of Elizabeth O'Kelly in 1978 during a conference for rural women in the Philippines at which she was a major speaker. My introduction to Hasina Khan took place in 1980 at the UN Decade for Women Conference in Copenhagen, where we presented a series of workshops together at the forum of nongovernmental organizations. After the book was under way, I had the opportunity in March 1986 to accompany Elvina Mutua on a tour of her programs outside of Mombasa, Kenya. And, finally, I was fortunate to see Reyna de Miralda in her home in Juticalpa, Honduras, in March 1985 and to accompany her to several of the villages in which the Honduran Federation of Peasant Women is active.

I interviewed each of the women several times, with the exception of Hasina Khan, whose interviews were recorded by Phyllis Forman, wife of the Save the Children director in Bangladesh. All of the interviews were designed around the same series of questions, for I wanted each woman to tell in her own words about her childhood, her family, the society she lived in, and her early education. I wanted to know whether she felt different from her peers, which people were the most influential in her life, and what her choices at critical moments had been. The responses to the questions are directly quoted throughout the text when other sources are not given. I was fortunate to have (and to be able to quote from) the letters that Elizabeth O'Kelly wrote from Cameroon and Sarawak as well as the extensive writings of Aziza Hussein. As all of the women had connections with NGOs, I was able to interview the people with whom they worked and to read some of the evaluation reports of their projects. For further insights, I spoke or wrote to their personal friends as well.

I asked each woman about the steps in her career. If there is a generalization that can be made about all five, they came from families that placed the highest value on education for their sons and daughters—a factor that, more than anything else, set them apart from their peers. For

Hasina Khan, Aziza Hussein, and Reyna de Miralda, school was the liberating experience that put them on a course different from that of most girls they knew. Elizabeth O'Kelly, too, used formal education to open up a career although her experiences in Africa were her greatest teacher. As a result, the lives of these women broadened and went in directions their mothers had never dreamed were possible.

A man's support was important to two of the women. The fathers and husbands of Aziza Hussein and Elvina Mutua were critical to their success. For Hasina Khan and Reyna de Miralda, their mothers were their champions. Elizabeth O'Kelly was essentially on her own. All were caught up in changes that rocked the countries in which they worked—changes, wrought by national independence, political upheaval, or natural disaster, that compounded the stresses on those societies caused by modernization. Each woman was exposed to situations in which she had to learn tolerance of different religions or different points of view, and each had an active empathy with other people's sufferings.

Their approaches to their work were as varied as the women themselves. Hasina Khan brought the idea of self-realization to her women's program in Bangladesh; Reyna de Miralda used the techniques of grassroots political organizing; Elizabeth O'Kelly ran a government literacy program before developing women's societies; Elvina Mutua brought entrepreneurial skills to her craft groups; and Aziza Hussein was an advocate for women's rights and family planning with governments and other international bodies.

Leadership is always more difficult to define than program success; it is also more difficult to trace to its sources, aside from recognizing a common core of ambition. In my interviews with the women, two characteristics were most striking: They were all blessed with bountiful energy, and they all welcomed responsibility. They juggled competing claims on their time, undertook the most taxing travel schedules and field trips, and still seemed to have reserves. Most important, not one of them was afraid to take risks; each had a strong sense of determination to accomplish what she had set out to do, despite many obstacles and criticisms. I believe that all five women substantially changed their views over the years and became far more aware of the particular disadvantages that women endure. But they would not consider themselves feminists because that term has a Western identification and implies to them not only a woman's selfish view of life but also probable promiscuity. Yet they are firmly for the cause of women, call it what they may.

This book is not intended as a scholarly study, but I have included a bibliography for further readings in development and women's studies. I have also tried to provide a setting for each story by giving essential background information about the lives of women in the countries under study. The narratives speak for themselves, and I have chosen not to comment on them except for an occasional point of clarification. Other perspectives of the same events undoubtedly exist.

My own most vivid picture of the changing world for women came about during a brief field trip to the provincial city of Mahweit in Yemen. At the end of each working day, we joined different groups of Yemeni women during their customary afternoon visits at one another's houses between the hours of four and six. The women would have tea, chew *qat* (a mild stimulant), dance, and talk. Those occasions were among the warmest and most animated gatherings of women that I can recall. Except for those afternoon hours, women and girls were almost completely secluded in their homes. When they did go out, perhaps to bring water up from the well or to make an "approved" visit, they were veiled and covered by *chadors* (concealing cloaks). They had to walk through town on the separate, rocky paths reserved for women.

The women of Mahweit had experienced almost nothing of the modern world. On the last day of my visit, we attended an afternoon gathering at the home of the provincial governor's wife. When the electricity went on at five in the evening, as it customarily did, the governor's wife turned on her new television set. All the talk and laughter ended, and all eyes turned with wonder to watch an Egyptian soap opera. There on the screen, an unveiled woman was in conversation with a man who seemed neither husband nor kin. I will never forget the faces of the women. I can only imagine the effects that such an intrusion, repeated many times, might have had on their views of the world, and I can only hope that those wonderful afternoon gatherings will survive.

Marion Fennelly Levy

NOTES

1. Women's Research and Training Centre, UN Economic Commission for Africa, "Women and National Development in African Countries: Some Profound Contradictions," *African Studies Review*, vol. 18, no. 3 (December 1975), pp. 50, 62.

2. Mayra Buvinic and Nadia Youssef, with Barbara Von Elm, *Women-Headed Households: The Ignored Factor in Development* (Washington, D.C.: International Center for Research on Women, 1978), p. iii.

3. Mayra Buvinic, Margaret Lycette, and William Paul McGreevey, eds., *Women and Poverty in the Third World* (Baltimore: Johns Hopkins University Press, 1983), p. 64.

ACKNOWLEDGMENTS

Foremost among the people to whom I am indebted for their help during the writing of this book are the five women whose stories I tell. They have been unstintingly generous with their time, their encouragement, their willingness to share their confidences and doubts, and their hospitality. I have thoroughly enjoyed the time that I spent with each one of them. In addition, both Elizabeth O'Kelly and Aziza Hussein provided me with extensive documentation, which made my work far easier.

I must acknowledge, too, the generous assistance of the staffs of Save the Children, World Education, and PACT. No request for information or advice seemed too much for them. I valued the help of the United Nations Voluntary Fund for Women (now UNIFEM) and the International Women's Tribune Center. A special thanks must go to the Wilton Library for cheerfully searching out some rather obscure books from the colleges and universities of Connecticut.

The thoughtful advice of Dr. Noreen Clark, whose international work with women's groups is of the highest level, helped give direction to this work, and Carole Nichols brought me new insights about oral histories. Martha Keehn's editorial comments were most helpful, as were those of Constance Jewett. John Loeb was kind enough to give the earliest manuscript a sensitive hearing, and Dr. Charles MacCormack helped my understanding of the direction these stories might take. Phyllis Forman, a consultant with Save the Children's Bangladesh Program, provided me with invaluable help by conducting several interviews with Hasina Khan following the format I had used for the other interviews.

No list of acknowledgments would be complete without mention of my husband who was critic, proofreader, and support throughout the preparation of this book; my son, who helped me with some of the research and added his perceptive editorial comments; and my two daughters, who were constant sources of encouragement.

I have benefited greatly from the extensive editorial comments of Sue Ellen M. Charlton, and, as an admirer of her writings on Third World women, I am honored that she has written the introduction to this book.

INTRODUCTION

by Sue Ellen M. Charlton

In the narratives that follow, Marion Levy shares with affection the lives of five leaders of social, economic, and political development in the Third World. These women are leaders because of their courage and stamina, their understanding of the unique conditions of their compatriots, their commitment to improving those conditions, and their willingness to innovate. They are courageous also in their ability to challenge the historical traditions that subordinate women's interests to those of men. Their efforts to alter the conditions of poverty and powerlessness in their countries have necessitated physical, intellectual, and emotional strength over long periods; but, in time, they have all come to understand that eliminating poverty entails change that is simultaneously cultural, social, and economic. Often their work has generated suspicion and hostility, which have been expressed even by those who claim to share the desire for development.

It has become commonplace to write about the special needs of women in development and to decry development patterns and projects that either ignore these needs or actually disadvantage women—but it is easy to forget how recent is our sensitivity to the issues of women in the Third World. The roots of our sensitivity lie in the intellectual currents of criticism that have emerged over the past thirty years. First and foremost, that criticism has been leveled at a course of development that has benefited industry to the detriment of agriculture, cities to the detriment of rural areas, the middle class and well-off to the detriment of the very poor, and men to the detriment of women. Our sensitivity was foreshadowed, moreover, by attacks on the status quo that were waged by Western feminist movements in the 1960s and early 1970s. Indeed, feminists in North America and Western Europe have raised questions about the structure of power, the distribution of work and wealth, and the efficacy of many social policies.

I am indebted to the encouragement of my colleagues, Carol Cantrell and Pattie Cowell, and to the assistance of Earlene Bell. —*Sue Ellen M. Charlton*

The processes of reexamining development priorities and rethinking the implications of gender converged at a time when other criticisms of the established orders of the world had begun to undermine assumptions about the meaning of development and who should benefit from it. Voices from the less developed countries made themselves heard in varied (and sometimes contradictory) ways. For example, the policies of the Organization of Petroleum Exporting Countries (OPEC) threatened Western dominance in energy and ultimately affected political matters, especially in the Middle East. The demands of Third World governments for a restructuring of international institutions produced gradual, but perceptual, changes in the United Nations system, the World Bank, and a wide variety of nongovernmental organizations (NGOs). The rapaciousness of some "development" projects has opened new debates about the environmental benefits and costs of standard practices. Persistent malnourishment and even famine have made it clear that development has not helped hundreds of thousands of people in the world, and it is equally clear that those most severely plagued by food shortages are women and children. Civil strife and war have contributed to these problems, as refugees have massed in camps or moved across national borders; and it is certainly no accident that the refugees in many areas have been predominantly women and children.

Under these conditions of dramatic change, women in Third World countries have risen to positions of local, national, and international leadership against odds virtually unimaginable by Western leaders. Although such fortitude is not unknown in cataclysmic times, the structure of the international system in the late twentieth century has given the experience of these leaders new importance. The technologies of modern transportation and communication have made it possible for the stories of the five women in this book to be recounted and to inspire across international boundaries. The political structures and priorities of international institutions created the United Nations Decade for Women, and the three UN conferences in Mexico City (1975), Copenhagen (1980), and Nairobi (1985), along with the NGO forums, have legitimized the desires and activities of millions of women from hundreds of cultures.

Remarkable women, like remarkable men, have always existed. What is significant about the five women portrayed here is that they are not the most famous women of their age and, in fact, are very different from the Margaret Thatcher, Indira Gandhi, or even Mother Theresa and Corazon Aquino of our decade. In many ways these five typify the invisible leaders of international development efforts: invisible to the mass media, yet well known to those whose lives they have touched and, thanks to

Marion Levy, to those of us who have an opportunity to learn from their successes and failures.[1]

What follows in this Introduction is an attempt to sketch a comparative picture of these women. Their experiences are common in some respects, unique in others. Taken together, they raise a number of questions about effective leadership, the strengths and weaknesses of women's organizations, and the contradictory effects of state institutions on the efforts of women to participate fully in the search for life-enriching development strategies.

In the first two parts of the Introduction, we shall look at the tension between tradition and change. The discussion in the first part emphasizes the role of cultural constraints on women's roles and options, using a comparison between Egypt and Bangladesh for illustration. It is here that we also get our first glimpse of the unique circumstances that propelled Aziza Hussein and Hasina Khan into positions of leadership. The second part reveals some of the massive changes engendered by international war, decolonization, and civil conflict that affected the lives of the five leaders portrayed here. The third part focuses on what is commonly known as the private/public distinction or dichotomy, and on the role of the government in supporting, hindering, and/or manipulating women's causes and organizations.

The fourth part of the Introduction looks at women's organizations and leadership, and asks what we can learn about these from the five women described here. What makes them exceptional in the context of their countries and their times? What are the similarities and differences in their efforts to build and use organizations for development? Finally, the concluding section explores briefly the potential for a new *international* feminism, by whatever name it might be called. As Marion Levy notes early on, these five women—like many Third World leaders—eschew identification with Western feminism. The experience of the UN Decade, however, suggests that popular images of feminism are in need of dramatic revision as "Westerners" and "Easterners," "Northern" women and "Southern" women, argue, share, and learn from each other.

Culture, Gender, and Class

Peoples' lives—what they can do, how and when they can do it, the choices they can and want to make—are circumscribed by culture, gender, and class. Although it is true that gender often seems the most predictable of these factors in defining opportunity around the world, gender never operates independent of class or culture. Moreover, even when gender, class, and culture all conspire to limit opportunity for a girl, her personality—or a single individual who reaches out to her—can transform that opportunity. Here we have five women we would have expected to be confined to traditional household roles in their respective societies; yet none was so confined. Before looking at their unique attributes, we need to understand how the interplay of traditional society with socioeconomic and political change set the context for their lives.

Hasina Khan of Bangladesh and Aziza Hussein of Egypt come from cultures that to Westerners probably appear to be the most structured along gender lines. Both Bangladesh and Egypt are predominantly Muslim countries, and there is little doubt that Islam has contributed to gender distinctions in these countries, just as Buddhism, Christianity, and Judaism have in others. Yet the connections among culture, gender, and religion vary; indeed, there are significant differences between the roles and status of Muslim women in Nigeria, Tunisia, Iran, and Indonesia, to say nothing of countries as diverse as Sudan or Turkey.[2] One important source of difference between societies with Islamic traditions and those that are non-Islamic is the degree to which the culture observes Islamic law (or the Shari'a), at the heart of which is family law governing marriage, divorce, and inheritance. Legal systems based on Islamic law differ from those with secular (Western) legal codes, and the rights of wives and daughters vary accordingly.[3] Religion and law thus interact with each other; they interact also with preexisting cultural systems[4] and, of course, are influenced by government policy. All of these factors, in turn, are affected by work patterns and control of resources, and hence class.

The traditions of seclusion for women, found throughout most of the Middle East and South Asia, characterize the cultures within which Hasina Khan and Aziza Hussein were raised. Seclusion, or *purdah* as it is also commonly known in South Asia, is a system of physically secluding women (typically within the household) from contact with men and thereby maintaining high standards of female modesty. As part of this tradition, women may be veiled in public, or at least required to wear head scarves and modest clothing that covers their arms and legs. Seclusion is widespread in both Muslim and Hindu cultures, but it varies according to geographical locale, class, and even individual family.[5] In general, it is stronger in Bangladesh than in Egypt, a point that makes Hasina Khan's accomplishments all the more striking.

There are several reasons for the differences between Egypt and Bangladesh in the norms governing women's behavior: the level of industrialization and urbanization, and hence women's work patterns; the emergence of a large middle class; the history of women's education, women's organizations, and female political activism; and, of course, laws and government policy. A few illustrations suggest the way in which these factors could account for the differences in gender roles between Bangladesh and Egypt, or between these and other countries.

Urbanization, at least initially, may have contradictory effects on women's options. Middle- and upper-class families sometimes practice seclusion more extensively as a way of demonstrating higher class status (for poor women forced to work outside the household, seclusion is impossible to maintain) and/or to protect wives and daughters from the increased threats to modesty accompanying the density of large towns and cities. But the same population density facilitates the spread of education and intellectual movements, including those championing social causes, and makes it easier also to sustain the kinds of organizational efforts typical of reformers. It is not surprising, therefore, that women's movements have generally arisen in urban areas sooner than in rural areas.

Industrialization often creates new job opportunities for women (and men), either in factories or in service occupations. Elizabeth White has argued that enforcement of traditional Islamic restrictions on women is greater where women's participation in the nonhousehold labor force is lowest. Even though Islamic laws do not prohibit female education or participation in economically productive activities, those nations that are unwilling to reform the Islamic laws are also apparently unwilling to provide equal educational facilities for women or to encourage the entry of women into the labor force. The nations that have reformed those laws most inequitable and restrictive to women exhibit higher female literacy, school enrollment, and reported female participation in economic activities.[6] In the long run, then, it seems that urbanization and industrialization (when it draws women into the labor force) break down the physical conditions that make it possible to maintain *purdah* in a rural society.[7] And where these socioeconomic changes are accompanied by government policies to remove inequities in women's legal status and access to education, women's life choices and status improve even further.

By the early 1980s, approximately 45 percent of all Egyptians lived in cities.[8] In contrast, although the population density of Bangladesh is very high, it is still basically a rural society, with only 8 percent of the population living in urban areas. Moreover, proportionately more females than males live in the rural areas of Bangladesh.[9] Consequently, there have been relatively few inroads into the traditional, rural-based, cultural norms that dictate an inferior status for women in Bangladesh, and seclusion has maintained a stronger hold on Bangladeshi women than on their Egyptian counterparts.

Man is the dominant figure in the society. The continuity of society is preserved through the male line. Children are known because of their father, and a wife because of her husband. A woman has no place in the scheme of social identification. She exists not as an individual but as a wife and mother. She is considered physically, intellectually and emotionally inferior to man and incapable of protecting herself. . . . She is considered incapable of freedom and independence throughout her life. . . . In such a situation, home must be the only world of a woman.[10]

Under these circumstances, it is not surprising that Hasina Khan found one of the greatest desires of the village women she worked with was to be called by their own names, rather than being known simply as "Ahmed's daughter," "Halim's wife," or "Yousef's mother."

Given the traditional culture of Bangladesh, that Hasina Khan could be educated through the university level, teach in college, and then work as a family-planning and rural-development organizer seems at best improbable. We can only begin to imagine the obstacles confronting her work when we realize that she had to walk from village to village, and from house to house. Until the early 1980s, when bicycle rickshaws appeared, rural transportation in much of Bangladesh consisted of bicycles and motorbikes, which women by tradition could not use. The problems of transportation and communication were compounded by the absence of any tradition of women working with women outside their own households. Thus, all organizational efforts had to overcome both technological and cultural barriers to create linkages among women.[11]

Unlike Bangladesh, Egypt has a long tradition of female political activism and of women serving in positions of prominent leadership. Feminist thought and debate emerged at the end of the nineteenth century, particularly among members of the new upper-middle class— "members of large landowning families who had acquired a Western education or at least had some acquaintance with European thought and culture."[12] The Egyptian Feminist Union established in 1923 helped set the stage for the relatively widespread participation of Egyptian women in public life.[13] This is the tradition into which Aziza Hussein was born.

In contrast to Hasina Khan, who had to walk through villages as recently as the 1980s, Aziza Hussein was traveling internationally by the 1950s. Aziza, who grew up in the 1920s, is the older of the two; Hasina grew up in the 1950s. Another important difference was family background: Both sets of parents supported education for their children, even the girls, but Aziza Hussein's parents came from relatively wealthy landowning families and her father was a highly educated physician who had studied in Dublin and Paris. The women in Hasina Khan's family, by contrast, generally observed *purdah,* and it was only through the intervention of a friend of one of her maternal uncles that Hasina's intellectual promise was actually rewarded with the opportunity to attend an outstanding girls boarding school. The fact that Aziza Hussein was being educated some thirty years earlier than Hasina Khan thus says a great deal about the importance of class and family background, as well as about the more progressive political conditions in Egypt.[14]

The gains for Egyptian women from the post–World War I period were largely confined to elite groups. In the 1950s, these gains began to spread to middle-class women and, in limited measure, to poor rural women. The formal British protectorate over Egypt, dating from the 1882 British invasion, ended in 1922, but British occupation was not actually terminated until the 1936 Anglo-Egyptian Treaty. In fact, British troops stayed through World War II, while Egypt functioned as a base for Allied military operations. It was partly as a reaction against Western influence that a group of disaffected army officers, led by Gamal Abdul Nasser, took over the government in a coup in 1952. For nearly twenty years, until his death in 1970, Nasser was Egypt's paramount political leader. Nasser and the other men who came to power in the 1950s were determined to modernize the country and reduce class inequities through such strategies as expanding access to public education and undertaking land reform in the rural areas. Women benefited from the expansion of public education, the formal granting of suffrage in 1956, and improved employment protection; they also began to play a role in government during the 1950s.[15]

Cultural Constraint and Political Change

A quick glance at the non-Muslim societies represented by the studies in this book bears out the importance of class and unique opportunity (such as schooling) in enabling women to move beyond the restrictions that are embedded in culturally defined gender roles. In contrast to Egypt and Bangladesh, where there is considerable ethnic and religious homogeneity, Kenya is an amalgam of diverse ethnic and religious groups. Muslims constitute less than 10 percent of the Kenyan population; the majority are nominally Christian. Elvina Mutua, who grew up in the culturally diverse region of Mombasa, Kenya, came from a family that reflected a mixture of Christian and indigenous religions. Because her father was trained as a health inspector, Elvina was raised with a high degree of consciousness about standards for health care (such as the importance of boiling drinking water), even though she lived in a village. Advantaged by comparison to many village children, Elvina had substantially more schooling than girls her age and, at the age of fourteen (when most of her friends were married), found herself in a boarding school. As with Hasina Khan in Bangladesh, her life broke free of the social norm because of unique family circumstances. This pattern was all the more unusual for Elvina Mutua, given that she began her education in the 1940s.

Like Hasina Khan and Aziza Hussein, Reyna de Miralda has lived in a society where cultural and religious norms reinforce gender segregation in family, household, and work activities. But unlike Elvina Mutua, Hasina Khan, and Aziza Hussein, Reyna de Miralda came from the poorest class of peasants in Honduras; recollections of hunger are a vivid part of her childhood remembrances. Following a pattern common to poor women in much of Latin America, she engaged in street trading, selling a variety of items to help support her family and to pay for the items she needed, such as school supplies.[16] Clearly it was a "hand-to-mouth" existence. Yet she pursued what public education was available and, at the age of fifteen, was able to take a job as a teacher. Her ambitions provoked conflict with her husband years later, when she sought a job as a volunteer community health worker, because the job required training and travel—to which her husband objected. Reyna herself attributes her husband's objections to deeply ingrained cultural patterns:

> The man, as head of the household, wants his wife to depend on him and wants her at home. . . . He doesn't want to be competing with her on the outside or to feel that if she gets a higher education he will become inferior to her. . . . Men don't want to see you talking to strangers as your reputation is of most concern to them. . . . Men believe they can do everything but women can only do limited tasks, below men's level. That's a sign of machismo. This is all part of our culture.

The term *machismo* has been widely used to explain the cluster of cultural attitudes that sustain the inferior status of women in Latin American countries.[17] Virility and strength in the man have their counterparts in the passivity, submissiveness, and self-abnegation of the woman. Home is the sphere of the woman, and the ideal woman is a mother; in some rural areas even today, the proper woman will not leave her house except to run necessary errands or to make family visits. Thus Reyna de Miralda had to challenge barriers of both culture and class.

Elizabeth O'Kelly's story differs from the other four. Although she, too, broke with conventional cultural expectations and class barriers, she came from a socioeconomic environment that, despite the limitations it placed on women, nonetheless presented far more options for a girl growing up between the 1920s and the 1940s. Great Britain, after all, was still an economic leader of the world in the period between World

Wars I and II, whereas Kenya, Bangladesh, and Cameroon were all poor colonies, and Egypt and Honduras were quasi-colonies, heavily influenced by Western culture, capitalism, and politico-military intervention. There were economic and political opportunities available to Elizabeth in the United Kingdom that would have been unimaginable for nearly all the women of her generation in Africa, Asia, or Latin America (recall that only education and class background made it possible for Aziza Hussein to take advantage of the rapidly changing social conditions of interwar Egypt). British women, for example, received full suffrage rights in 1928, whereas female suffrage came to Egypt and Cameroon (with independence in the latter's case) in 1956, Honduras in 1957, and Kenya (also with independence) in 1963.[18]

Elizabeth's life nevertheless reflects the importance of unique family conditions. Despite the relative advantages of British citizenship, her family's poverty forced her to leave school at the age of fourteen and, while still a teen-ager, to work. She later pursued her education in music, although this training never led to a career. Her real opportunity came with World War II, when she joined the military effort and, after the war, the Cameroons Development Corporation.

Elizabeth O'Kelly's career path also highlights for us the importance of the broader political changes occurring in the five countries under review here. Even though tradition set "acceptable" limits for the activities of the leaders portrayed by Marion Levy, tradition itself was being undermined by changes that were sometimes global in nature, sometimes regional. Egypt after World War I was caught up in nationalist ferment; Britain's "great power" status was confirmed, then undermined, by the events of the war and postwar periods; and Cameroon, Kenya, and Bangladesh (the last of which was originally part of India) were shaken by the process of decolonization. In addition, Bangladesh itself was born of the civil war within Pakistan in the early 1970s.

Deep and widespread political change, often accompanied by violence, takes its toll on every individual, and women often suffer directly. The war between West and East Pakistan and the birth of Bangladesh, for example, set the stage for Hasina Khan's work. Her family was forced to flee from town to village to escape the war, and it was in the village that she confronted the extreme poverty and suffering that would kindle her social conscience. A common abuse of women in time of war—rape—was widespread in Bangladesh; the war also created a large class of homeless women.

Grim though they are, war and revolution also create opportunity. As Barbara Jancar writes:

In such a situation, women have easier access to political roles, since dominant institutional patterns are weak. Moreover, social change affects women directly in every aspect of their lives. Hence, there is a greater likelihood of political interest and political response. . . . role differentiation according to sex tends to diminish as women find they have to perform tasks formally considered male, such as waging guerrilla warfare or working in armaments factories. Finally, because the new order has not yet been established, the real possibility of change still exists.[19]

In Bangladesh, war and revolution created a massive need for educated Bangladeshis to staff the programs of recovery. The war was followed by the monsoon of 1974, which led to severe famine throughout the country. Thousands of women had to work outside their homes, and women were needed to help run the programs designed to benefit poor women. This was Hasina Khan's opportunity.

Revolution in twentieth-century Egypt began at the end of World War I, when a newly formed nationalist group, the Wafd, agitated for independence from British rule. The British authorities sent the leaders of the Wafd into exile and met public demonstrators with gunfire. The political elite of Egypt joined the Wafd, and their wives formed a women's committee that organized strikes, demonstrations, and boycotts of British goods. Upper-class women thus became politicized, and, as Marion Levy points out, this movement of women into public life led to social activism. Demands for the emancipation of women were part of this ferment.[20] Aziza Hussein's life also reflected this time of transformation: She attended American University in Cairo, took an office job during the war, and joined organizations that had grown out of the movement of elite women after World War I.

World War II also meant a job for Elizabeth O'Kelly. When she joined the Women's Royal Navy Service, she started on a government career that would take her to a position in the British Colonial Service, as well as to work in Asia and Africa. Decolonization and independence for Cameroon forced the end of her work there, but decolonization created an opportunity for Elvina Mutua in Kenya. Elvina started secretarial training in 1963 and was well placed to profit from the trend to replace British personnel with Kenyans in Kenya's private and public institutions. Her job with Home Industries became the launching pad for a twenty-year commitment to income-generating activities for poor Kenyan women.

Honduras, like other Latin American countries, suffers from extremes of poverty and wealth, few natural resources, and incipient political conflict. As Marion Levy notes, the combined effects of natural disaster and endemic poverty exacerbated conflict throughout the country in the mid-1970s. Peasant groups were radicalized, dissidents were arrested, and the Catholic Church moved to separate itself from social-welfare programs viewed as too closely linked to political activism. Reyna de Miralda was one of those who lost her job when programs were changed or dropped. The experience was a blow, but it marked a turning point in the focus and scope of her work, as she became a national leader in the Honduran Federation of Peasant Women (FEHMUC).

Reyna's experience in FEHMUC raises important questions about the impact of political instability on women's opportunities. The need—and therefore the potential—for leadership is pressing, and talented, energetic women can move quickly into positions of influence. But the dilemma for these new leaders then becomes acute, especially if fundamental change does not occur or is very slow. Governments trying to stabilize explosive situations (e.g., in Central America) are quick to try to exploit or co-opt opposition leaders. Nevertheless, women like Reyna de Miralda, Elvina Mutua, and Hasina Khan, understanding the fact that government policy invariably influences the masses of poor people who have little or no say about the nature of that policy, have chosen explicitly or implicitly to become transmission channels between public decision-making and private lives. In effect, they recognize that private lives can no longer be insulated from public decisions and officials: Everyone is touched by the tax collector, the soldier, the extension agent, the social-welfare worker, or the public-works official. Villages may be isolated from wealth, but they are seldom isolated from the effects of the state. How, then, do those seeking fundamental change in their societies approach or view their government agencies—agencies that can block or facilitate their efforts (and sometimes both simultaneously)?

Private and Public: The Role of Government

The process of development as we know it transforms our definitions of what constitutes private versus public matters. In traditional societies, however, there is often no effective distinction between private and public; that is, people do not think in terms of a dividing line between the family or household on the one hand and a community of people unrelated by ties of blood or marriage on the other.

One of the prevailing characteristics of development is that human activities become more specialized. Like early family farms in the United States, subsistence farms provide for a complete range of family needs; although farming and household tasks are divided within the family by gender and age, there is little or no specialization in the sense that we know it today. An important change comes with the introduction of cash, which must be earned through the sale of one's labor or commodities, and which is then exchanged for goods and services that formerly were produced by the family for its own use.

Not only economic activities become specialized; political activities, too, become more complicated and differentiated from other kinds of activities. In a primitive, communal society, people may govern themselves, but as societies grow in size and complexity, a state emerges and people are increasingly governed by others—and, historically, the vast majority of human beings have had little or no control over these "others." Development as it has occurred in the nineteenth and twentieth centuries has been accompanied by two contradictory political tendencies. On the one hand, government bureaucracies (both civilian and military) have been created and have expanded to foster and control economic development—a trend facilitated by modern technology. From the building of railroads and the financing of state-owned industries to the fostering of public health and education, development has developed governments as much as it has developed economies and societies. On the other hand, however, the nineteenth and twentieth centuries have constituted a great era of political liberation: Slaves have been freed, working classes and even women have been enfranchised, nations have been released from colonial control, and hunger and human rights abuses have generated international publicity. As recently as two centuries ago, most of this was unthinkable, but today mass politics and populist politics (though not necessarily democracy) are the norm. People may be mobilized by governments and they may also be mobilized *against* governments. Governments both manipulate and exploit people, but they also underwrite programs for human well-being. This is the late-twentieth century political contradiction within which the five women in this study have spent their lives working.

Most of the problems of rural poverty that our five leaders have confronted have existed in one form or another throughout most of recorded history. The conditions of our era have guaranteed that these problems can no longer be considered private matters: Our reevaluation of human life combined with modern communications technology means that hunger in Honduras or rape in Bangladesh now exists in the arena of public consciousness. In the past, decisions about giving birth to children (insofar as such decisions were made at all) were made in the privacy of the family, but now they form a part of the national and international debates about family-planning policies. Governments are expected to address these kinds of issues, even when they handle them badly or want to avoid them. It is therefore not surprising that, in their individual efforts to address the problems of rural poverty, the five leaders discussed here have drawn on government resources. Their contacts with their governments, while inevitable, have both hindered and facilitated their development efforts, for governments are both part of the problems and necessary to the solutions. The experience of the *harambee* movement in Kenya illustrates some of the dilemmas that typically present themselves to women mobilizing for change.

Harambee (which literally means "let us all pull together" and is usually translated as "self-help") refers to the program for social welfare and development that emerged from the Kikuyu, one of Kenya's dominant ethnic groups and the one from which Kenya's first president, Jomo Kenyatta, came. *Harambee* was highly politicized and, in the view of some scholars, was designed as much for keeping power in the hands of Kikuyu as for developing Kenya as a whole.[21] Marion Levy points out that the government's effort to involve women's groups in development was an offshoot of the *harambee* movement. If women's organizations want to benefit from government assistance for their projects, they must register with the government. Even with registration, however, the proportion of government funds they receive is minimal and the women themselves must sustain the community projects with their own scarce funds and labor.[22] As community development priorities become more consistent with broader national-development priorities, women and their organizations become, in a sense, part of the "raw material" mobilized for state-defined objectives. In this respect, *harambee* is typical of community-development projects in many parts of the world where local "initiative" is stimulated from the top down. Yet, although women may benefit from social-welfare projects, they are not necessarily the *primary* beneficiaries and have little autonomous control over the overall direction of development planning.

The tension generated by the government role in development is even more striking in the case of Honduras. One could easily argue that in a country such as Honduras—where the government has historically sustained or accommodated foreign intervention, inequitable distribution of wealth, corruption, and political repression—the government is as much, if not more, a source of development problems as it is a potential problem-solver. Reyna de Miralda's entry into social activism came through the Housewives' Clubs in Honduras. Created by CARITAS, the Catholic welfare agency, the Clubs offered health and family-welfare programs in poor villages. When the government repressed peasant organizations in the mid-1970s, members of some Housewives' Clubs were among those arrested. CARITAS ceased funding the Clubs and Reyna lost her job. Subsequently, she became an organizer for the Honduran Federation of Peasant Women (FEHMUC). Despite this legacy of political opposition to the government, within two years FEHMUC obtained government help to run short training courses on health for village women. The contradiction lay not only in dependence upon government funds for projects but also in the potential implications of FEHMUC's activities: The goals of community development for women entail organization, and organization ultimately risks challenging the established hierarchies. This is one reason for which women's groups often rely on external, nongovernmental support, as noted below.

The relationship between women's organizations and government policy is difficult both to understand and to prescribe. Women must work with and within government agencies and attempt to influence government policy, while simultaneously building a power base outside of government. Even "bad" governments may yield good policies when the conditions are right. Elizabeth O'Kelly, for instance, was an officer of a colonial administration at a time when the legitimacy of colonies was under attack around the world. Yet her position, coupled with her sensitive insight into the conditions of farm women in Cameroon, led her to take the initiative in the introduction of a simple technology—a corn mill that lightened the daily workload occasioned by the need to grind maize.

The experience throughout the past two decades of women's organizations seems to confirm this dual strategy: Work with government and organize outside it, using whatever resources are available. The duality of the UN Decade and its conferences, on the one hand, and the dynamism of the NGO Forums (whose meetings overlapped those of the official UN conferences in 1975, 1980, and 1985), on the other, symbolizes this strategy. Representation in official UN meetings is intended for *government* delegates. Thus, for example, Aziza Hussein had no choice but to represent the position of the Egyptian government when President Nasser appointed her to the UN Commission on the Status of Women. Her position gave her an opportunity to educate Commission members from Western countries as to the realities of the status of women in Egypt—but she simultaneously became more introspective and sensitive to her country's problems. Her prestige and leadership position permitted her to push both for family-planning programs and for legal reform of women's rights in Egypt. She both served her government and used her government to serve the interests of Egyptian women.

Not every leader can hope to be an official UN delegate. What has been so remarkable about the UN Decade for Women and the accompanying NGO Forums is that the latter have offered the opportunity to thousands of women to be unofficial UN delegates. More than 2,000 official delegates representing 159 governments gathered in Nairobi for the third UN Conference on Women in July 1985, but the corresponding Forum attracted nearly 14,000 women from well-known, established nongovernmental organizations and from new, nearly ad hoc women's groups. The Forum participants shared ideas in 1,500 planned workshops as well as in discussions organized on the spot by the NGO Planning Committee.[23]

The mobilization of women's organizations dates back to the first UN Conference, when more than 6,000 women attended the Tribune—a meeting that paralleled the official conference. This number rose to 8,000 at the NGO Forum in Copenhagen in 1980, and then jumped again to nearly 14,000 in 1985. In view of the fact that forty years earlier (when the United Nations was founded) only half of its 51 members gave women the right to vote, the events of the UN Decade represented an astonishing testimony both to government recognition (if only "lip-service" in practice) of women's issues and to nongovernmental initiatives taken by women who were unwilling or unable to work through government channels. It is this simultaneous within government–without government, within nations–across nations movement that characterizes the work of the five leaders in this book. And it is in this regard that their lives exemplify the thrust of women's organizations at the end of the twentieth century.

Organization and Leadership Among Women

The central challenge for development strategies designed to improve the social and material conditions of rural women is to engage women's participation in decision-making about their own lives and about their communities. In other words, the goal is to transform women from objects of development to subjects or participants in the development process. Clearly, women's interests are not identical across time, culture, and class; but economic development as it has occurred in most countries, and coupled as it is with the expansion of state bureaucracies, has had the effect of creating more uniformity among women's interests within different countries. Kathleen Staudt argues that it is difficult to locate societies in which women, *because they are women*, do not face

- less access to agricultural and vocational opportunities, training, and support services than men;
- less access to education than men;
- stereotyping in schools, resulting in unequal skills between the sexes and a narrower range of occupational choices for girls than for boys;

- an imbalance between the sexes in domestic work and compensation;
- legitimacy of overt physical abuse toward women, or of covert abuse perpetuated through a reluctance of political authorities to interfere in "private" matters; and
- underrepresentation and nonparticipation in the political, institutional, and bureaucratic structures of the nation-state.[24]

Individual women, as the five in this book demonstrate, can escape restrictive conditions, but changing those conditions for the majority of women requires some kind of group action. There is no "formula" to define what kind of group and what kind of action will have the highest potential for success in improving women's lives in general; much depends on the specific nature of the obstacles involved. We can say, for example, that women throughout the world need better access to education and to resources, but the kind of education and the type of resources depend on local conditions. Similarly, we know that when women organize, their chances of improving their lot go up, but it is difficult to generalize about how they should organize. Even so straightforward a question as to whether women should organize around a specific task or around multiple goals, alone or with men, is still open to debate.

Nevertheless, a few facts about the potential power of organizing have been reaffirmed by the research of social scientists over the past two decades: (1) Effective organization can overturn a sense of isolation and fatalism about the possibilities of improving one's life; (2) groups of some kind are a necessary intermediary between the human beings who are the presumed beneficiaries of development projects and the project initiators—be they governments, nongovernment organizations (NGOs), or public international agencies; (3) the sense of participation and efficacy that comes with successful organization is necessary to counteract the dependency that easily results when the impetus for development comes from outside the community; and (4) organizations can help compensate for the lower access to resources that prevails among the poor in general and among women in particular.[25]

The five women portrayed here are all builders and users of organizations. In the following section, we shall look first at the qualities that made these women leaders and discuss why their lives failed to conform to the dominant patterns for women in their countries. We will then look at what they have learned in the course of their work about organizations and development among the poor, and at what, in turn, their experiences suggest about the general role to be played by women's organizations in the context of the global transformations described at the beginning of this Introduction.

Leadership

Marion Levy's portraits suggest that, despite significant differences among the five women, they have shared some important traits and circumstances. All have been blessed with relatively good health and physical stamina. Elvina Mutua, it will be recalled, came from a family that practiced good health principles at a time when most rural Kenyans were unaware of basic sanitation and nutrition practices. Both Hasina Khan and Aziza Hussein attended schools at which physical activity was encouraged among the girls, who were accustomed to this activity and genuinely enjoyed it. Reyna de Miralda survived the extreme conditions of poverty in her native Honduras, and Elizabeth O'Kelly managed to work effectively in rural Africa under conditions that left many people ill or dead.

Native intelligence and ambition also characterize all five women; these qualities, plus courage, are what made it possible for them to take advantage of the opportunities they perceived to move beyond traditional barriers to women. For example, Hasina Khan and Reyna de Miralda, despite the differences in their class and cultural backgrounds, were able to distinguish themselves in school very early in their lives. The narrative also makes it clear that family members—fathers or mothers, or occasionally an uncle or grandmother—are an important source of support for children who excel, especially in ways that are atypical relative to their societies. The one woman who had virtually no family support, Elizabeth O'Kelly, came from a society that, compared to Egypt, Honduras, Kenya, and Bangladesh, offered greater opportunities—both because of the greater freedom in gender roles and because of the greater wealth and power of the country itself.

Four of the five leaders married, but it is difficult to generalize about the role of the husbands in their wives' accomplishments. At one point or another, each husband appears to have supported his wife's education and community involvement. Elvina Mutua, for example, stressed that her husband was not typical of Kenyan men because he wanted an educated wife and tolerated her independence. Hasina's husband met her in college and married her despite the fact that she did not have a dowry, which is the traditional prerequisite to a good marriage in Bangladesh. Both her family and her husband's family, however, had concerns about the marriage, and the tension Marion Levy describes between Hasina and her in-laws weaves in and out of her story. When Hasina left her position with Save the Children Federation in 1983, it was largely because of family obligations and her husband's concern that she was spending too much time away from him and their children.

Aziza Hussein married a German-educated agricultural economist who began his career in community development and went on to become Egypt's ambassador to the United States under the Nasser government in the 1950s. His encouragement and his own leadership role became the catalyst for Aziza's involvement in the problems of the rural poor in Egypt. In contrast, Reyna de Miralda's husband—though tolerant of some of her activities, which brought in money for the desperately poor family—was "jealous" (in her words) of her training and drive for self-improvement. When they had been married about fourteen years, he died, and she was left with seven children and no family support.

As suggested at the outset, these are courageous women. Whether we are reading of Reyna de Miralda's near-heroic efforts to keep her family together while pursuing community goals, or about the day-to-day courage that permitted grass-roots family-planning workers in Bangladesh to talk to hostile villagers about birth control, it is clear that only conviction and dedication to specific objectives made it possible to sustain the kind of long-term efforts needed to break the cycle of poverty in these countries. But these women are not only courageous in pursuit of their causes; they are also patient and persevering, trying one approach or another as the occasion warrants. Moreover, their commitments are long-term: Elvina Mutua, for example, has been with Tototo Industries in Kenya for twenty years.

Although each woman has her own leadership style, the central concern of all five is the ability to hear and see what poor women want. Hasina Khan and Elvina Mutua, for example, have spent hours listening and talking to village women in order to understand their needs. Because Reyna de Miralda herself came so directly from the culture and class of women who needed help in Honduras, she plunged into any activity that would help earn a little money for her family; in addition, because of her experience in teaching and in running a village cooperative, she was able to develop the skills that made her a candidate when CARITAS and the Housewives' Clubs in Honduras were looking for village leaders. She learned as she taught, but, given her background, it is not surprising that her style has been the most personalistic and aggressive of the five women described here. Elizabeth O'Kelly's approach was different in the sense that she was not only an outsider to the culture in which she was working but also a representative of colonial authority. What she lacked in terms of shared cultural roots she made up for by drawing on the work of an anthropologist who had studied the Nsaw people, with whom Elizabeth was working, by consulting with village leaders, learning from her own mistakes, and making careful observations.

Organization

Each leader relied on, helped create, and fostered village-level women's organizations at some point in her work. Like many leaders, these five began their public lives by joining groups that gave them skills and contacts; thus it was a logical step to move from being member to being leader. As a young mother, for example, Elvina Mutua says that she joined a number of women's organizations—the Women's Guild, the Women's Fellowship Union, Maendeleo Ya Wanawake (Progress for Women), the YWCA, and the Girls' Guides—and went on to become a volunteer discussion leader for the YWCA. Her career/leadership pattern, in other words, would be familiar to those American women who have moved from home to club membership to community volunteer to initiator and leader.

For each woman, organization was the key to success. Aziza Hussein worked with the Cairo Women's Club to set up a children's center in the village of Sandyoun. Elizabeth O'Kelly's international reputation came from her success in setting up cooperative groups known as Corn Mill Societies, each of which consisted of seventy to eighty women who shared the cost of buying and maintaining the mills. Elvina Mutua's efforts to create income-generating opportunities for village women have always relied on the women's willingness to organize themselves for cooperative projects. Reyna de Miralda's first community activities took place in the context of the Housewives' Clubs, and it was through the Honduran Federation of Peasant Women that she helped initiate village training and health projects. The first major challenge to Hasina Khan's village work was simply to get women to come together and talk about their needs. These meetings then became the basis for subsequent efforts at health education and training.

The tradition of women's organizations varies among the five countries under study here, and each manifestation of that tradition clearly influences the nature of the barriers to women's projects encountered by the five leaders and their co-workers. Sub-Saharan Africa, for instance, is notable for the women's multipurpose groups that have emerged in recent history. Kathleen Staudt notes that "these organizations reflect the division of labor and interest of women in those societies, and foster women's management of their 'own affairs.'"[26] Elizabeth O'Kelly found that the concept of women's groups was natural to Cameroonians because women had long been organizing savings and social-assistance groups (as well as traditional secret societies) for themselves. Elvina Mutua, too, drew on an indigenous tradition of women's groups—a tradition enhanced by the *harambee* movement.

In contrast to those areas in which there is a strong tradition of women's groups are the areas in which the tradition of organization exists among women but the initiative has come from above, from the government, an NGO, or an institution such as the Catholic Church. In Honduras, for example, the Church-sponsored social-action agency, CARITAS, initiated the Housewives' Clubs (clubes de amas de casa, or CAC) in 1967. And in 1970, Church activists concerned with the condition of the rural poor, and imbued with the Christian Democratic philosophy of political and social reform, inspired the founding of the National Peasants' Union (UNC), with which the Honduran Federation of Peasant Women (FEHMUC) is affiliated.[27]

In the absence of an indigenous tradition or strong initiative by a widely accepted social institution such as the Church, government, or NGO initiative becomes the norm for grass-roots organization. Thus it is not surprising that village organizations in Egypt and Bangladesh were the result of government-sponsored community-development activities. Although government intervention subjects such efforts to external manipulation, it represents the only option in the absence of other prominent social institutions committed to social reform. The "Mothers' Club" effort in Korea provides an illustration of the importance of this external initiative from a region of the world not touched on in this study. In the late 1960s, the Planned Parenthood Federation of Korea established Mothers' Clubs to encourage family planning and, subsequently, provided nutrition classes, credit unions, and other community-development activities. Reports in the 1970s suggested that the clubs were generally successful.[28] But their success did not come easily: The organizers often met with resistance in rural communities where male dominance was strong and traditionally unchallenged. In one instance, an organizer was beaten by village elders when she talked about contraception; in another, the establishment of a club was opposed by the elders until the government ordered them to accept it.[29] Women's organizations mean women's power and, as such, pose a threat to the traditional order. Similarly, as organizations of the rural poor always threaten those who hold power and wealth, it is not surprising that violence sometimes accompanies rural movements when they begin to be effective, as in Honduras. Under these circumstances, the attitude of the government becomes critical in determining success or failure.

Generally a local organization by itself cannot produce development in most countries today, because the process of development—however defined—is exceedingly complex. As noted earlier in this Introduction, development involves change that is simultaneously cultural, economic, social, and political, and it engages numerous "actors" both private and public, including regional and national government officials and often international groups and agencies. Milton Esman and Norman Uphoff summarize the prerequisites for rural development as follows:

1. *Public investments* in physical and social infrastructure
2. A *policy environment* that is responsive to the interests of rural constituencies, including the poor
3. *Technologies* suitable to the circumstances and capabilities of small farmers and other rural producers
4. *Effective institutions* operating at various levels and enhancing capacities in the public and private sectors, including (a) a *network of government agencies* providing the public services necessary for higher productivity and improved quality of life (e.g., school systems); (b) *private enterprise* or *private voluntary agencies* (nongovernmental organizations), which may undertake some activities that elsewhere are left to government initiative; and (c) *local organizations* that provide direction, define priorities for rural development, and implement specific projects.[30]

The recognition that local organizations, including women's groups, exist within this broader context helps balance our expectations and evaluation of them: They are necessary but insufficient for development. Indeed, they form a necessary linkage among the private and informal spheres of individuals and family/households on the one hand and the public domain of development projects on the other.[31]

Some general observations can also be made about the strengths and weaknesses of women's groups based on the national context and the individual experience of our five leaders. Whatever the broader environment, the following seem to be the minimum necessary for any level of effectiveness:

1. The groups must reflect the needs and desires of rural women, and these needs and desires are not necessarily self-evident—hence the importance of the patient communication practiced by each of the five leaders.
2. It follows logically that any organization must appeal to the self-interest of its participants. Self-interest is certainly the reason for which indigenous groups in Sub-Saharan Africa have lasted so long, and for which it is more difficult for outsiders to find the right "incentives" for village women there to organize themselves.
3. The organizational effort must have its own legitimacy, especially where there is no indigenous tradition of women's groups. This is especially true when culture and women's productive roles have combined to keep them segregated in the public sphere and

physically isolated in the private sphere (i.e., the household). The Catholic Church provided some legitimacy in Honduras, and the role of government has been critical in Egypt and Bangladesh.

4. Every new endeavor requires that people overcome their suspi- cion of new ideas, new technology, new foods or ways of pre- paring old foods (where improved nutrition is the goal), and new roles. Change does not come easily to most people, and when it demands new resources (such as time) or challenges traditional assumptions about what is appropriate behavior for women and men, resistance is inevitable. As agents of change, the five leaders and their organizational co-workers found culturally acceptable ways of using need and self-interest to overcome barriers to change.

5. The pattern with regard to women organizing alone or with men is less clear. In cultures strongly segregated by gender, such as Bangladesh and Egypt, contact with women exclusively seems necessary to the initiation of improvements in family planning and health, and even in efforts to help women earn cash. Female groupings (i.e., the Corn Mill Societies) also tend to work in the case of organizations designed to address a specific need or task that is performed solely by women, given the gender distinctions in productive activities. When the need for change is defined in more far-reaching terms (such as land reform), however, either integrated or collaborative male-female efforts are called for. Thus FEHMUC in Honduras is affiliated with the National Peasants Fed- eration. Of course, the potential—or "danger"—of men co-opting women's efforts is very real, particularly where a group has undertaken a successful income-generating project. Readers will see the nature of this "danger" in the efforts of Kenyan women to start and control a ferry service from Mombasa.

6. The organization must become self-sustaining; that is, it must be able to survive financially and continue to attract support with- out outside leadership or money. The experience in the five countries seems mixed in this regard; it may simply be too soon to judge the long-term viability of several of the groups discussed in Marion Levy's narrative.

Of the six criteria noted above, the last merits further discussion in the context of the role played by NGOs. As stressed earlier, local groups must appeal to their members' self-interest; in development, their pri- mary utility (in these cases) is to help women get more leverage over scarce resources or to help them create resources. In the past quarter- century, NGOs have come increasingly into prominance precisely because of their grass-roots focus—a focus created at a time when government and public international institutions (such as the UN agencies and the World Bank) were concentrating on macro-level development and large, expensive projects. NGOs obviously couldn't compete in large-scale development activities; what they have attempted, instead, is to act as catalysts for projects that would benefit the poorest of the poor, those people typically bypassed in the development efforts of the 1960s and 1970s. NGOs have become the levers encouraging grass-roots self-help projects because they can be more innovative and flexible than government agencies. Careful readers will note that the NGOs mentioned in this book include those both very well known and very little known to many Americans: Asia Society, Bread for the World, CARE, CARITAS, Centre for Development and Population Activities (CEDPA), International Planned Parenthood Federation, OXFAM, Save the Children Foundation, Trickle-Up, and World Education.

Nongovernmental organizations are particularly important for women; they are often staffed predominantly by women; in development efforts they have been more sensitive to gender issues than have many public agencies (which are staffed predominantly by men); and by focusing on local issues and the poor, they have come to understand the special roles and needs of women. One of the shared characteristics of the women leaders under discussion is the way they have used and (in the most positive sense) been used by NGOs. Aziza Hussein achieved international prominence as president of the International Planned Parenthood Federation. Both Elvina Mutua and Hasina Khan benefited from training courses run by the Centre for Development and Population Activities in Washington, D.C. Aziza, Elvina, Hasina, and Reyna witnessed the financial support provided by NGOs for development efforts in their countries. After one of her "retirements," Elizabeth O'Kelly became general secretary of the Associated Country Women of the World (an umbrella organization of NGOs) and later became a consultant to NGOs working in development.

The first international linkages between private organizations, including women's organizations, were created in the nineteenth century.[32] What is unique about our era is the pivotal role some of these groups have come to play in development around the world and the special meaning they have taken on for women, whether village women or national leaders. The five women in this study are special for many reasons, but one of those reasons is the way in which, as individuals, they symbolize the interrelationships of the world, from village to United Nations, through their lives and their work. Their lives and work, in turn, raise provocative questions about the potential for a truly international feminism.

Conclusion: Toward International Feminism?

Published in 1984 was an anthology of writings from what its editor called the "international women's movement." Some may object to the selection of authors or to the writings themselves, but it is still a remarkable compilation—one, in fact, that would have been surprising, if not unthinkable, twenty years earlier. The anthology, in which seventy countries are represented, was long in the making and, in its very existence, represents the global awareness that has influenced women around the world. As the editor, Robin Morgan, notes in her preface, "in 1968 a consolidated feminist network on the cross-national front did not yet exist. That was to require years of hard work, patience, travel, meetings, and changed sensibilities on the part of all of us."[33]

In the past twenty years, thousands of women have come to think the thoughts that only a handful of women (such as Aziza Hussein and Elizabeth O'Kelly) were thinking in the 1950s. On many questions they do not agree, and on some there is hostile disagreement. This is not surprising. What *is* surprising is the increasing scope of relative agreement, even consensus, that has emerged rather clearly in the lives of the five women discussed in this book. The consensus may seem obvious to many Americans, but it verges on the revolutionary in some settings: (1) Women have a contribution to make, and obligations to fulfill, to their local and national communities; (2) there are important gender differences, but whatever their origin, women as women have unique skills and concerns that must be accommodated in the process of development; (3) the notion of a dichotomy or separation between private and public may have more validity in our ideologies than in reality; (4) differences between women that are based on class and culture are critical, but they do not necessarily represent insuperable barriers to cooperation (all the women portrayed here worked across class and cultural boundaries); and (5) despite these differences, women and men must work toward agreement on ways to remove the vestiges of colonialism, to address inequities between and within nation-states, and to reduce the burdens of domestic civil conflict and international war. Both feminist scholars and political activists in Western countries seem to be listening to the voices of Third World women and contributing to this growing consensus with new energy. Robin Morgan's anthology is just one illustration of this listening and learning process.

In 1984, a group of women met in Bangalore, India, to talk about "Development Alternatives with Women for a New Era" (DAWN). The collaborators in the project cut to the heart of the debate about women and development that had been growing for ten years, arguing that the debate was not increasing women's access to or participation in development activities as they had been fostered by national and international agencies. The development process as it has evolved in most Third World countries, they argued, cannot be considered to have been beneficial or even harmless.

> We see crises of growing impoverishment and inequality, food insecurity and famine, financial and monetary instability, environmental problems and population pressures in Third World countries. Among the reactions to these pressures are increased militarization, domestic repression and foreign aggression. We also see both a growing sense of hopelessness about the world's poor and cutbacks in aid to multilateral agencies by some of the richest, most powerful and most militaristic nations. We argue that human survival is now the world's most pressing problem, that women's contribution as workers and managers of human welfare is central to the ability of households, communities and nations to tackle the crisis of survival, and that the empowerment of women is therefore essential for the emergence of new, creative and cooperative solutions to the crisis.[34]

The DAWN manifesto links the global with the local, focusing on the problems of development from the vantage point of poor women. As suggested in Robin Morgan's *Sisterhood Is Global* and many other writings, it is hard to imagine that DAWN's project could have been conceived two decades earlier.

Anthologies and manifestos are but an initial step toward changing the realities that trap poor women around the world. They cannot and should not paper over the individual and collective struggles that bring women, as well as their menfolk, into conflict with each other. We do not have a *single* international feminism but, rather, *many* women's movements and many feminist ideologies. Moreover, there are numerous questions still to be asked about the meaning or desirability of something called feminism. But despite the questions and the hostilities, feminist concepts seem to have become much more widely accepted than they had been even a decade ago—in part, precisely because Third World women themselves have added the force of their voices to the debate. For many Third World women, the term *feminism* has been closely associated with parochial, radical feminism in Western Europe and North America; that is, Western concepts have seemed unacceptably bound by culture and class, and they have reflected Western assumptions about what was good for the rest of the world. Hence Muslim feminists, for example, have struggled to free themselves not only from Western economic and political influence but also from Western modes of thought, ideologies, and discourse. That struggle has entailed a reexamination of their Islamic traditions, for it is these traditions that provide their identity in the face of the tidal wave of westernization that has swept the world in the nineteenth and twentieth centuries. The process of reexamination, in turn, means asking hard questions about sexual oppression in Muslim societies and about the potential for a redefined Islam in the hopes of providing cultural identity without subordination of women.[35]

The five leaders studied here are not theorists but practical women—at one and the same time, both grass-roots and elite activists. But their lives are both a product and a source of the rethinking about development and the roles of women that is taking place in virtually every society in the world. They might be reluctant to identify themselves either as development experts or as feminists, but each in her own way is both.

NOTES

1. There are relatively few studies of female leaders below the highest level of media prominence. A recent exception, in addition to Levy's work, is Mae Handy Esterline, ed., *They Changed Their Worlds: Nine Women of Asia* (Lanham, Md.: University Press of America, 1987). The women in Esterline's collection have all received the Ramon Magsaysay Award in one of a number of categories (community leadership, international understanding, public service, etc.) The award is named in honor of the Philippine president who was killed in a plane crash in 1957.

2. See the comparison provided by Elise Boulding in Chapter 8 of *The Underside of History* (Boulder, Colo.: Westview Press, 1976). The UNESCO study, *Social Science Research and Women in the Arab World* (Paris: United Nations Educational, Scientific, and Cultural Organization, 1984), contains a number of articles examining the research on women in Arab, predominantly Islamic, societies. Note particularly Amal Rassam's introduction in "Arab Women: The Status of Research in the Social Sciences and the Status of Women" (pp. 1–13) and her "Towards a Theoretical Framework for the Study of Women in the Arab World," in which she focuses on the family/household as a "system of structured cross-sexual relationships underwritten by a specific Arab-Islamic ideology" (p. 127). Nikki Keddie and Lois Beck contrast the status of women in Muslim countries in their introduction to Beck and Keddie, eds., *Women in the Muslim World* (Cambridge: Harvard University Press, 1978), pp. 1–34.

3. Traditionally, the primary role of women in Muslim society has been that of wife and mother, and Islamic laws set the norms for women's rights and duties. As John L. Esposito notes, in *Women in Muslim Family Law* (Syracuse, N.Y.: Syracuse University Press, 1982), there is considerable diversity within Islamic legal traditions. Moreover, as David Waines points out in "Through a Veil Darkly: The Study of Women in Muslim Societies, a Review Article," *Comparative Studies in Society and History*, vol. 24, no. 4 (October 1982), pp. 642–659, the tradition of the Shari'a is so diverse in both legal interpretation and practice

that it can be viewed as either liberal or conservative. See also Elizabeth H. White, "Legal Reform as an Indicator of Women's Status in Muslim Nations," in Beck and Keddie, *Women in the Muslim World*, pp. 52–68.

4. Germaine Tillon, for example, argues that the inferior social position of women in Mediterranean countries has roots that predate either Christianity or Islam. See Tillon, *The Republic of Cousins: Women's Oppression in Mediterranean Society*, translated by Quintin Hoare (London: Al Saqi Books, 1983).

5. See the studies in Hanna Papanek and Gail Minault, eds., *Separate Worlds: Studies of Purdah in South Asia* (Delhi: Chanakya Publications, 1982).

6. White, "Legal Reform," pp. 65–66.

7. Generalization is risky, of course; for example, most women would find *purdah* preferable to prostitution (another typical by-product of urbanization and industrialization). In addition, both the source and nature of urban growth or industrial development are critical in assessing changes in women's status. Urbanization can deprive women of some resources, such as farmland, without providing new productive activities. Historically, this has happened to African women in many areas. See Esther Boserup, *Women's Role in Economic Development* (New York: St. Martin's Press), Chapter 10. Research on Latin America has revealed that the position of women tends to deteriorate with development. Latin American economies are subjected to a type of development that is dependent on external finance capital and advanced technologies. The women there constitute a marginal, unskilled labor force, working at the lowest levels of productivity, pay, and status. See the analyses in June Nash and Helen Safa, eds., *Sex and Class in Latin America* (New York: Praeger, 1976); and Heleieth I. B. Saffioti, *Women in Class Society*, translated by Michael Vale (New York: Monthly Review Press, 1978).

8. Richard F. Nyrop, ed., *Egypt: A Country Study* (Washington, D.C.: American University for the U.S. Army, 1983), p. 76.

9. Mahmuda Islam and Perveen Ahmad, "Bangladesh: Tradition Reinforced," in *Women in the Villages, Men in the Towns* (Paris: United Nations Educational, Scientific, and Cultural Organization, 1984), p. 28.

10. Ibid., p. 30.

11. In their study of the early phase of the Women's Program of the Integrated Rural Development Program of Bangladesh, Tahrunnessa A. Abdullah and Sondra A. Zeidenstein found all the culturally based problems confronted by Hasina Khan, including those of transportation, to be widespread. See *Village Women of Bangladesh: Prospects for Change* (Oxford and New York: Pergamon Press, 1982), especially pp. 135–136.

12. Juan Ricardo Cole, "Feminism, Class, and Islam in Turn-of-the-Century Egypt," *International Journal of Middle East Studies*, vol. 13, no. 4 (November 1981), p. 392. The early feminists were both women and men, Muslim and non-Muslim.

13. Earl L. Sullivan, *Women in Egyptian Public Life* (Syracuse, N.Y.: Syracuse University Press, 1986), p. 22.

14. Sullivan's study of female political and business leaders confirms the importance of class and education as explanations for the emergence of influ-

ential women. See Sullivan, *Women in Egyptian Public Life*, Chapter 6. When Aziza Hussein was maturing in interwar Egypt, Bangladesh was still firmly under the imperial control of British rule in India.

15. See Sullivan, *Women in Egyptian Public Life*, Chapter 2. Dr. Ann Lesch, Universities Field Staff, lecture on "Women in Egypt" (November 15, 1985), Alexandria, Egypt.

16. In 1980, the U.S. Agency for International Development found that between 20 and 50 percent of people working in cities were employed in the "informal sector," often running tiny businesses such as street vending. Women and children form the majority of the people working in this informal sector. See Lee Mullane, "The Urban Poor: Making It on Their Own," *Agenda*, vol. 3 (November 1980), pp. 16–20. See also Lourdes Arizpe, "Women in the Informal Labor Sector: The Case of Mexico City," in Wellesley Editorial Committee, ed., *Women and National Development: The Complexities of Change* (Chicago: University of Chicago Press, 1977), pp. 25–37.

17. See Ann Pescatello, ed. *Female and Male in Latin America* (Pittsburgh: University of Pittsburgh Press, 1973); Audrey Bronstein, *The Triple Struggle: Latin American Peasant Women* (Boston: South End Press, 1983); and Lois Paul, "The Mastery of Work and the Mystery of Sex in a Guatemalan Village," in Michelle Zimbalist Rosaldo and Louise Lamphere, eds., *Woman, Culture, and Society* (Stanford, Calif.: Stanford University Press, 1974).

18. Ruth Leger Sivard, *Women . . . A World Survey* (Washington, D.C.: World Priorities, 1985), p. 28.

19. Barbara Wolfe Jancar, *Women Under Communism* (Baltimore and London: Johns Hopkins University Press, 1978), pp. 113–114.

20. Afaf Lutfi al-Sayyid Marsot, "The Revolutionary Gentlewomen in Egypt," pp. 261–276, and Thomas Philipp, "Feminism and Nationalist Politics in Egypt," pp. 277–294, both in Beck and Keddie, eds., *Women in the Muslim World*.

21. See Jomo Kenyatta, *Harambee! The Prime Minister of Kenya's Speeches, 1963–1964* (Nairobi, London, and New York: Oxford University Press, 1964); and the analysis of *harambee* by Barbara P. Thomas, *Politics, Participation, and Poverty: Development Through Self-Help in Kenya* (Boulder and London: Westview Press, 1985).

22. See the related discussion in Jeanne McCormack, Martin Walsh, and Candace Nelson, *Women's Group Enterprises: A Study of the Structure of Opportunity on the Kenya Coast* (Boston: World Education, Inc., 1986), pp. 10–17, 46–50, and 88–89.

23. Margaret E. Galey, "The Nairobi Conference: The Powerless Majority," *PS*, vol. 29, no. 2 (Spring 1986), pp. 255–257.

24. Kathleen A. Staudt, "Women and Participation," paper presented to the Technical Assistance Bureau/Rural Development, US Agency for International Development (Washington, D.C.: AID, n.d.), p. 37.

25. In particular, see Norman Uphoff and Milton J. Esman, *Local Organization for Rural Development: Analysis of Asian Experience* (Ithaca, N.Y.: Cornell University, Rural Development Committee, 1974); Esman and Uphoff, *Local*

Organization and Rural Development: The State of the Art (Ithaca, N.Y.: Cornell University, Rural Development Committee, 1982); Esman and Uphoff, *Local Organizations: Intermediaries in Rural Development* (Ithaca and London: Cornell University Press, 1984); and Staudt, "Women and Participation."

26. See Staudt, "Women and Participation," p. 37. Kathryn A. March and Rachelle L. Taqqu provide numerous examples of traditional informal associations among women in *Women's Informal Associations in Developing Countries: Catalysts for Change?* (Boulder and London: Westview Press, 1986).

27. Sally W. Yudleman, *Hopeful Openings: A Study of Five Women's Development Organizations in Latin America and the Caribbean* (West Hartford, Conn.: Kumarian Press, 1987), pp. 35–36.

28. See Baick Lee, "Village-Based Family Planning in Korea: The Case of the Mothers' Club," in Richard O. Neihoff, ed., *Non-formal Education and the Rural Poor,* report of a conference and workshop (East Lansing: Michigan State University, College of Education, Program of Studies in Nonformal Education, 1977); pp. 106–109. Esman and Uphoff, *Local Organizations,* pp. 321–323.

29. Esman and Uphoff, *Local Organizations,* p. 187.

30. Esman and Uphoff, *Local Organizations,* pp. 17–18 et passim.

31. March and Taqqu, in *Women's Informal Associations,* Chapters 6 and 7, discuss this linkage role for indigenous informal groups. Externally inspired organizations designed for development are created with this linkage in mind, whereas indigenous traditional organizations may or may not be "convertible."

32. Boulding, *The Underside of History,* pp. 674–683.

33. Robin Morgan, ed., *Sisterhood Is Global* (Garden City, N.Y.: Anchor Press/Doubleday, 1984), p. xiii.

34. DAWN, *Development, Crisis, and Alternative Visions: Third World Women's Perspectives* (New Delhi: Development Alternative with Women for a New Era, 1985). This book has been republished by Monthly Review Press (New York, 1985). The quote here is taken from the introductory summary (p. 1).

35. See Caroline Ramazanoglu, "Gender and Islam—The Politics of Muslim Feminism," *Ethnic and Racial Studies,* vol. 9, no. 2 (April 1986), p. 259.

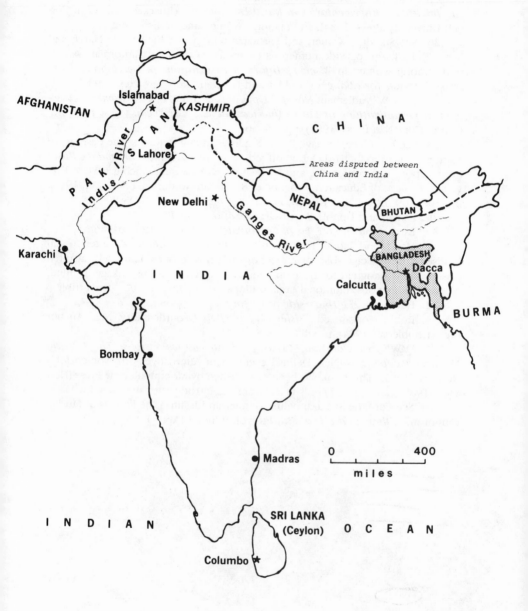

30

HASINA KHAN
Women and Community Development in Bangladesh

Hasina Khan, when she was in school, wanted to be "the first girl in everything." She had the advantage of coming from a family that believed in educating girls. Her mother was highly regarded within the family for her sound judgment and noted for her skill at getting what she wanted. Hasina inherited both of those qualities. A fortunate contact and her own quick intelligence brought her, as a scholarship student, to an outstanding school in Dhaka with a mixed student body of Hindu and Muslim young women. This was her first lesson in tolerance and diversity.

After graduating from Dhaka University, she found a job teaching in a college in the Comilla district of Bangladesh. She avoided an arranged marriage by marrying a man she had met at the university, much to her parents' consternation. When she and her husband left the teaching profession after nine years, they and their two children moved to Dhaka, where Hasina took a job as a trainer for the government's newly organized Rural Women's Project. She found her way into community-development work and became the women's program officer for the Save the Children Federation in Bangladesh. She was the despair of her family as she traveled through the rural villages meeting with groups of women. For a Muslim woman married to a man of conservative family, such traveling about, let alone working outside her home, was considered reprehensible behavior. She was also the butt of the antagonism of many of her male colleagues and of the men of the community because of the women's program she was undertaking. But Hasina prevailed, at considerable personal cost, and in five years had won a substantial victory. Women from dozens of the villages in which she worked had, indeed, joined together in a series of successful educational and economic projects.

Hasina's earliest experiences as a teacher and later as a women's program director persuaded her that a critical starting point in the learning process for women was awareness of how they thought about them-

31

selves, because it underlay any efforts for positive change. Encouragement of such self-awareness had to be given with exquisite care to avoid
the more active forms of male resentment. Her tools were pictures and
games and the techniques of nonformal education, which emboldened
women to describe the conditions of their lives as they had never done
before. Her goal was to ensure that women could express their needs
and that their concerns would be taken into account in the planning of
community-wide development programs.

Hasina posed the critical question: Who decides what constitutes
community improvement? If not the community itself, such improvement becomes imposed. If women do not have a voice in that community, others speak for them. Hasina succeeded most notably in helping
women in Bangladesh find their voices and press for changes in accor-
dance with their best interests.

1

Hasina Khan fulfilled the dire prediction of traditional Bangladeshi society: If a woman is given an education, it will render her unsuitable for
her natural role and make her difficult to control, less compliant, and
more likely to arrange her own marriage. Every aspect of that prediction
proved true for Hasina, although she could not have foreseen that outcome when she joyfully immersed herself in her early schooling.

She was born in Brahmanbaria in 1947, in what was then East Bengal. For India it was a time of partition, when Bengal and its Muslim
majority were severed from predominantly Hindu India. By 1948, the
new state was called Pakistan, divided into East and West Pakistan, and
separated by 1,000 miles of Indian subcontinent. Hasina's family escaped
the terrors of partition, and she remembers hearing little about that traumatic period as a child.

Life for Hasina revolved around the *bari*, or family compound,
where the Wahed family had lived for generations. Recollecting her early
years, Hasina says, "Let me describe my paternal grandmother. I remember her proudly telling us how she brought up her three sons and a
daughter as a widow. She was seventeen when her husband died—only
seven and a half when she was married." Hasina guesses that her grandmother had her first child when she was twelve. Her second son—Hasina's father, Quazi Abdul Wahed—left school when he was twelve to
become apprenticed to a tailor.

Hasina's mother, Halima Karim, came from a more prominent family
than that of her husband; her father held the prestigious post of police
inspector.

My grandfather was always honored and taken care of as the king of the family. And the best part of it was that his name was Badshah, which means emperor! And his personality was also like that. My grandmother was always careful about his likes and dislikes. I remember how she used to help him put on his uniform, belt, and shoes before he went to the office. In the evening she would massage his limbs with mustard oil. She'd sleep only after her husband fell asleep. She never expressed her emotions or any discomfort or sickness. Maybe she thought that, being a woman, she shouldn't, that it would be a discredit to her.

Hasina's grandmother had been married when she was nine years old, just as her new husband was entering college. "At night she used to sleep with her mother-in-law. She had to wait until her pre-teens before she could live with her husband. Once my grandmother told me that they had to find chances to stare at each other. Thus, they fell in love after marriage."

Hasina's mother, who also married before puberty, was the first of eight children, born when the police inspector was assigned to the city of Chittagong in southeast Bangladesh. The women of the family were not required to remain in the family enclave or be completely veiled in public, which are the traditional observances of a strict *purdah* (a system for the seclusion of women). "My mother had a very good childhood. Her father's job was such that, due to a lot of transfers, she had the opportunity to see many districts of the country and could learn different dialects and the cultures of different regions. After completing sixth grade, she had to stay at home to learn the art of housework." Hasina believes that the experiences of travel gave her mother a broader perspective than that of many women of her age and status. She was married when she was twelve to Abdul Wahed. Hasina describes both families as members of the village elite—not especially well-to-do but of high reputation.

Hasina was the first of ten children (two died in infancy) born to Halima and Abdul Wahed. She speaks of her mother as a strong woman of sound judgment, respected and listened to within the family. "My father was always ready to accept the ideas and plans of my mother. He felt that my mother always made wise decisions." Hasina was close to her mother and, as the firstborn, "was very important to her. My mother tried her best to bring me up differently than my traditionally brought up cousin-sisters. She didn't want me to lead the same life as them, or even herself." Both her mother and father had high goals for their children and apparently recognized the unusual promise of their intelligent and energetic eldest daughter. But there were difficulties in arranging for her education. "My mother was very interested to send me to school, but a lot of strong objections were raised by my uncles."

One of Hasina's maternal uncles, however, had a rich Hindu friend, R. P. Shaha, well known for his generous philanthropy and for the school he had founded to encourage education for girls. Bharateshwari School for girls in Tangail was famous in Bangladesh and the "best boarding school of that time," says Hasina. Her mother was convinced that this was the place for Hasina. Her father's family, however, feared the Hindu and foreign influences that pervaded the school. After protracted debate (during which Hasina missed the first term), "my mother somehow convinced my father to sell a part of his land and then buy land in the city [Dhaka, the capital] so that I could go to school. That's how I was saved!" The Waheds moved to Dhaka, where Hasina's father started a new cosmetics business. At the age of six and a half, Hasina was enrolled in kindergarten. From class five through high school, the bright, ambitious Hasina received a full scholarship, as did other promising students who were the fortunate recipients of Mr. Shaha's philanthropy.

Hasina excelled at the Bharateshwari school and credits it for whatever success she feels she has achieved.

> It has ornamented my whole life. This school is very different compared to other schools in our country. Children of different religions and castes and from different backgrounds live together. This is the only place where students don't have a chance to think of caste and creed. The founder of this school was a great social worker, and he had a special concern for the education of women.

Mr. Shaha and his daughter, Mrs. Poti (her favorite teacher), took a special interest in her, Hasina believes.

Thinking about her years at Bharateshwari, Hasina says she had

> a peculiar interest . . . at least it may seem peculiar. I was always ambitious. I always wanted to be the first girl in everything! I used to be the vice-captain in school and when I was in the tenth grade, I became the school prefect. And when I was in the twelfth grade, I was selected captain of the school. When I graduated in 1965, I won one of the school's highest prizes. Not only that, I was the physical-education instructress, and I tried my best to participate in every activity like drama, debate, and essay competitions.

The school was famous for teaching classical Hindu dance, for which Hasina discovered she had talent. She became well known as one of the stars of the school's dance dramas, an unusual accomplishment for a young Muslim woman. She apparently was exuberant and headstrong, always pushing the limits: "I was considered witty and naughty in my school."

Hasina lived at the school eleven months out of each year, spending one month at home. "My parents came only once a year to meet me. They kept in touch through letters. My parents were always in touch." She believes, however, that being away from home so much and mixing with girls of different castes and religions caused her to question the more traditional values of family and friends. It also gave her a strong sense of self-reliance and independence, setting her apart from many of her peers.

Upon Hasina's graduation from Bharateshwari, her parents determined that her education was complete and that the time had come for her to marry. Hasina, however, hoped to become a teacher, one of the few options open to her as a woman. Extensive discussions about her future took place between her family and Mr. Shaha, the founder of the school. "Mr. Shaha used to tell my parents that although they had given birth to me, he had nurtured me and brought me up, so they should not think about my marriage until I had completed my university education." The Waheds finally dropped their opposition and agreed to allow Hasina to attend the university, encouraged no doubt by Mr. Shaha's offer to pay her tuition. Hasina entered Dhaka University in 1965, when she was eighteen.

2

Hasina is petite, with shining eyes and great vivacity. At college, she attracted friends easily. Female students generally kept aloof from men; they had separate reading rooms and lounges, but they did share some classes. Hasina, like many other young women, had a few male acquaintances. During her freshman year, she met Abdul Halim Khan, who was six years older than she and in his final year at the university. He showed particular interest in her over the next several years, and Hasina seemed to enjoy his attentions.

When Halim proposed, they consulted their families. According to friends, the members of Halim Khan's family agreed that Hasina had come from an educated family that was well regarded in its own town and that she was quite beautiful. However, the Khans were reported to be angry that they had not had an opportunity to arrange a marriage for Halim themselves, and, even more disappointing, that Hasina did not have a dowry. She maintains that her mother and father spent all their money on their children's education. The lack of a dowry was considered a major drawback, and Hasina says she is still reminded of it by Halim's family.

Hasina acknowledges that her family was opposed to the union, believing that she might have married more advantageously. They also questioned the lack of education of Halim's family and their rather narrow conservatism. But Hasina's parents could not persuade Hasina to change her mind, try as they might, and she and Halim were married in 1968. Hasina was twenty-one years old and still attending the University of Dhaka, where she was completing her Bachelor's degree and about to start on a Master's.

After their marriage, they lived with Halim's family, as was expected of them. Hasina admits that she had had no experience of life in a traditional family because both her mother and her father had held advanced views about the education and social role of girls. She was horrified to discover that she was expected by her new family to wear a *burqah*.

> And everywhere we went I had to wear it! One day my father-in-law was very sick and I took great care of him. During this period, while I looked after him, he became very close to me and he asked, "Do you like our place?" I said I liked everything except wearing a *burqah*, which made me sick! And he just smiled and didn't say anything.

Eventually, Hasina confides, she and her father-in-law reached an agreement. She would wear a *burqah* when she left the Khan house to placate her mother-in-law, but when she arrived at the university she would remove it.

As Hasina came to realize, far more was at stake than wearing a *burqah* or being chaperoned in public. Her whole style of life was at issue. She retells, with anguish, some of the steps taken by her in-laws.

> Something I want to tell you. I had an album which had all the photographs of my growing-up days, pictures of me as the physical-training instructress at school, wearing P. T. clothes, and another one of me dancing in a dance drama. They were nice pictures and I was proud to show them to my in-laws because my family was always proud of me and my activities. The day I showed my in-laws the album, I found out that instead of being proud, they were shocked! Why? Because I had danced like a dancing girl. My husband took the album and all the pictures. I can't forget that. Still now I remember that, because after the Liberation War many of the negatives were lost and now I cannot show them to my daughters!

In 1969, Hasina received a Master's of Arts degree from Dhaka University with honors in English. Halim, who had received an M.A. in philosophy in 1968, had accepted a job as lecturer at the coeducational Comilla College and Hasina had followed. English teachers were in great demand at Comilla. "Educated ladies didn't want to teach there as the place was far from urban facilities—no electricity, no gas, no water supply, no clubs, and no cinemas to enjoy. But we—my husband and I—were delighted to go there for I wanted to free myself from the stern grip of my traditional in-laws!" Hasina was greatly relieved not to be asked to wear a *burqah* at the school. The Khans did not approve of Hasina's teaching job; they considered it a disgrace that she would work. Hasina's family, on the other hand, was proud of her new post. Hasina's mother said to her about the job at the Comilla College, "You will get two things. One, you will be free of your in-laws; two, you will make my name shine with my in-laws. They will admit and agree that I did the right thing in educating you!"

Hasina is a spirited and warm woman who develops a quick rapport with the people she meets. Perhaps because of these qualities, she was asked by the principal if she would visit local families and try to overcome their resistance to sending their daughters to a coed school. The college did not have enough female students, and Hasina must have seemed a likely recruiter. Halim was not happy about the prospect of her traveling around the neighboring villages, but Hasina was eager to try her skills at persuasion and welcomed an opportunity to visit the countryside. Although she did not travel alone (other school staff members accompanied her), such behavior departed from strict convention. Hasina and Halim found working at Comilla College sufficiently satisfactory that they remained there for almost nine years, during which time Hasina believes she learned to be a skillful, sympathetic teacher.

3

While Hasina and Halim were teaching in Comilla, the East Pakistan Liberation War was sweeping over the country in waves of extraordinary violence and cruelty. After years of agitation and protest, East Pakistan was struggling to separate itself from the more powerful West Pakistan, where the seat of government was situated. The East Pakistanis, by far the poorer of the two, felt that West Pakistan had preserved for itself the greater share of governmental power and an unconscionably larger portion of the nation's scarce financial resources. East Pakistan was taxed highly on its limited income and received few governmental services or amenities in return for its disproportionate contribution. The West Pakistanis had fought off the independence move for years but could no longer contain the rebellion. Riots took place involving thousands of East Pakistanis in 1968 and again in 1969, and were contained only by strong military intervention from West Pakistan. When free elections were finally held in 1970 to elect a joint federal parliament for both portions of the country, the Aswami League of East Pakistan won the largest number of seats. West Pakistan could not tolerate such a situation and refused to abide by the results of the election. Rebellion in East Pakistan and repression from the west followed quickly.

In the Comilla district, where Hasina and Halim were living, a Pakistani brigade killed all the local Bengali soldiers and as many Hindus as it could find. Similar scenes were reenacted in other parts of the country as rage grew among the Bengalis. By 1970, East Pakistan had enlisted the help of India and full-scale war had erupted; West Pakistan troops poured into the country.

Dhaka felt the greatest brunt of the war, and the city was in turmoil. Most people who were able to had fled to the countryside during the worst of the upheaval. Hasina's parents, brothers, and sisters came to Comilla to join Hasina and Halim. Soon, however, the Pakistani army overran Comilla, too, and seized the school as a barracks. This time, Hasina and Halim joined the family in its flight to a village in the interior, where an uncle still lived in a family home. "Money and ornaments were in my father's hands," Hasina recalls. "I carried all the certificates. My brothers carried the bedding and blankets. . . . My uncle, however, was threatened to see us and was unwilling to allow us to stay. But we did not make him angry. We had money with us and bought bamboo, fencing, nails, etc., and the villagers helped us to construct a house within a week."

The family remained in the village for eleven months. As Hasina's father did not want his children to be idle, he provided the older boys with funds to start small businesses: The smaller children studied, whereas the girls did the cooking and sewing, and learned crafts from village women. They lived with the sound of bombs and bullets nearby, but the village was not attacked. Hasina heard regularly about the arrests or deaths of young men from the village, but she did not know until afterward the full extent of the war's ravages. A daily horror to Hasina was the visible suffering and even death of the poor and the fleeing. "Each day I could not finish my meal because the knocks of the beggars would begin on our door." She watched with grief as a young boy of five or six ate dust and mud from the street. When Hasina gave him some food, he mixed it with dirt to make it go further. It was a traumatic period for her that brought her face to face with extreme suffering and heightened her natural empathy and altruism.

Dhaka fell to the Indian and East Pakistani forces on December 16, 1971, and the new nation of Bangladesh came into being. It had been almost completely devastated by the civil war. Many civilians had been killed or wounded and displaced from their homes and land. It was variously estimated that 1 to 3 million Bangladeshis were killed by Pakistani troops and their agents during the strife. Ten million had crossed the border to India as refugees, many of them educated and skilled, leaving a crippling shortage of trained people in government service and business. Road and rail transport was severely disrupted, creating serious barriers to food distribution. Most terrifying, people were armed and the government had no control over them. The violence continued.[1] Bangladesh was in turmoil.

The suffering that resulted from the war took its cruelest form for some Bangladeshi women. The stories of atrocities during the fighting abound, but perhaps the most devastating concerned the widespread rape of Bengali women—the ultimate violation in Muslim society. According to one observer, "A significant proportion of the unknown number of girls and women raped by Pakistani soldiers during the 9 months of army terror and 3 weeks of war have not been accepted back by their families because of the shame their presence would bring."[2] The occurrence of this outrage could not be documented nationally, but every social-welfare agency was besieged by a stream of women, many with children, who, having been turned out of their homes, begged for help. The presence of so many homeless women caused a major crisis of policy in the government.

> While the plight of women is all too obvious in the stream of unattached mothers and children who pour into the towns to beg; in the growth of prostitution; in the desperation with which rural women have left the seclusion of their homes to seek work in road construction, in the construction of urban housing, in factory employment; official attitudes are still governed by the notion that all women are necessarily attached to men and that their needs are taken care of through their links with their husbands, fathers and brothers.[3]

The international-aid community responded actively to the crisis caused by the Independence War, and the plight of the abandoned women touched a new chord. There was an outpouring of funds to agencies such as the Bangladesh Women's Rehabilitation and Welfare Foundation, which provided immediate care for the most destitute of the women. The U.S. government supplied surplus food to those most in need in exchange for their labor through its Food for Work program, which was implemented by UNICEF and the Bangladesh government. International medical groups made abortion services available to women seeking an end to pregnancies that had resulted from rape. Other agencies, with substantial financial support from the international community, provided shelter and income-producing opportunities for thousands more.

When the monsoon of 1974 led to a severe countrywide famine, almost everyone in Bangladesh was affected. It brought even more women into the workforce, especially through Food for Work programs, providing thousands of women their first opportunity to work outside their homes. Women were leaving their family enclaves in unprecedented numbers to earn money, but many were reported scarcely able to afford clothing that would properly cover them. It was a time of radical uprooting, continuing the dislocations caused by the war and changing the relationships of women to their families.

4

When the war was over in 1971, Halim and Hasina returned to Comilla. In 1974, Halim became vice-principal of the college, and their daughter Rumana was born. Hasina continued her teaching after the birth and was in charge of the school's extracurricular activities. At the end of 1977, Hasina says, "suddenly my husband wanted to leave that place and come to Dhaka and so, according to his decision, I too came to Dhaka." By that time, the country had settled into a more stable political condition under General Ziaur Rahman, then president.

Dhaka was a center for massive foreign-aid programs. Although the economic situation had improved perceptibly, Bangladesh continued to be one of the world's poorest countries. It is the most densely populated country in the world, almost overwhelmed by its staggering population growth. The number of Bangladeshis grew from 50.8 million in 1961 to an estimated 107.1 million in 1987.[4] The low-lying delta regions are regularly flooded, causing major loss of life and crop damage. The landless poor constitute as much as 48 percent of the population, and the country is unable to feed itself.

Dhaka had attracted a rapidly increasing cadre of development workers as dozens of government and nongovernmental organizations (NGOs) set up offices in Dhaka. In addition to the UN agencies— UNICEF, the UN Development Program, FAO, and the UN Fund for Population Activities, governments and NGOs had responded to the crisis in Bangladesh with high levels of aid. In the forefront of the NGOs were CARE, the Red Cross, the church agencies, the population and family-planning groups, the Ford and Rockefeller Foundations, and small agencies such as the Save the Children Federation and OXFAM. It was the place to be for educated Bangladeshis looking for new ventures.

Whether they intended this effect or not, outside agencies were bringing with them foreign values and standards. The idea of proposing that women work together in organized projects away from home—in either agriculture or road construction—was itself revolutionary. The agencies were able to take approaches to solving problems that the government could never have initiated, although the government, of course, had to give its approval for any NGO program.

5

On their return to Dhaka, Halim and Hasina lived in their own house but did not escape the critical surveillance of Halim's family. "My family was run under the remote control of my in-laws, to whom my husband was very obedient and humble," Hasina says. They now had a second daughter, Selina, born in early 1978. Halim started a business, but it was unsuccessful; Hasina hints that he lost a significant proportion of the money they did have in the venture. As he could not find other employment, Hasina decided to hire a maid to look after Selina (still an infant) and Rumana (then four years old) and look for a job.

At that time there were not many jobs that an educated woman would be considered for or allowed to accept. There were almost no women in sales work and few in clerical or office positions because of the possibility of contact with men. Even primary-school teaching was

Hasina Khan at the training program of the Centre for Development and Population Activities, Washington, D.C., 1979

dominated by men. Hasina found her way to the newly formed Bangladesh National Women's Organization, which had been advertising for trainers for a proposed Women's Development Academy.

> I had originally applied for the job of trainer but then, after my interview, Dr. Amina Rahman [ex-minister of women's affairs in Bangladesh] told me to apply for the post of project director for Rural Women's Projects. I was very reluctant as I wasn't experienced in such a job, but she was insistent, pointing out my village experience and my understanding of village women's problems. So I applied and I got the job.

Hasina was a rare find for such a job among educated Bangladeshi women. She had traveled through the villages in the Comilla district when she was recruiting female students, and she was willing to do so again. She also had an easy rapport with rural women. A co-worker noted that she combined the more liberal thinking of the Dhaka woman with a true understanding of the basic values of a village girl.

The Rural Women's Project received project money from an American agency, Family Planning International Assistance, and had the strong support of the government. Its goal was twofold: to encourage family planning in order to control population growth, and to improve women's health. The health of girls and women was particularly precarious in Bangladesh because boys, strongly favored at birth, were given extra food and care. Serious malnutrition in the country was reported in 1982 to be four or five times more common among girls than boys, and yet there were fifty times more boys than girls treated in hospitals for the condition.[5] As a result of such discriminatory care, Bangladesh is one of the few countries in the world in which the infant mortality rate for girls is higher than that for boys. Compounding their health problems, girls are married in their early teens and are expected to have as many children as possible. Such early and frequent pregnancies lead to a range of physical difficulties and contribute to the country's high maternal mortality rate.[6]

The Rural Women's Project was designed to reach down into the villages and persuade women to accept family planning. Thousands of women were given training and brought into the rural areas as family-planning motivators, while a complementary effort was undertaken to provide rural women with income-producing skills to lessen their dependency on children as a means of support. To prepare her for the job as project director, Hasina was sent to the Centre for Development and Population Activities in Washington, D.C., where women leaders from developing countries were being trained.

She had never been out of Bangladesh before, and there were serious conflicts at home about the propriety of her traveling abroad without her husband. She was willing to risk family disapproval, however, for what she saw as a unique opportunity. She was never sorry to have made the trip and says she was transformed by the experience. "It was a golden chance to exchange ideas with women of different countries who were also involved in women's development," said Hasina. "That training equipped me with lots of ideas on program planning. It also fixed in my mind that as a project director, I should meet directly with women to know their problems and that all ideas should come from the village—from the grass-roots level. It also trained me to 'start small and think big.' " This participatory approach appealed to Hasina. The idea that people should assess and articulate their own needs was to become the core of Hasina's philosophy.

Her eyes were opened to the special difficulties to which women were subject in all societies, and she began to see far more clearly the constraints that women faced within the cultural context of Bangladesh. In her own life, she had resented the restrictions and hardships she faced as a woman. When she entered the Bharateshwari School, she had her first glimpse of a more diverse and questioning society than her village life had led her to expect. The war had provided its own terrible lessons, deepening her awareness of the misery of its victims. Her exposure at the Centre to dozens of other Third World women—women who were leaders themselves and shared her concerns—gave her a new sense of community and commitment. She discovered, too, that there were other women in Bangladesh who were thinking along the same lines, women with whom she might work. She was energized by the experience and through the training found important reinforcement for her ideas and for herself personally. She was seen by her colleagues as a "woman with a vision to do something innovative, something different."

When Hasina returned to Bangladesh, she approached her field-work as a project director with new fire and heightened sensitivity. Although she had lived in villages and observed the never-ending tasks of a woman's daily life, she was startled at what she discovered now, listening with a newly attuned ear.

Typical of the stories that she and the field-workers heard was this one, related by a fourteen-year-old girl:

The whole day passes in work. In the morning I get up from bed, do the bed, sweep the rooms, house, verandah. After washing the dishes I have to make bread and serve food to all. I collect fruits from the garden for the market. Then I have to cook at noon for 10 to 12 people. After cooking I take my bath. Then I feed everyone. After everyone, I eat. Sometimes there's no curry left for me. Then I wash the dishes, sweep the kitchen and plaster it with mud. Then I sweep the house in the afternoon again. I light the evening lights. Sometimes I bring in the cows and goats. Otherwise my mother-in-law does it. Then I go to the kitchen to cook dinner. After cooking I feed everyone. Then I sit with my mother-in-law to eat. After I eat, I put the pots and dishes in the big room and then go to bed. . . . I have to supervise when the crops from the field are stored. . . . My husband does everything according to his parents' wishes and I have to obey his words. . . .

My parents married me young. They never thought about education. They were relieved to marry me. . . . If I don't obey my husband or father-in-law or mother-in-law, they will give a divorce without any further question. They threaten to send me to my father's place. And if I go to my father's place, then he will give me in marriage again. They won't let me stay there forever. So I have to listen to whatever they say. We don't have any way of earning our own income but are totally dependent upon men so we have to stay as simple as possible.[7]

The young woman had been married at ten and was now pregnant at fourteen. She was relieved to have a new, younger sister-in-law in the family who could share some of the work.

Hasina observed the same pattern over and over again. It was actually not so different from that of her grandmothers, although they had apparently been better off than many of the women with whom she spoke. On the other hand, one of Hasina's aunts, having returned home as a widow, was forced to marry against her will. The pattern was in sharp contrast to her own unusually independent life.

After her training at the Centre, Hasina was more troubled than ever by the hierarchical style of her superiors. They believed in traditional social-welfare programs in which they would make the decisions about what should be done for their beneficiaries. The latter did not participate in those decisions—a situation Hasina found unbearable. "I couldn't do anything for the rural women because ideas didn't come from them but from the sophisticated *begums* [high-ranking Muslim women] and I was there only to do their bidding. They had no regard for the ideas and thoughts of the rural women." In her view, the *begums*, as she called the elite women for whom she worked, knew almost nothing of the rural life of their own country. When Hasina did go to the villages with them, she complained that they never went to anyone's home but instead sat in the community center and met with those women who were willing to come there to speak with them. "There was no chance of seeing the real village women for whom we were working." She believed there was a significant discrepancy between what the *begums* thought they knew and what women's lives were really like. In frustration, Hasina resigned at the end of 1978, barely a year after she had joined the project.

6

Hasina heard about an opening for a women's program officer with the Save the Children Federation, an international voluntary child-assistance and community-development agency with headquarters in the United States. With a grant from the U.S. Agency for International Development and with its own private funds, the agency had initiated its program in Bangladesh by providing aid to the victims of the cyclone of 1970 and then to those who suffered the devastation of the Liberation War in 1972. In contrast to many of the international agencies that provided food and medical help, Save the Children quickly redirected its efforts to village-development programs. Its goal was to upgrade community life—particularly the lives of children—through community organizing, training, and project funding. Strongly oriented toward participatory development, it introduced a program of balanced economic and social development that grew out of the needs expressed by the community.

The agency had begun a concerted effort to upgrade the condition of the women in its programs and was looking for that unique Bangladeshi woman who was a natural leader, had a sufficiently strong character to withstand the inevitable resistance she would face, and was allowed by her family to travel. It found that rare combination of attributes in Hasina. Indeed, Hasina had long maneuvered to circumvent the cultural restrictions placed on her as a woman and had the courage to take on jobs and activities that were often controversial. She applied for the job and was hired by Save the Children in January 1979 as its first women's program officer in Bangladesh.

The most challenging aspect of the agency's criteria for community organization was that all members of a community—including the women, the landless, and the poor—be represented in the power structure and be part of the program. Redistribution of power is always controversial, but in a highly stratified and male-dominated society, any attempt to expand that power to include women runs against the most deeply held values. The agency proposed to each community that there be a subcommittee of women under the supervision of the all-male Village Development Committee. In that way, women would be assured of at least indirect representation and their groups could become the focal point for learning about health and nutrition. This approach was buttressed by the government's active promotion of programs and training for women. If villagers wanted the help of Save the Children, they had to accept the women's subcommittees—and so they did. When Hasina was appointed to the newly created post of women's program officer in 1979, the agency had had seven years' experience in community development in Bangladesh and believed that villagers were ready to take the next steps toward including women in development projects.

At that time, Save the Children was working in twenty-seven villages within four regions of Bangladesh. As part of its early program, the agency had hired men and women to work as family-planning motivators, sharing the government's concern that rapid population growth would undermine development efforts. The first women hired to go from house to house to speak for family planning had to be uncommonly courageous, for such a course had not been tried before. Before the war and the famine of 1974, women did not customarily leave their household compounds. They could not be sure how the villagers would react to them, and they risked being ostracized—a terrible and sometimes lifelong catastrophe, for such ostracization could mean being shut out of village life and even employment. These early women workers were often widows who, in Bangladesh society, were considered to be without status and thus were freer to walk around the village for they had little to lose. They were desperate enough for the small income they received to risk the social stigma. By the time Hasina joined the agency, the women family-planning motivators had established a solid reputation for performing their jobs well and for encouraging a high percentage of contraceptive use among the village women.

Hasina's first assignment was to learn about the villages involved in the Save the Children program. Following not only the participatory development theory she had learned during her training at the Centre for Population and Development Activities but her own instincts as well, she spent many hours encouraging the village women to talk about their lives. In hearing the repeated details of the poorest women's lives, she learned of a level of despair that she had previously only guessed at. "You do not have to stay in a village very long to know what real pain is," she commented.

A village woman from the very beginning of her life is neglected. When a child is born, people ask whether it is a boy or girl. If the midwife replies "girl," suddenly all the faces become pale and the *azan* [prayer of blessing] is not said. . . . The *azan* is recited only when a boy is born because it is through boys that honor comes to a family. A girl grows up with dreams and hopes. She may go to school and be a bright student. However, as soon as she reaches the age of eleven or so, she is prevented from going on to further study by her family and society. She might have been a better student than her brother, but it was useless for her. She must now remain inside the house to assist her mother and to receive training to become a housewife. Her brother is the future father and head of the house. So he receives special care in the form of food and education.

The time comes, at about twelve years old, when she will be married, and she enters another world. She is now a woman and living a life like a caged bird, imprisoned in her husband's house and strictly ruled by her in-laws. She is forbidden to go anywhere outside, except to haul water from the pond with her face covered. As the new daughter-in-law she assumes a large part of the household chores and also contributes to her husband's professional activities such as rice processing, weaving, pottery, and drying fish. She is the last to eat and [eats] only what remains after everyone else has finished. Often she keeps several diseases within her because she may not consult a male doctor.

Not only her new family, but a stern society is there to frown at her. She is under constant threat of being cast out from society if her conduct is not the traditional model. On top of all this she has to follow the moral advice that "heaven lies under the feet of her husband." Often she is victimized because she is not aware of her legal rights. In a word, for rural women, surviving is the challenge.

What the neighbors might say about a family, especially about the girls and women, was of the greatest importance to villagers—for a family's status had to be carefully guarded. Hasina confronted this conviction frequently as she tried to persuade village women to participate in special programs. What would people think? As women could only do what the men in the family allowed, the men would have to be persuaded that such activities would not discredit the family. Hasina would not permit herself to be discouraged by the suspicion she encountered in those early visits. A colleague reported on one such encounter:

When we reached Muslendapur there was already a large gathering of men. Hasina and I, however, were led to a schoolroom where we found a small group of sad-looking and nervous women waiting. We spent maybe fifteen minutes talking to them and discovered that they were VDC [Village Development Committee] subcommittee women members, a literacy teacher, and the family-planning and nutrition workers. I will never forget that occasion and the bitterness of those women. They spoke about the humiliations related to their work, of village politics, and [of] Hindu/Muslim factions. Then the old family-planning worker said, "We are not Hindu or Muslim—*we are women*." . . . They felt equally downtrodden and powerless. Hasina's presence and her position as a women's program officer was like an infusion of hope. They all began talking, and Hasina knew how to listen. "Yes," they said, "when someone comes from Dhaka, they parade us out and make us sit on a bench; but after the visitors go, we are sent back to our houses and nobody thinks about us."

That discussion made an indelible impression on Hasina's mind. One of the male community leaders informed Hasina and her colleagues that the last time a delegation of women had come to the village, "we had floods and a plague of frogs. We don't want to suffer more by the arrival of women and women's development in our village." Hasina regularly went to see that man on subsequent visits to Muslendapur. "She wanted to win him over, knowing that the blessing of this scowling, disapproving village leader was vital for the women's program. She succeeded."[8]

Hasina was assisted in her work by four women called social-development coordinators, hired by Save the Children to implement the women's programs in the four major project areas. They traveled with Hasina on her visits to the villages in their regions, and they all found the job both emotionally and physically draining. In spite of Hasina's intermittent successes, she realized that introducing a women's program to suspicious villagers and agency field staff members was more of a hurdle than she had anticipated. Promoting a new role for women, even though it had been officially sanctioned, was disrupting. Her workers reported that when they made their house-to-house visits in the villages, some women shouted insults at them, said they were shameless, and refused to talk to them.

Hasina herself reacted strongly to her travails. "I had to endure a lot of mental torture to win the confidence of men. I had to bear and tolerate scandals and physical torture. The physical torture that I faced covering all the villages on foot cannot be expressed in words!" At that time roads were fit only for motorbikes. As women were prevented by custom from riding bicycles or motorbikes—and as there was no other transport—they had to walk. When rickshaws drawn by bicycles appeared in the countryside in the early 1980s, Hasina rejoiced because women were allowed to ride in them. "My social-development coordinators and I had to walk from one village to another. Now, with the rickshaw, our communication with the villages has improved."

Almost no women's societies of any kind existed in the villages of Bangladesh, due primarily to the seclusion of women. Because women worked in their own households and rarely ventured outside, Hasina and her staff had to create the base from which to construct a program. They had to start by visiting individual households and meeting with the women of each family. Any long-range plan for a women's program would demand even more efficient efforts and the synergism of groups.

7

In her trips through the villages, Hasina encouraged the women to talk about their lives. As their stories unfolded, an underlying sense of worthlessness was expressed again and again. A woman might have value as a thing, but not as a person. Some of the women confided to Hasina that what they wanted most was to be called by their own names: They had always been Ahmed's daughter, or Halim's wife, or Yousuf's mother. If a woman was called by her own name, she could think of herself as a separate person with the right to be respected. Nor had women any hope for changing their situation—a fact that reflected in part, the society's sense of fatalism. It was difficult to overcome their inertia, their lack of mobility, and the absence of free time. Hasina was able to arrange small gatherings of women, to which she would bring drawings of women and children from similar villages. She encouraged the women to make up stories of what those other lives might be like. Soon, women were describing their own lives, their own needs. They realized that they might be able to grow more food and store it for seasons of scarcity; they recognized their need for basic health care; they wanted education for their children, many of whom were school drop-outs by the age of seven; they had to find a way to earn money. Hasina began to put together a list of their most compelling needs.

With a well-mapped agency strategy and the agency's full support, Hasina developed a plan for a women's program. As such a program could be only as good as its reception in the villages, she wisely scheduled an initial meeting with the men of one village. She started by giving them a draft of the plan, which she reported, "they read . . . minutely and carefully, with the help of dictionaries; but they did not want to sit and talk about it. They felt threatened and thought that all their power and authority would be snatched away by women." But her most dangerous opposition came from some of the male Save the Children program staff. Hasina was stung by their sabotage.

> I should be frank to say the truth—these men, with the help of the field coordinators, created a kind of fire which spread to the village men also. They lit fires here and there, by which village men were made to believe that this women's program was "separate" from the major interest of the Save the Children program and that village women were being manipulated to go against society and religion. They were trying to tell them that all these activities for women's development were actually for women's liberation. The men were angry.

At the same time, in almost all the villages, women themselves had overcome their initial wariness and wanted to learn how the program could benefit them. Hasina called a meeting in the Mirzapur area to discuss the representation of women on a primary-health committee. "All of the women of the area, about 300, gathered in the community center to discuss this issue." The issue was critical. In the absence of female health workers, women could not receive the care they needed because they were not allowed to consult male doctors. During the meeting,

Hasina noted that the village men were standing outside the community center, listening. At a second meeting, several hundred women again appeared. The report back at headquarters was that the size of the first meeting was a tale made up by the women and that the second meeting was a fiction. But in the village itself, the meeting was taken very seriously by men and women alike. The men were astonished and not a little alarmed to see the number of women who had congregated to press for inclusion in the health program. The women realized how keenly they felt about health care and how dramatically they had made that point by gathering together.

The challenge to Hasina and her field-workers was to demonstrate to the communities the effectiveness of their program. The lack of support from most of their male colleagues only stiffened their resistance. Some of the women workers were not given access to simple supplies in the field offices. Even their requests for reimbursement for expenses were ridiculed: One worker slept on the floor of the local community center because a bed had not been ordered for her. On several occasions, Village Development Committees were known to deliberately lock the community building just before a scheduled women's meeting.

Hasina had to work closely with each of her staff members to buoy up their flagging spirits and reinforce their determination to go on. Save the Children's country director tried to ease the conflict by bringing together the entire field staff, all of whom were Bangladeshi, for several open discussions about the women's program. Finally, he made it unmistakably clear that the women's program was an essential element in community development and that it would increasingly receive the resources and staff necessary to make it work. The recalcitrant male staff members would, with time, learn to adapt. Those who objected most vigorously left the agency.

The disputes with the Save the Children male staff subsided as Hasina's success with the program grew, but they never disappeared. Hasina was furious over the disruptions they caused and threatened to leave. When the women's program was made a separate entity by the director in June 1980 (thereby allowing its funding to go directly to the women's groups rather than through the male Village Development Committees and the male field directors—a great victory for Hasina), there was near mutiny among the male staff members. But the program was too well-entrenched to suffer more than a temporary setback. Its value had been amply demonstrated to the village leaders, to the staff, and to the women themselves.

Hasina and her staff were deeply moved by the response of the women to any promise of help. They started their work within a small cluster of related households by demonstrating basic health and nutri-

*Women discussing pictures of village life with a Save the Children field-worker,
Bangladesh, March 1984 (photographer: Mike Novell)*

tion skills, child care, food processing—whatever the women themselves responded to with the most enthusiasm. These were the
traditional interests of women, understood by the community. The
longer-range goal was to help women move toward addressing the wider
range of needs that they had expressed. Hasina drew them into the program with activities that she hoped would begin to build their sense of
self-esteem. It was difficult at first to encourage women to express opin-
ions because they were so unaccustomed to being asked what they
thought. "Men were shocked to see women holding meetings in their
house yards with no men to rule and guide them," Hasina recalls.

Small neighborhood savings groups were promoted by the agency
as a way to move from helping individual women in isolated households
to encouraging group activity. Women had borrowed from one another

within the family, but now that pool was expanded to include the women of a neighborhood. The agency made a small contribution to the capital of the loan fund, helped the women develop guidelines for its use, and encouraged investment in small-business enterprises. Women welcomed the savings groups as a way to put money aside not only for the needs of their families but also as security for their own futures. As the threat of divorce loomed over them always (their husbands could exercise that threat whenever they chose to), the women had to be prepared to fend for themselves. As Muslim women they could have their own money, but it was far safer from the demands of men if it could be banked.

Larger meetings of women were much easier to arrange following the success of the savings societies. Nevertheless, many of the first women who came forward were widowed or divorced, separated or abandoned; many of them were young, and almost all were nearly destitute. They represented almost 20 percent of all the women in the Save the Children project areas. Those with no men present were usually the poorest villagers. One young mother in a training course wept when she was served a snack of puffed rice and yoghurt. She said, "I have food and my children are hungry."[9] Some women tucked the food away in their *saris*; others were too hungry to save it.

Eventually, other women gathered courage and came out of their houses to attend the training sessions and meetings. One of the earliest signs of encouragement for Hasina was the unexpected appearance of several women at a village meeting for men. The women stood silently outside the community center in the dark, listening to every word of the discussion. When an issue came up of direct importance to them, one would quietly knock on the center's shutter until it was opened and then whisper to her husband the recommendations of her group.

It was the promise of quickly realized economic help, slight as it might have been, that encouraged most of the women to take part. It was the promise of money, too, that persuaded the men, after their early fears, to allow their wives and daughters to join the groups. In exploring ways for women to earn money, both the agency staff and the village women had much to learn. One early project in cotton processing, before Hasina arrived at the agency, demonstrates the initial difficulties. Because women were rarely allowed to go to market themselves, they sent an emissary to buy raw cotton from a river merchant. They hoped to buy it at a low price, have it processed, hold it until the price rose, and then resell it. On this occasion, however, they were charged an exorbitant price for the processing and then overcharged again by the intermediary. There were endless delays. When they were ready to sell the cotton, the price had plummeted, their profits had disappeared, and

their meager capital was tied up in a crop they could not bring themselves to sell at a loss. This experience was repeated often enough that
Hasina dared to suggest that the women must have their own network
through which to negotiate.

Other projects were undermined by village men for their own gain.
An example was a loan society set up by the agency to provide destitute
women with the means to begin to raise poultry or make fishnets and
thus some cash. Hasina discovered that the women selected by the Village Development Committee were not the poorest in the community
but, rather, were women who had connections with committee members. She was furious. When she called a meeting of those women to see
for herself who they were, she found that her transportation to the
meeting had been canceled by the village men. Undaunted, she made her
way there by "running most of the way," knowing that the women were
waiting for her. The best compromise she could arrange was that a few
of the neediest women would be included, too.

8

With the expansion of the women's program to forty-two villages under
Hasina's direction, Save the Children needed an increased cadre of
women to work part-time in the villages to help staff field-workers. Still
available were family-planning motivators who could be trained to do
broader tasks, but there were too few of them. When the agency called
for applicants, months passed in some villages before any women came
forward. Those who did were often the wives of Village Development
Committee leaders, obviously pressured by their husbands to cooperate
with the agency. Most women would have welcomed the small stipend
the job provided, but some feared the social risk or felt inadequate. Hasina did not despair. She said, "A woman with her head bent, looking
down, must slowly lift her head. If she stands erect immediately, the
neck, being brittle, will break." Finally, as the program gained credibil-
ity and acceptance, a few women not connected with the development
committees did apply for the jobs. By the second year of the program,
fourteen women in one village had applied to be development workers.

Hasina was seeking those women who were respected in the community and who did not have serious personal problems with their families, for such problems could destroy any chance they might have to be
effective. She carefully researched each prospective candidate, asking the
opinion of village leaders. She also interviewed every candidate herself.
Observers of the program have noted that the women workers were well
chosen and highly motivated. They were given extensive training in

nonformal education by an expert team that included Hasina, who was considered superb at this type of instruction. Her instinctive ability to communicate effectively had been honed to a fine point by her years of teaching and training. She was meticulous in keeping track of her staff, the projects, and the funding. She made sure that all her staff members had courses in bookkeeping and, in turn, could train other women in keeping accounts.

Hasina brought in a staff doctor and other specialists so that the development workers would have the best technical information about health, nutrition, and family planning. Others learned how to supervise the neighborhood savings societies themselves, instead of relying on the Save the Children field-workers; they even began their own small-business enterprises. It became increasingly apparent that the women could manage their own affairs with greater skill than anyone had expected. This, Hasina believed, was always the critical issue and the one most questioned by men, although it was an accepted fact that there were women in every village who were naturally entrepreneurial.

As the trust in Hasina grew and the program developed, workers began to report that when they walked through the village neighborhood, women called them to come in. "They say, 'Are we sinners that you are not visiting here?'" When women encountered problems in their projects, Hasina was sought after as a mentor and mediator. She infused them with new spirit. One of her colleagues described her as "diplomatic, creative, manipulative, extraordinarily reponsive, fearless. . . . She relates wonderfully to people, from a minister to a village woman. She really loved the village women." Hasina also brought about a cohesiveness in her groups that transcended the moment and left the women stronger for her infusion of spirit.

9

In a welcome respite, Hasina was asked by Save the Children to attend the UN Decade for Women meeting in Copenhagen in July 1980. It was an unparalleled opportunity to gain perspective by meeting with women from all over the world who were struggling with similar problems—an expansion of Hasina's experiences at the Centre for Development and Population Activities in 1978. She met Elizabeth O'Kelly, who had prepared a highly useful set of manuals on technology and income-producing ideas for women in Bangladesh for UNICEF. She shared a room with a woman who had helped to organize loan programs for women in Colombia and met with Indian women who had successfully marketed village crafts. She herself presented the programs she was shaping in Bangladesh in a series of workshops and was now able to look at them from an outsider's point of view. Perhaps the problems she faced in Bangladesh were more complicated and intractable than those in other countries, but she was reinvigorated by the ideas and support she received from so many of her peers. It was just the moment for a bit of distance from the dynamic but sometimes turbulent development of her work.

In assessing what the women's program had achieved, as she was asked do at the Copenhagen conference, Hasina realized how much had been accomplished. The program had actually taken root in most of the villages. In most agency project sites, there were pairs of trained women development workers who organized the meetings now held monthly by village women. There were greatly expanded opportunities for women to earn money by raising livestock and poultry, making fishnets and ropes, cultivating fish, working with bamboo, cultivating and processing rice, sewing, spinning, knitting, processing cotton, and growing and selling lentils and mustard. After meeting with considerable resistance from some community men, a few groups had set up their own networks to sell products instead of going through emissaries. The villages were witnessing the emergence of women who were themselves starting up neighborhood savings groups, requesting literacy and numeracy training, and seeking information about their legal rights in divorce and inheritance cases. There was no doubt about the changes that had taken place.

The growth of the program had been slow and the numbers small, but Hasina and her colleagues knew that they had tapped a significant force, ready to be channeled. Hasina was given full credit for the extraordinary diplomacy and persuasiveness she exhibited in her dealings with the rural hierarchy of men. She was said to have taken the vision of a women's program and brought it alive.

"Now," Hasina claimed, "if men want to reach the grass roots, it is not enough to have a motorcycle to get there. They have to go through our channel of workers. This is my greatest achievement." She also notes that when she started her work for Save the Children, "the meeting places were filled with men, with one small corner of women in black *burquas*. But now, half the place is filled with women wearing multicolored *saris*. They plan their own projects, count their own money, keep records of their own expenditures, and have learnt the language to prevent themselves from being exploited by men." As one village woman said, "We were seeds under the dirt, in the darkness. Now we are coming out."

When Hasina came to Save the Children as its first women's program officer in 1979, there were perhaps 400 women involved in activities organized by the Village Development Committees. By August 1987, 410 groups with 4,200 members had emerged. Most remarkable to observers of the program were the changes in women's behavior in many of those villages. In the winter of 1987, Save the Children established a women's work camp, to which it invited four or five women from each of seventeen villages near Rangunia to help one community build a road. The women, a mix of poor and elite from the villages, camped out in tents for five days, worked on the road each morning, and attended workshops each afternoon concerning the role of women in development. To the agency's knowledge, such a gathering had never before taken place in Bangladesh and would have been unthinkable five years earlier.

10

Hasina was in the vanguard of the changes occurring for women in Bangladesh. Those changes had been carried forward by many currents, not the least of which was the increasing number of people living in poverty. A higher percentage of married women were becoming household laborers, a dramatic change from the past, when those jobs were filled by women who were usually older, widowed, or destitute, "for whom the social conventions of *purdah* could not be met because of economic need. . . . For more than 60 percent of all families in Bangladesh, the observance of *purdah* has, in fact, become a luxury."[10] Women began to talk of "inner *purdah*." There are those who believe that the Liberation War opened women's eyes to the true dimensions of their insecurity, just as it had done for Hasina. Rehabilitation efforts directed toward the thousands of women who had been violated or widowed during the war brought many of them to economic independence for the first time in their lives. Contributing to the swift flow of change was the increase in secondary-school education for girls, brought about by government design and popular acceptance. Education for a girl was increasingly thought to improve her marriage chances and to add to the family status. The delay in the age at which girls marry was also changing traditional behavior. Although laws against child marriage had been on the books for years, a poor family was now loath to add a new mouth to feed by taking on a young bride for a son.

Hasina had great dreams for the expansion of the agency's women's program, but by the middle of 1983 her personal life had become too complicated for her to continue to work full-time. Although she was able to arrange satisfactory care for her two daughters when she was away, she endured constant criticism for not remaining at home. Halim had frequent objections to her job; "staying in a village, traveling with men in a car, going outside Dhaka—all this, he thought, was destroying his family prestige." Whatever her difficulties, Hasina had never demonstrated any sense of self-pity; on the contrary, she seemed to have a steel core that kept her from being overcome by circumstances.

Now, however, Halim was working with Hasina's brothers in a prosperous company and Hasina's salary was no longer required for maintaining the family. Their daughters, then almost eight and eleven, demanded more attention—a fact that Halim expressed clearly to the members of both families. Hasina says that "the remark against me was that 'she is saving the children but killing her own.'" Even Hasina's own family began to complain that she was away from her girls more than was advisable, now that their future education had become an issue. Hasina's mother-in-law suggested a possible marriage of the older daughter to a cousin. The pressure became too intense. Hasina, too, was worn out from the physical exertions and emotional tensions of her unorthodox and controversial job. Without the support and encouragement of her own family, which she had always counted on, Hasina gave in. In the spring of 1983, she formally retired as women's program director for Save the Children while maintaining a link with the agency for another year as a consultant.

Hasina helped to select and train her successor, Jebunessah Lily, who herself had an unusual background. She alienated her family by refusing an arranged marriage and now supports her divorced sister and her children in an independent household—a highly irregular arrangement. But, like Hasina, she has the experience and courage that is needed to continue the program and a personal and deep commitment to the improvement of women's lives.

In 1984, Hasina accepted a teaching position in an international secondary school in Dhaka attended by her daughters. It is supported by Saudi Arabia and is strictly Muslim, unlike the Bharateshwari School Hasina so loved. After a brief two years, Hasina was appointed the acting headmistress. She says she was astounded to be asked to head the school because she considers herself weak in ideological matters. But she has quickly made her mark. She has insisted that the girls participate in physical education classes, a startling departure for the school and one that was strongly resisted. Although Hasina must cover her head when she leaves the school, her veil rests around her shoulders when she is in a classroom, a laxity permitted her ostensibly because she suffers keenly from the heat. When her hennaed hair drew criticism, she quoted a line from the Koran that she believes supports the practice of coloring one's hair.

It is a testimony to Hasina's political astuteness that she has advanced so quickly and has been able to make changes in the school's programs. Her friends believe that Hasina's new post has revitalized her and has given her a cause and a zest that she seriously lacked for a while. The reformer and the rebel still live in her, and when her daughters are settled, she will undoubtedly find new challenges. "I miss the women's program. . . . I'm still in touch with some of the village women. Even now I have deep feelings and concern for them."

When she was working on a family-planning project in Dhaka, Hasina wrote a song that she liked to sing to women who came to the gatherings. It is far more feminist than any song she would sing in a traditional village, but it clearly expresses her own deep feelings.

Women of Bangladesh

Here and there we the women are awakening
Our actions will make history. We are awakening.
We don't care and fear for superstitions. And don't
    care for criticism.
We are no more in the corners of our houses.
Mothers! Sisters! No more sitting idle. The
    hopeless
    night is ended.
We, the mothers and sisters of Bangla, have come
    out
    of the corners of houses.
And proved before the world our unity.
We, the Bengali women, are tearing away the veils
And proving to the world our strength and power.
All around the country we are awakening.
Awakening even in the villages, suburbs and
    towns.
No more sitting idle.
Mothers! Sisters! The hopeless night is ended![11]

NOTES

1. Taluker Maniruzzaman, *The Bangladesh Revolution and Its Aftermath* (Dacca: Bangladesh Books International, Ltd., 1980), pp. 164–165.

2. Janet Zollinger Giele and Audrey Chapman Stock, eds., *Women: Roles and Status in Eight Countries* (New York: John Wiley & Sons, 1977), p. 112.

3. Sultana Alam, "Women and Poverty in Bangladesh," *Women's Studies International Forum*, vol. 8, no. 4 (Oxford and New York: Pergamon Press, 1985), p. 361.

4. UN Statistical Office, *Population Vital Statistics Report* (data available as of January 1, 1987).

5. Stan D'Souza and Abbas Bhuiya, "Socioeconomic Mortality Differentials in Rural Areas of Bangladesh," *Population Development Review*, vol. 8, no. 4 (New York: Population Council, December 1982), pp. 753–769.

6. *Women in the World: The Women's Decade and Beyond* (Washington, D.C.: Population Reference Bureau, April, 1986), p. 4.

7. Tahrunnessa Abdullah and Sondra A. Zeidenstein, *Staff Training Manual*, for the Women's Programme of the Integrated Rural Development Programme (IRDP), Interview taken by D.P.O. Kohinoor in Jhigorgacha (Bangladesh: IRDP, 1981), pp. 209–211.

8. Phyllis Forman, consultant, Save the Children, Bangladesh, letters to the author (1985).

9. Phyllis Forman, "Save the Children Community Report" (Westport, Ct.: Save the Children, September 1983).

10. Florence E. McCarthy and Shelley Feldman, *Rural Women Discovered: New Sources of Capital and Labor in Bangladesh,* Working Paper no. 105 (Ithaca, N.Y.: Cornell University, November 1985), p. 15.

11. Song printed in *International*, newsletter of Family Planning International Assistance, vol. 2 (New York: October 1978).

SUPPLEMENTARY READINGS

Abdullah, Tahrunnessa, and Zeidenstein, Sondra A., *Village Women of Bangladesh: Prospects for Change* (New York: Pergamon Press, 1982).

Baxter, Craig, *Bangladesh* (Boulder, Colo.: Westview Press, 1984).

Chowdhury, Anwarullah, *Agrarian Social Relations and Development in Bangladesh* (New Delhi, India: Oxford & IBH Publishing Co., 1982).

Integration of Women in Development (Dhaka: United Nations Information Center, 1985).

Islam, Mahmuda, "Child Wives of Bangladesh," *People*, vol. 12, no. 3 (London: Longman Group for International Planned Parenthood Federation, 1985).

Islam, Mahmuda, "Social Norms, Institutions and Status of Women," *Situation of Women in Bangladesh,* Women For Women Research and Study Group, (Dacca: BRAC Printers, 1979).

Karim, A. K. Nazmul, *The Dynamics of Bangladesh Society* (New Delhi: Vikas Publishing House, 1980).

Roy, Manisha, Bengali Women (Chicago and London: University of Chicago Press, 1977).

Women For Women Research and Study Group, *Women For Women* (Dacca: University Press, 1975).

CEUTA
MELILLA
Tunis
Algiers
TUNISIA
Rabat
Benghazi
MOROCCO
Tripoli
Cairo •
El-Ayoun
ALGERIA
LIBYA
EGYPT
WESTERN
SAHARA
CAPE
VERDE
IS.
MAURITANIA
Praia
Nouakchott
MALI
NIGER
CHAD
Khartoum •
SENEGAL
Bamako
Niamey
SUDAN
Dakar
THE
GAMBIA
BURKINA FASO
DJIBOUTI
Banjul
Ouagadougou
Ndjamena
Djibouti
GUINEA-BISSAU
GUINEA
Conakry
BENIN
Bissau
Porto Novo
ETHIOPIA
Freetown
SIERRA LEONE
IVORY
COAST
GHANA
NIGERIA
Addis Ababa
Monrovia
Abidjan
Accra
Lagos
CENTRAL AFRICAN
REPUBLIC
SOMALIA
LIBERIA
TOGO
Lome
CAMEROON
Bangui
EQUATORIAL GUINEA
Yaounde
UGANDA
Malabo
Kampala
KENYA
Mogadishu
SAO TOME E
PRINCIPE
Libreville
GABON
RWANDA
Nairobi
Kigali
CONGO
ZAIRE
BURUNDI
ZANZIBAR
Brazzaville
Bujumbura
Dar es Salaam
Kinshasa
TANZANIA
Luanda
ANGOLA
Lilongwe
ZAMBIA
MALAWI
Lusaka
Harare
MOZAMBIQUE
NAMIBIA
ZIMBABWE
BOTSWANA
Windhoek
Gaborone
Pretoria
Maputo
SWAZILAND
SOUTH
AFRICA
Mbabane
LESOTHO
Maseru

THREE

ELVINA MUTUA
Small-Business Enterprises for Women in Mombasa, Kenya

Elvina Mutua of Mombasa, Kenya, speaks with pride of the rural women in her program who have "come up," but she worries that outsiders will never understand how far they have come. "I know how they started. I have watched them from nothing." Elvina refers to the nearly 2,000 women from the poorest villages around Mombasa who are participating in Tototo Home Industries, a project that teaches women how to earn income. The women are primarily traditional farmers, as are 90 percent of Kenya's rural women.

Elvina Mutua herself was born in 1933 to a farm family of modest means. Her father, a firm believer in education for girls, allowed her to leave the village so that she could attend secondary school. She had hoped to complete her course and graduate. Her father had a change of heart, however, and at age sixteen she was married. While at home with her five children, she became a dressmaker to add to the family income. Blessed with abundant energy, she made time in her busy life to work as a volunteer with several women's organizations that helped disadvantaged women. When most of her children were in school, she earned a degree from a business school.

It was Kenya's independence from Britain in 1963 that brought many women like Elvina into the paid workforce for the first time. After a series of office jobs, she found an assignment with a handicrafts shop sponsored by the National Christian Council of Kenya which was looking for a Kenyan to replace its British manager. This was just the springboard that she needed. She created a series of village handicraft groups that became Tototo Home Industries and went from village to village training women in crafts and marketing skills. The handicrafts they made were sold successfully in shops in Mombasa and Nairobi. But Elvina realized that crafts could not generate enough income to change families' standards of living, and that sales were too dependent on the vagaries of the tourist trade. Although the money that the women earned did

61

give them status in the family, they were in danger of being segregated permanently in a marginalized, poorly paid occupation.

Elvina found support and funding for her beliefs from successive international voluntary agencies. She was able to launch a network of women's groups engaged in small businesses such as poultry raising, ferry-boat service, sale of water, food processing, bakeries, and tea shops. It took years of nurturing and the careful development of leaders who could carry the projects forward. Elvina traveled tirelessly to the villages—difficult, tedious travel, to meet with women's groups grappling to make a success of their work but uncertain as to how to proceed. Elvina needed all of her inspirational and conciliatory talents to hold the program together. In fact, it has flourished—not only because of her extraordinary leadership but also because of her unusual business acumen. She is providing a steadily increasing number of rural women with long-range income-producing skills and the capacity to "come up" in all aspects of their lives.

1

In the villages around Mombasa, Kenya, where Elvina Ikumi grew up, women were proud of their traditional farming skills. But, as Elvina had heard them say, it was easier in their mothers' time to feed their families well. Some of the good land that the women had used for growing food was taken over by men for cash crops. In addition, they had to divide their land into smaller and smaller parcels to accommodate the increasing number of family members. Few of the women had the tools, seeds, fertilizer, or loans that would allow them to improve their production. Their men continued to flow into the towns and cities where paid employment was available, leaving them in the villages to manage their families and farms alone. Some women, of course, were better off financially with the income contributed by their absent sons and husbands, but the cost of town living was high and the men had limited cash to send home.

Elvina remembers when money first became a part of the family's economic life. Her grandfather would call her "to come and count the money." He told her to pick whatever she wanted from the big pot in which the money was kept. The family did not yet know how much money they had, nor did they fully comprehend its uses. The village had been more self-sufficient then, trading for needed goods before money became the common medium of exchange. Although money had been introduced by the British early in their colonization of Kenya, its spread to the villages had been a slow process. As more and more men earned money for the cash crops they grew or through outside labor, women were disturbed that they rarely earned any money from their food crops, except for the small amount they could market.

As the economy became widely monetized, rural women faced mounting problems. Achola Pala, the prominent Kenyan scholar, quotes a Luo woman as saying, "In the past all you needed was a piece of land and one cow for milk. But today, wherever you go, you need money." Women continue to produce most of the family food, but they need cash for soap, clothing, cooking oil, salt, sugar, and medicine. They also require money to pay for their children's education and for food when the surpluses run out. As the Luo woman said, "Tell me of a place where you can mine money from the ground."

Elvina Ikumi, who ultimately helped shape a movement to provide thousands of rural women with the chance to lift themselves out of poverty, knew firsthand the life of a farming woman. She grew up in the village of Mariakani, in the Kilifi district near Mombasa, and worked on her mother's farm—as was expected of a girl. Her grandfather had been a chief in the Akamba tribe from Kitui, in the eastern part of Kenya. She surmises that an inland famine caused by one of the frequent droughts drove many of the Akamba tribe to the coast, where they became traders.

Elvina was the first of nine children, born on February 19, 1933, to Ikumi Nzou and Mutethya Nzomo. She lived in the village of her mother's father, contrary to custom, as brides generally moved to the villages of their husbands' families. None of the elders in her family, including her mother, had ever attended school. Her father, however, had run away from his village to go to school in Mombasa, persuading his mother to send him what money she could. After lean years and long struggle, working at odd jobs as he could find them, he completed his course. He was one of the few of his dozens of siblings and step-siblings (his father had ten wives) ever to attend school. His father had been considered wealthy, but little of his wealth was passed on to his son Ikumi following its division into so many portions. "At eighteen he was forced to marry since it was traditional to marry at that age. My mother was about sixteen. There were no birth records so no one was sure." Elvina's mother's family was Christian, "though most people were nothing," and the expectation was that the young couple would remain monogamous.

After Elvina and her brother John were born, their father, a health educator, decided that he wanted to become a fully accredited health inspector, for which he needed a college degree. "When my father went away, we were left in the village of Mariakani. I remember that time. It was very difficult because he had no money and the government couldn't pay him while he was training. . . . We had a lot of struggle. My father was able to return home only at Christmas." After several years, he finally completed his degree and received a coveted appointment as health inspector.

The village of Mariakani comprised about a hundred houses; Elvina's house, as she remembers it, was the best cared for because the family believed it had to set a high standard. Elvina and her brother were not allowed to drink water in anyone else's house because it was almost certainly not boiled and they had to be very careful of what they ate or drank. They were not allowed to swim in the local river, a source of schistosomiasis, "unless we cheated and ran with the other children. In the evening, I had to have a bath. That was a family rule even when we were short of water. You can take a bath in a very little bit of water if you have to." Elvina believes that she and her brother escaped many of the diseases that other children contracted. The girls and boys in the village played together until they were about ten years old; thereafter, "we were told 'don't play with boys!'. . . I never told my children that." But the girls had their own lively society.

Elvina's routine during her early school days was to arise at 6:00 in the morning and,

> while my mother was cooking breakfast, go out to the *shamba* [farm] during the rainy season and do some cultivating. Then I would come back, wash my face and feet, put on a uniform, eat breakfast, and go to school. I would take a water vessel to school with me so that on the way back I could collect water for the household from the river. We helped a lot. On Saturdays, I went to collect firewood with the other girls, walking about 2 to 4 kilometers. We had to grind corn on Saturdays, too. Although I went to school, I learned every process of village life.

Although Elvina followed the pattern of other village girls, her father had set higher sights for his children, as expressed most visibly by their meticulous health practices. The family was also slightly better off than most of their neighbors and could afford to educate the children.

When Elvina was thirteen, she completed primary school—the first girl in the village to do so. Her father insisted that she continue her schooling even though that meant attending a boarding school, a most unusual step for a girl from Mariakani. He had struggled for years to complete his own schooling, and he had vowed that his children would become educated, too. But Elvina realized how contrary that was to village tradition. "At thirteen you were a big woman and most of the girls got married at eleven, twelve, or thirteen. . . . Families who sent their girls to the village primary school wanted them to be able to write letters, read a bit, but not much more."

Elvina was sent to Ribe School, in the Kilifi district, and found herself one of a small minority of girls.

> Many students came from the upper coastal areas, where families were a bit better off and education was valued more; but the girls weren't taking the school very seriously. . . . I was a small girl going to school with very big girls. . . . I felt lost in school at first and cried a lot. School was very tough, too. The girls had to get up early, fetch water, and help cook before school. The boys bullied the girls—they would pinch you or, if you made a mistake, they would laugh at you. The older girls made the small ones do the chores. . . . It was a very strange experience going to a boarding school but it was very, very good. I think that's where I learned independence, where I learned to think for myself and take care of myself.

Girls played out their female roles, even at school, by helping with the cooking and cleaning, whereas the boys had no such responsibilities.

When Elvina's father was assigned to a post in the district of Taita six months later, the family moved and she was relieved to transfer to Murray School, a boarding school for girls near their new home. As one of the quickest and best of the students, Elvina was encouraged by her teachers. Just as Hasina Khan in Bangladesh experienced a separation from her village friends as she advanced in school, so Elvina found that when she visited Mariakani, she had little to say to the girls with whom she had grown up. "Somehow they felt I was not part of them, and they resented me and were moving apart from me. I was not comfortable with them." Most of her friends were already married, and she had momentary qualms about whether she should remain in school. A girl her age, almost fourteen, was "something terrible if she wasn't married." But she held on to her vision of a life for herself different from that of her village friends.

Security, marriage, and having children to support you were what every girl hoped for—but "if you weren't lucky you could find yourself in a bad situation." Some of Elvina's friends became co-wives when nothing better could be arranged; she knew one girl of twelve who had to become one of many wives when she married a rich man of seventy. "If you're rich you can marry and marry and marry." Men of Elvina's tribe, the Akamba, were expected to give their prospective in-laws cows as the bride price, sometimes working for years to afford them.

Among the Akamba, a young widow might still be expected to marry her late husband's brother, who would then take care of her and her children. If she is older,

> she is left alone and her children must take care of her. If a woman doesn't have children, it is easier for her to marry. Also, her children

may not be accepted by her new husband. Or she may leave her children at her family's home and go to her new husband's home; for not only might her children not be treated well by her new husband and his family, but they would not be able to inherit any land or money from them.

In Kenya, marriage is a complex set of social arrangements based on lineage alliances and property. A family's wealth is often measured by the number of its members who can work; women are a major component of that labor pool. The more wives a man can afford, the more wealth he controls. Neither the husband nor the family of the wife is eager to see a marriage dissolve, for if a woman leaves her husband for any reason, he loses her services and her family must return the bride price to him. Most families make every effort to urge a woman to remain in the marriage so as to avoid such a repayment. For the unhappy woman determined to flee from an intolerable marriage, it is easiest simply to disappear. When the tribes were strong, especially before the colonial period, they would bring pressure to bear on a man who was treating his wife poorly or unfairly. As Mumbi Gakuo notes, "One man's problems was the community's problem and . . . the community or clan carried out disciplinary measures against the offenders of the social rules."[1] During the colonial period and afterward, those restraints began to ebb away.

2

Elvina spent three years at Murray School, finishing the equivalent of two years of American high school. During that time, her father retired from the government health service and opened what was called a ration shop in Mombasa, selling wine and beer. Elvina was called on, whenever she was home, to help her father keep the accounts, a job she liked and did easily. It was a useful skill, and an uncommon one for a woman. She was looking forward to the next level of school, and had passed the exam and been accepted, when, to her surprise and utter perplexity, her father would not allow her to continue. "Perhaps he wanted me to do something else than prepare for teaching, such as nursing or another course, but I've never been sure. I did not know at all why he changed his mind." As she loved her father and admired him, she did not argue (she would not have dared to). But she was angry. Although Elvina has learned to accept those situations about which she can do nothing, this reversal was too disturbing. She had been encouraged to be different from the girls in her village, to have ambitions for herself, and now the door had been shut in her face. Elvina was provoked to take a dramatic course of action. She had met Benjamin Mutua (the brother of one of her school friends) while visiting the family, and a romance had started. Now that she had to leave school, she decided to marry Benjamin. He was twenty-one; she was seventeen.

Elvina's father was furious about the marriage, apparently understanding the nature of Elvina's defiance. He had not been consulted; in fact, he had never even met Benjamin Mutua. He did, however, know the Mutua family and consented to meet with them to work out the marriage agreements. The bride price was six cows, and the wedding celebration took place on November 14, 1950. Benjamin had graduated from the Alliance High School in the Kikuyu district, was working with Nairobi Railroads, and had good prospects in business. He had received a good education, as had his three sisters and two brothers, and he wanted an educated wife. Elvina points out that "not many girls had been to school."

The couple lived in Nairobi during their first year of marriage and enjoyed going to movies and occasional dances. Elvina did not find much else to admire in Nairobi. There was "no sense of togetherness . . . people have no time for one another; they just pass one another." Neither she nor Benjamin felt comfortable there. She describes her husband as a quiet type; he did not mind if she chose to go out with friends when he preferred to stay at home. She believes that he was not a typical husband in allowing her such independence, but he understood that she was not the sort of person who "only wanted to sit at home and cook and all that. . . . I wanted to do things. He was not the kind of person who wants to put you down. I knew this from the beginning." They had their first child, Janet, in September 1952 and shortly afterward moved to Mombasa, where Benjamin had taken a job with the Municipal Council.

Elvina was glad to be back in Mombasa. She preferred the climate of the coast, to which she was accustomed, and she was pleased to be close again to her family's village. She had not realized how much a part of the coastal culture she was. She found a diversity of people there, and a tolerance of those from different backgrounds and different tribes. Centuries of migration had brought people from the Arabian Peninsula, India, and Persia when Mombasa was a major trading port. It had been influenced by more than a century of Arab domination, which also accounted for the prevalence of Islam in the area. Elvina had heard in Nairobi that the people from the coast were lazy and lacked initiative. "Not so. They move more slowly because it is hot. They are resourceful in their own ways when given a chance. Women from the coast have a reputation of being dangerously independent and hard to control."

After the birth of their first child, Elvina settled into a period of quiet domesticity, bearing three more children—Albert, Myra, and Edward—at two-year intervals. After her fourth child, Elvina decided that her family was complete and broached the subject of contraception with her husband. "Family planning was still very secret at that time, and my husband was unusual in agreeing that we should stop having children. Many of my friends had ten or so children, and that gave them terrific prestige." In spite of their precautions, they did have one more child. Simon arrived in 1961 but the Mutuas were still a small family by Kenyan standards.

Elvina stayed at home during these years of childbearing, but after the arrival of her last child, she set out to find something to do with herself. She did not think she could find a conventional paying job because "I didn't have any training . . . so I joined a lot of women's organizations—the Women's Guild, the Women's Fellowship Union, Maendeleo Ya Wanawake (Progress of Women), the YWCA, and the Girl Guides. I wanted to keep myself very busy." She was free to join the various groups because there was a day-care center in the house in which they lived. In the mornings she did her housework, and in the afternoons she helped at the clubs. Maendeleo, one of the most famous women's groups in Kenya, was teaching sewing and cooking, hygiene, nutrition, care of the sick, and literacy to its members. As Elvina had been well trained in basic health as a child and knew how to sew, she was appointed a volunteer teacher as well as group leader of Maendeleo for her neighborhood.

Elvina's volunteer activities gave an invaluable boost to her self-confidence and were an important stepping-stone in her discovery and use of her own talents. She also discovered that the skills she had sharpened as a volunteer could provide her with a source of income to supplement Benjamin's salary, which barely met their needs. "I had developed into a very good tailor, so I did a lot of sewing for people and made dresses and sold them." At first she sewed by hand; then she bought a small sewing machine; and eventually, as her business prospered, she was able to buy a larger and more professional machine. The money she made allowed her to pay the children's school fees and to buy clothes that she couldn't make herself. She chose to do her sewing at night so that she could continue her volunteer work at Maendeleo. She had been deeply touched by the misery she had seen. "The women there really needed to be helped in so many ways. By comparison, I was so fortunate."

The women who came for courses at Maendeleo and the YWCA spent part of their time in Mombasa, returning to their home villages during the rainy season for planting and then later for harvesting. But the food they grew rarely provided for the family year-round. Unable to find paid work in town, they felt useless and newly dependent on their husbands. Many of the men worked irregularly and for low wages, providing at best only partial support of their families. The women in families living in desperate circumstances were driven to find ways to survive. "You will rarely find a woman just sitting around waiting for her husband to bring home the cash. She'll try anything to earn money." Women sold prepared food and vegetables. They sewed, made handicrafts, or traded. But there were far too many women trying to earn a few pennies through the same undertakings and with inadequate skills. Others, unable to support their families through such projects, turned to prostitution. Elvina taught them to become seamstresses, food purveyors, craftswomen, and better managers at home. The women rarely complained, but as she got to know them, she became increasingly distressed by their hardships. Despite a demanding schedule, she found herself being drawn into the work that would become her lifelong commitment.

Elvina's own income through dressmaking was really not sufficient for the growing needs of her family; nor was the work adequately rewarding as her own interests expanded. Accordingly, she decided to go back to school. In 1963, with her husband's encouragement, she entered Pioneer College in Mombasa, a commercial training school. In classes that lasted four hours every morning, she studied English, math, typing, bookkeeping, and secretarial skills. In addition, she signed up for a correspondence course in English at the British Tutorial College. Her older children were now in primary school; the youngest, who was three, attended the day-care center in their building; and Benjamin agreed to keep an eye on the children in the evenings when she was studying.

Midway through her course, Elvina took a job with the Extramural Department of the University of Nairobi in Mombasa. The department offered courses for adults pursuing higher degrees while they worked. Elvina did typing, arranged classes for the students, received fees, and kept the books. It was a full-time job but she kept on with her courses at Pioneer College, leaving the office at 4:00 to attend her own classes from 4:30 to 5:30. Her salary allowed her for the first time to hire household help, thus easing her burden; but she was forced to give up teaching at Maendeleo. Even then, she kept her ties with the YWCA. "I've never stopped doing volunteer work all my life."

Elvina is grateful that she was born with a prodigious supply of energy that allowed her to meet the demands of both school and job while maintaining a tightly knit family life. It was a help that the children went to boarding school at the age of twelve or thirteen, and that Benjamin shared in the supervision of those at home. She admits to only one difficult period, when several of the boys were in their teens and were more rambunctious than she or Benjamin knew how to handle. Fortunately, that period was short-lived.

In 1966, she received a certificate in secretarial duties from Pioneer College. She promptly applied and was hired for a job as claim officer with the Port Authority of Mombasa. She considered it only temporary because Benjamin worked in that office, too—not the best of arrangements for either of them. Despite her misgivings, she stayed at the Port Authority for a year, until she was offered the post of secretary in the office of the Lint and Cotton Marketing Board. This was a more responsible job, a step up, but not much more satisfying than her work with the Port Authority. Of all the work she had done, she had most enjoyed the teaching and counseling at Maendeleo and at the YWCA.

3

An unexpected opportunity came to Elvina as a delayed result of Kenya's independence from Great Britain in 1963. She claims that the independence movement of the early 1950s barely registered with her in Mombasa. It had centered in the highlands of Kenya, among the Kikuyu. But its effects had important repercussions for her. There was a gradual move among institutions to replace English personnel with Kenyans. Elvina heard about such an opening in the fall of 1967 at Home Industries—as noted, the agency established in 1963 by the National Christian Council of Kenya. After one year at the Lint and Cotton Marketing Board, Elvina was ready for a change. She applied for the job she had heard about at Home Industries, replacing the English director who was leaving. The job promised to use her designing skills, her management talent, and her basic interest in working with disadvantaged women.

The women from the coastal area around Mombasa were even poorer than those of the highlands. The area was never one of highly productive farming, because the soil is poor and the climate arid. Tourism replaced commerce as the lifeblood of Mombasa, whose beautiful beaches stretch along the Indian Ocean. Tourism, however, has not been able to provide enough jobs for those who live there. Inland from the coast, where Elvina's work would eventually take her, the villages were remote from one another, transportation was inadequate, water sources far away from most homes, and government services few. Illiteracy was as high as 90 percent among the women, and only one out of four families had sanitary facilities as compared with the national average of one out of three.[2]

Elvina believes that Kenyan independence played a vital role in the advancement of women. Opportunities opened up that had never existed before for women, such as the one at Home Industries. "It had not been thought that women could run these kinds of things." Men, too, had new openings, replacing some of the retiring British—but they also had prior experience in the bureaucracy, limited though it was by colonial control. Kenyan women, by contrast, had been effectively closed out of most formal business enterprises and government posts. Elvina speaks excitedly about that period as one of true liberation, one that had encouraged her and others like her to come into the formal workforce for the first time. The government-inspired self-help movement, called *harambee*, did indeed provide a strong impetus to the activities of women's groups too.

Harambee is unique to Kenya. Begun by President Jomo Kenyatta in 1964, shortly after independence, the movement had a political as well as an economic basis. It brought together in common purpose conflicting tribes, regions, and ideologies, mobilizing the people to plan, build, and finance social-service and public-works projects in rural areas. Coinciding with the *harambee* movement was a government initiative to encourage women's groups. When a Women's Group Programme was set up in 1971, thousands of government social-development assistants spread throughout the rural areas organizing women. Although Kenyan women had long been accustomed to working together in farming and crafts groups, the network of associations was not as advanced as that in Cameroon, where Elizabeth O'Kelly esablished the Corn Mill Societies. Nevertheless, the time was ripe for such a movement, and it grew at an extraordinary rate. By 1984, there were thought to be as many as 15,000 women's groups, most of them registered with the Department of Social Development—a requirement if they wished to be eligible for government grants.[3]

The women's groups in Kenya have taken on community projects such as construction of nursery schools, water-supply systems, roads, and clinics. Only a small percentage of the funds for such projects is supplied by the government; as much as 90 percent may come from *harambee* fund-raising events organized by the very women's clubs that do the work. According to the authors of an evaluation study of women's group enterprises, "women's groups are mobilized at every possible opportunity to contribute labor and scarce funds to other community development projects. . . . It is women, not men, who are the target of state policy with respect to social welfare and who are organized into groups for the purpose of carrying out this work."[4] Although the *harambee* movement in Kenya is singular in that it calls on women to generate funds for community projects, the Housewives' Clubs in Honduras, the Corn Mill Societies in Cameroon, and the crafts groups in Egypt are all encouraged by the government to achieve social-welfare benefits such as improved health and child care through women's efforts.

Elvina traces some women's groups to the occasion of Kenya's independence, not just to the *harambee* movement. "Women got together to practice dances to perform before the president at the celebration of Kenyan independence. Though they got together for dancing, they went on to do a lot of things together, but they didn't have the training to make them successful." In Mombasa, the dancing societies (*Lelemama*) preceded independence and were well known and highly developed from the 1920s through 1945. They were famous for their dancing competitions, which were marked by high rivalry and even conflicts. Almost exclusively composed of Muslim women, they are believed to have evolved after World War II into the Muslim Women's Institute and the Muslim Women's Cultural Association, which are known for their philanthropic works.[5]

Home Industries, Elvina's new employer, trained women to improve the quality of their handicrafts to make them more salable in its Mombasa shop. Run by British women with an eye to the export and tourist markets, this shop was the centerpiece of the agency's activities. Home Industries had successfully developed color and design standards and was hoping to expand sales. Elvina was a novice at marketing, but she knew that her experience in bookkeeping and handling accounts would be a valuable asset. She also knew how to drive, a useful and uncommon skill that her husband had taught her in their recently purchased automobile. Part of her job was to collect crafts from the artisans in the outlying districts. By 1968, her three oldest children were in boarding school, thus somewhat decreasing her responsibilities at home.

In 1969, a private voluntary American agency, Bread for the World, had given Home Industries a two-year grant for Elvina's salary and that of two staff members. Elvina believed that the shop should stop depending on subsidies and either become self-sustaining within that time or close down. She was meticulous in her efforts to master her new job, spending a minimum of two days learning each function performed by workers in the organization. In the process, she discovered that the craftswomen were not paid for their pieces of handiwork until the shop sold them, causing great hardship for some of the women. Elvina quickly arranged for payment upon delivery of the crafts, on the grounds that the work was of sufficient quality to be readily salable. This innovation also eliminated many of the shoddy goods accepted by the shop on consignment.

Elvina was in her element at Home Industries, and she shared its goal of improving women's skills. As the new director, she planned to expand the program to the rural areas beyond Mombasa where some of the neediest women lived. She also wished to strengthen the trend toward traditional handicrafts, which the women already knew how to make, rather than having them construct "foreign things for export," such as toys. Toys were not natural to the Kenyan culture, and the women's version of them was unsalable. Traditional handicrafts, however, were quite marketable when upgraded in design and quality.

In 1972, Home Industries became Tototo Home Industries so that the name would include a Kenyan symbol. *Tototo* means "perfect" in Giriama, the language of the Kenyan coast. Under Elvina's direction, Tototo was no longer an agency that worked only with individual craftswomen; it had become a network of groups of women working and learning together. Their collaboration helped them maintain a quality of craftsmanship through the example set by the most skilled workers; it also provided them with a strong underpinning of mutual support. This bonding of women, which sprang from their own shared interests, was to become a powerful impetus to their advancement.

Welcome assistance came to Tototo from an American Peace Corps volunteer, Holland Millis, who was talented in design and had a good sense of what would be marketable. He was also fluent in Swahili, knowledgeable about Kenya, and easily accepted in the villages. Elvina and Holland toured the villages around Mombasa, examining the traditional crafts. Women were making baskets and fans of sisal and palm leaves, and weaving highly decorated floor mats that were used to cover marriage beds. A strong tourist market of Germans, Italians, Swiss, and Americans eagerly bought the well designed traditional crafts. Elvina and Holland taught the women to produce a new line of high-quality, handsomely designed table mats, lamp shades, handbags, and letter trays that were successfully sold in the Home Industries Shop. They also developed a tie-dye project for the women, whose tie-dyed goods continue to be among the finest in Kenya.

Elvina spent the next several years mastering the skills of running a shop and developing a proficient cadre of craftswomen. She visited Greece to study their cottage industries and spent several months during 1976 at the International Training Center in Haifa, Israel, learning marketing, promotion, and the development of small-scale enterprises.

Tototo had gone about as far as it could go, even under Elvina's inspired direction, but it was not yet either self-supporting or able to expand. It continued to rely on funds from its sponsoring agency, the National Christian Council of Kenya. For most women's groups in Kenya and elsewhere the move from small projects that provide intermittent profits to stable enterprises is almost insurmountable without sufficient capital. As women themselves rarely have access to adequate funding, their enterprises tend to remain marginal. Elvina despaired that this wonderful structure she had helped to create would remain a miniature—unknown and irrelevant, although its potential was great. She had reached an impasse. The women who worked with Tototo had been helped, but their needs were still acute and there were so many more women even worse off, still to be reached.

4

The Peace Corps connection with Tototo, which had lasted for six productive years, finally brought Elvina in contact with some of the major international agencies interested in community development and in promoting the role of women. Among them was World Education, an American NGO highly regarded for its programs in functional literacy and nonformal education in developing countries. Through the Peace Corps staff, World Education had learned of the work of Tototo Home Industries and of its director, Elvina Mutua. Elvina had become convinced that most rural women did not have a way into the economic system and that selling handicrafts could benefit only a few. It was difficult to compete with the handicraft collectives, and so many women were trying to sell their handiwork that the market was glutted. When she heard of World Education's integrated approach to development and its goal to train women to do what they themselves wanted to do, Elvina became interested. World Education invited her to a workshop they were running, and she accepted because she intuitively felt that their approach to reaching the poorest rural women had a good chance of success.

In 1977, World Education proposed to Elvina that they collaborate on a program to expand nonformal education and training for the women with whom Tototo was already working. World Education had a grant from the U.S. Agency for International Development that would underwrite the intensive training necessary for the program, fund the start-up of pilot income-producing projects, and provide for careful documentation of what actually happened in the course of the project. As that sort of information was rare, few groups were able to learn from the successes or failures of others.

Elvina was elated at this new opportunity and set out to take the first critical step involved in initiating the project—the selection of appropriate villages. She chose villages with women's groups

> that had not done very much or whose projects had not gone very far. I felt that such groups would provide more measurable results. If I take a group that is already very strong and has already done quite a bit, we

Elvina Mutua, Director of Tototo Home Industries, Kenya (photo courtesy of Ray Witlin of the Ford Foundation)

may not be able to see the results of what we do. It is good to work with different kinds of groups, some compatible and stable, and those that have conflicts, those of differing religious backgrounds.

Working with the very poorest of the villages posed particular problems. "It can be very, very difficult. . . . You are working with people who are desperate, and even to get women to come to meetings is almost impossible because they have to look for food. They need first of all to be helped to get something to eat." Elvina could not offer direct funds to the participants, for the limited funds directed to Tototo's new Women's Rural Development Program were meant to be used for training. Whenever Elvina spoke with women about the primary needs of their villages, they would produce a long list of things that cost money. "I had to sit and think of how I am going to put it to them in a way that they will understand, that we don't have the money but we want to train them. It gave me a headache!" Elvina was able to persuade a sufficient number of groups—usually those that were highly motivated and ambitious—that the problem of funding had to be primarily their own responsibility. Fortunately, the *harambee* movement had made that issue more comprehensible.

Six small villages were finally chosen, and 180 members of women's groups were invited to participate. Anyone who wished to be a part of the program had to agree to be interviewed at both the beginning and the end of the program. Of the 180 women, 130 decided to participate in the three-week training course; the remaining 50 agreed to be interviewed but could not or would not be part of the project. Few literate women in the villages felt that they needed the groups.

From these interviews emerged a profile of the average participant. She was between twenty and thirty years old, had five children, had never attended school or had left after a few years, was illiterate, was more likely to be the only wife rather than a co-wife, and was Christian only slightly more frequently than Muslim. Approximately 45 percent of the women were Christian, 40 percent Muslim and 9 percent traditional. (In the coastal region around Mombasa, the ratio of Muslims to Christians is approximately 46 to 35 percent; 11 percent are traditional.)[6] The Muslim women generally do not observe *purdah* and are engaged in the full range of activities open to women. They have the advantage, by Islamic law, of being able to own and inherit property. In addition, as the bride-price payments are lower and therefore less difficult to repay, divorce is easier and more frequent among them.

One-third of the participants were co-wives, and another 20 percent were heads of their households through divorce or widowhood. More of the women received regular remittances from an adult son than from any other relative, including husbands. The fact that a woman was an only wife rather than a co-wife frequently indicated that her husband was too poor to afford more than one wife. The typical woman was responsible for raising food crops for the family (primarily maize and vegetables) and was already engaged in income-producing activities, which chiefly involved selling for pitifully little money the handicrafts she made or the crops that she grew. She was the ideal candidate for such an undertaking.

When asked why they joined Tototo, some members of the Majengo Women's Group explained:

> I joined the group because I had left school to get married and my husband turned out to be bad. I had a child and no work, and I heard that

Majengo was a way one could get money . . . I also wanted to get ideas
to get clever. Majengo offered different experiences.

Another noted that

> a woman does a project and gets money to take home. Also the women
> exchange ideas. She doesn't have to sit at home alone. Here she gets an
> education. . . . Majengo helps the relationships at home. Money always
> helps. . . . The people of Majengo used to be suspicious of what we
> were doing. A few still think we are witches, but most of that has
> stopped. . . . When we started providing the health clinic and the water
> kiosk, they were alerted that Majengo was a good thing.[7]

True to the participatory doctrine that had shaped World Education's training philosophy, the women who agreed to join the projects in
the six villages chose their village coordinator themselves. Elvina was
present at those crucial sessions. She asked the women to select a coordinator who was able to read and write, for reasons readily apparent to
the group. In certain villages, the chief's influence was ever-present and
unavoidable. That fact demanded great finesse on Elvina's part, as she
could neither offend the chief nor be saddled with a coordinator whom
the group could not truly respect or follow. In later evaluations it became
strikingly clear that the choice of a leader was critical to the success of
the project. Women simply would not learn from someone they did not
trust.

Six women were finally selected by their peers as leaders. These
were women twice as likely as other group members to be divorced or
to be living separate from their husbands—thus their greater independence. They were to receive a stipend of 150 shillings (US$9.00) a month
from Tototo for the work they would do.

The three-week training given the new leaders proved a real challenge. For Elvina it was training too, in the nondirective, participatory
approach that she had instinctively understood but could now articulate. In the beginning, few of the coordinators were effective in their
efforts to bring out group ideas or to plan lessons. As Elvina cautioned,
"You must be patient and very good at listening or you can end up with
a disaster." The coordinators gradually learned to tell stories and to do
simple tracings and drawings that could trigger discussion among their
groups. "You should see what they draw now—wonderful things. It's
really fantastic."

They also made up dramas that presented common problems, thus
further opening up discussion among the women. Elvina tells with pleasure of a play about two mothers—one with a few children, the other
with many. The first woman belongs to a successful group, earns money

through handicrafts and sewing, is able to send her children to school, and can provide them with adequate clothing. She asks the woman with many children why she doesn't come to the group's meetings. That woman's children are sick, her husband is drunk and demanding, there's no food in the house, and she's pregnant again! Elvina says that when enacted at the clubs, this drama was a great success. "It touches the women so much that they start discussing it very seriously. . . . 'If I have fewer children, I can do these things.'" Indeed, Elvina believes strongly that uncontrolled childbearing is one of the critical problems facing Kenyan women. Kenya has the world's highest fertility rate and its population is increasing at an annual rate of 4.2 percent, according to a World Bank survey in 1986. The number of children borne by the average woman over her lifetime is eight. Elvina understands the conflicting pulls on a woman about childbearing. On the one hand, she desires the traditional respect granted a woman who has many children; on the other, she must protect her own health as well as the health and educational opportunities of her children.

Tototo's newly trained coordinators sat with the assembled group of women, attempting to steer the discussion to what the women considered to be their worst problems. It was a long and sometimes bewildering process. Women were fatalistic about their lives and felt helpless to make any changes, caught as they were in a web of apathy, ill health, isolation, and years of deprivation. Lack of food and money was critical, but what could they, "poor ignorant women," do about that? Some of the women were as muscular and lean as men and had aged far beyond their years. It was not surprising when they did not object to their husbands' taking second wives; they had so much work to do, especially as they grew older, that they welcomed a younger co-wife to share the burdens and do the heavier work. They had long ago accepted the departure of their men from the village to find work. Most placed little value on their own experience or their ability to cope with adversity; nor did they recognize the skills that existed within their groups that might aid them. Elvina developed a deep respect for their wisdom and tenacity. With agonizing slowness, in the eyes of the eager coordinators, the women moved toward action.

They talked about raising chickens, or starting a bakery, or expanding their trading. But for each of these goals they would need capital. Perhaps they could sell crafts or the extra produce they raised in their gardens and save that money to use as capital—but that would take a long time. Most of the Muslim women did not farm. "They say they have never held a hoe in their hands," says Elvina, and "there's no way you can get them to farm." They did, however, have their own vegetable gardens and many other small projects. The discussions continued for weeks, and the slow pace of progress tried even Elvina's patience.

Elvina realized that, by training the coordinators in Mombasa she was losing a rare opportunity to involve the whole group of women in the experience.

> In a developing country like ours, a change cannot be brought in by one person in a village. One person coming back to a village trying to explain new things has a hard time persuading people; they take it up but very slowly. Sometimes training only one woman from a village can make her feel superior and antagonize the other women.

A far better solution, she believed, was to train the leaders in the village itself so that all could see and learn. The whole group could then join in the exercises.

The women and the coordinators spent months trying to identify the skills and resources they would need to start up small businesses and the potential problems they would face. Because the women had so little idea as to what to expect, this was a critical step. Elvina was considered a miracle worker in the way she created a spirit of common purpose among the women and among her own coordinators. She spent hours and days in the villages generating hope among the women and providing a model for her own staff. Here was a woman in control of her life. Her manner was ebullient, forthright, and vigorous. She rarely directed the discussions but often posed questions that provoked answers. Even then, the women needed more attention and encouragement than the program design allowed.

After almost a year of organizing and planning, five of the six groups were ready to initiate projects. None had access either to credit or to the small loans of $200 or $300 that they needed, except through moneylenders at exorbitant interest rates. Like most women who do not own property, they lacked the collateral to secure a loan. (The United Nations' estimate that women own less than 1 percent of the world's property is a stark reminder of the magnitude of the loan problem for women.) Several of the Tototo groups needed only very small amounts of money to launch their projects. Some groups held *harambee* events to raise funds for their projects, but such fundraising had its own handicaps. As it was a reciprocal activity, women had to contribute to others' *harambee* projects either with their labor or their contributions.

In addition to some loan money, Elvina managed to find $100 grants from such imaginative agencies as the American Trickle-Up Program. It was not the size of the loan that really mattered, she believes, but the timing, the demonstration of confidence, the push to get a group over the hump. Most of the time her methods worked. The telling point was that all the loans were eventually repaid. One group opened a bakery, and a second began to raise chickens. Two groups were growing and selling their communal farm produce, and another made straw mats for thatched roofs. The sixth had not decided on a project because the women didn't get along with each other and didn't like their coordinator, who had been imposed upon them by one member.

The weather itself was an added and sometimes insurmountable barrier to the success of the ventures. During the dry season, the women of the villages of Kayafungo and Vigurungani had to leave their homes at 1:00 in the morning to walk to a water source, not returning until 6:00 a.m. They had to do this every day, and with no time left over for anything other than their normal household and farming tasks. During the rainy season, when the women did have more time, the inland roads were impassable and no Tototo staff could reach them. There was little that Elvina could do to ensure that those groups had adequate supervision of their projects during critical stages; as a result, they experienced more setbacks than the others.

The communal farm that the women had set up in the village of Bomani was not going well at all because some of the women were unwilling to share the work. The demands of their own farming took precedence over the communal farms, and the women frequently didn't show up. A handicap of any voluntary effort is that it is voluntary, and women can't be required to work—just encouraged. Elvina suggested that the coordinator begin again with the women to explore projects they might like. This time, they unanimously chose a bakery instead of a farm. The bakery was, and still is, a success. It struggles to be profitable while coping with state pricing policies for wheat, flour, and the bread itself, but it has produced a regular income for its participants. The attached tea shop, which sells scones made by the bakery, is named for Elvina.

The women saw their increased income as the most direct answer to their needs, as indeed it was; but the Tototo strategy was broader. Elvina was eager to persuade women to improve the level of health in the villages—a difficult task to weave into the program when women did not understand the causes for illness. However, when a group of Tototo women began to build a nursery school, they realized that it had to have sanitary facilities to qualify for government certification (as did the bakery in Bomani). Most of the villagers considered such facilities to be almost irrelevant, even though poor sanitation is a major cause of infection and disease in Kenya. Nevertheless, the latrines were built and clean water was made available for both the nursery school and the bakery. After a few years, the same women claimed that they could see an improvement in their own health and were among the first to have their children vaccinated; they also started a drive for clean water in the village.

Elvina urged the women to put the money they were earning into a bank instead of hiding it or keeping it in a neighbor's shop. When the government mobile banks came to the village, the women tended to ignore them, not trusting their savings to anyone else. Elvina pointed out the dangers for women in not banking their money; a husband, for example, might insist on borrowing it. "If you're the treasurer of the club and your husband comes home drunk and says, 'Give me the money,' you'll give it. If you've put it in the bank, you can say, 'I don't have it.'"

Elvina discussing business with other members of Tototo Home Industries, Kenya (photo courtesy of Ray Witlin of the Ford Foundation)

A few of the men did, in fact, cause problems. They wanted to know what the women were doing with the money they earned. They tried to interfere if the money was reinvested and pressed for monthly distribution of profits. The same situation in other projects had provoked Mumbi Gakuo, an anthropologist of Kenyatta University College, to assert that the marriage relationship was a distinct detriment to such women. They had lost the independence they had known before colonialism, and the cash economy made them mere chattels of men. If a woman did not marry, Gakuo claimed, she then would not be required by law or current custom to account to her man for whatever earnings she had. And if he drank or treated her poorly, she could throw him out.[8]

How women chose to use the money they earned was described by members of the Mwamambi group of Tototo in 1985. One woman spent her money on treatment for spirit possession; another bought poles for building a new house after her old house had fallen down. Other women reported that individually they had contributed money to the school from which a son had been sent home for failing to bring a "building" contribution; had paid a traditional doctor to cure a husband who was ill and had not responded to hospital treatment; had bought bandages and medicine for a son who broke his leg; had paid for new crutches for a daughter; and had given money for treatment for a mother's spirit possession. The women running the Bomani bakery used their earnings to buy clothing, cattle, goats, and trees; they also paid their children's school fees.

There were times when the village women might have agreed with Mumbi Gakuo, but Elvina believes that they probably *wanted* to share what they had earned with their husbands. "The women who work with Tototo still think their husbands are the most important part of their lives. Perhaps there are a few problems." According to a World Education evaluation, the women's earnings in some cases

> may displace the income provided by a husband by alleviating the need for him to contribute to the household from his own pocket, thus leaving him with more income at his disposal. When income is handed over or otherwise finds its way back to husbands, there is no guarantee that women will play a role in determining how it is invested or whether it is invested in the household at all.[9]

It was common wisdom that younger wives were less able to control the way in which their earnings would be spent than older, more experienced women, and Elvina's campaign to encourage the women to bank their money was an acknowledgment of a general problem that some women felt helpless to address.

The Tototo program was evaluated two years later, in 1979, and the results, though not uniformly good, were encouraging. Although one group had failed and another had not found a satisfactory project after all that time, most of the women had grown significantly in confidence and competence. Many had learned better health and nutrition practices. They had increased their incomes and could provide more adequate food for their families; more of the participants had gone on to open bank accounts, and fewer were engaged only in subsistence farming. Their standard of living had indeed improved.[10]

The painstaking evaluation process confirmed many of Elvina's previous suspicions. Handling funds, for example, was almost always a problem because of inexperience and occasional misuse by the women. As the projects became more complex, the intuitive trading sense and everyday competence of the women were not enough. Every group had to learn how to handle and account for money more effectively, and every group needed more time to learn to manage its projects. Although the effects of the program were not as positive as Elvina or World Education had hoped, Tototo was increasingly attracting the interest of other agencies because its approach had resulted in documented changes and sustained results.

5

Elvina was selected to attend a training course at the Centre for Development and Population Activities in Washington, D.C., in 1983. It was the same leadership and program-management training course that had so inspired Hasina Khan of Bangladesh in 1978. The emphasis of the training is on the participatory process of community organizing; it is oriented toward women, and it proposes family planning as an integral element in development. Elvina's nondirective style was reinforced, and her interest in family planning was greatly heightened. Upon her return, she would have liked to have her coordinators dispense birth-control pills "as they do in India." In one Tototo village, where women had built their own small health dispensary, the government eventually sent two nurses, "neither of whom knew anything about family planning. I got the family-planning people to go to that village, too, and train the nurses to give pills." She also succeeded in bringing a mobile family-planning clinic to several villages on a monthly basis.

It is generally true in rural Kenya that even when a woman wishes to control the frequency of her pregnancies, contraceptives are not easily available; even the subject itself provokes suspicion and extravagent speculation. In the winter of 1986, rumors spread that the government was sending agents to the schools to give forced contraceptive injections to the children or to add contraceptive ingredients to the school-supplied milk. Panicked parents in one school district warned their children to run away from school if they saw a stranger come. When a car, driven by the new school-district supervisor, pulled into the school yard in Mugumoini in Thika, children leaped out of school windows and fled to their homes. Upon hearing of this incident, Kenya's President Daniel arap Moi was infuriated; he actively campaigns for family planning and had personally introduced the immunization and school milk programs. The government blamed the Catholic Church's anti–family planning campaign for spreading the rumors.[11]

6

After years of soliciting every possible donor and tirelessly pursuing leads to organizations in Kenya and beyond, Elvina managed in 1982 to locate funds for a revolving loan program from the Ford Foundation and Private Agencies Collaborating Together, an American NGO known as PACT. Additional funds from Lutheran World Relief enabled Tototo to expand its program to reach twenty new groups of women. The existence of the loan fund dramatically changed the potential of the program, allowing women to undertake an extraordinary range of entrepreneurial ventures. In addition to raising poultry, livestock, and produce, they could now build rental properties, operate day-care centers for profit, run tea shops, sell porridge, run motor boats for paid transport from the islands, and trade dried fish. These ventures, with careful planning and consulting assistance from Tototo, were bringing in more than pin money. According to Elvina, by 1986 many of the women were earning between US$12 and US$24 a month—a substantial supplement to the family income in Kenya, where the national per capita income is only about $390 a year.

The boat enterprise, one of the most intriguing to foreign donors, proved a success and a failure in almost equal proportions. The women of the Bogoa group, whose members were Muslim, lived on an isolated island off the coast of Mombasa. The island had irregular and risky ferry service, run by fishermen when they had the time. The women decided to operate a ferry service themselves, as they and their children were the most frequent travelers to the mainland. This venture went beyond any experience they had ever had before and was an activity unheard-of for Muslim women of that area. Elvina solicited funds from an international donor totaling US$2,555 for the purchase of a boat, the women's group at Bogoa raised $226 themselves by subscription, and they took out a loan from Tototo for $365. The boat went into operation in October 1983. The group had to hire the husband of one of its members to run the boat; group members took turns being conductors.

They paid a flat proportion of their income to the man who ran the boat (far too high a price, they later discovered); but the maintenance and gas cost more than they had expected, and their returns were woefully small. The process of dividing the income became progressively more confused, and the accounts were in a shambles. Some members of the group "bought a piece of black cloth and a chicken, with group funds, and took them to a traditional doctor on the mainland to provide the boat with protective medicine." This caused the resignation of some of the more progressive members of the group who had always disagreed with the direction of the project. Seven months after the ferry service started, the boat's engine was stolen. If the boat had been insured by an insurance company rather than by the local medicine man, the group might have collected money to buy another engine. As it was, the women had to go deeper into debt to buy a second-hand engine that kept breaking down. Men in the community who had searched for the stolen engine sent the group outrageously high bills for what they considered their services. Tototo came to the rescue in April 1986 with advice and funds from a new international donor. The finances were cleared up, and the boat has resumed its crossings. Although the enterprise is considered successful now in that it does earn money, it is believed to be at risk of being dominated by men because custom demands a male boat captain, men insure the boat, and men found the new engine and even keep their own accounts of the boat's earnings.[12] Elvina can do only so much to prevent that.

By October 1985, there were 45 groups whose membership came to more than 1,400 women, and the Tototo staff numbered 30. Thinking of Tototo's growth, Elvina says, "I just planned this and then this for tomorrow and tomorrow, and slowly I found myself really doing something. These small, small things which I do, and which I keep learning, . . . fill my days with satisfaction." Today, the first five remaining groups of the initial six are on their own, although Elvina keeps in touch with them and they continue to receive business training. The Tototo group experience has led some women to start their own businesses. Elvina thinks it's fine that these women have become individual entrepreneurs, even though they have left the group. Their independence is a sign of Tototo success. She makes sure that the women in the program have access to continually expanding opportunities for new economic projects. This means an unending search for support from local banks, businesses, and agencies—essentially the male bureaucracy. That search, in turn, presents its own problems. "It can never be easy," says Elvina.

Men will always think "What can you do as a woman?" . . . In the villages the men said, "What makes you think you can do these things? . . . Why do you think you can start a bakery?" You can't avoid the problem, but there's no law that stops you from going to ask. Sometimes you will meet a nice man who's interested in helping and you work with that one. Sometimes you meet a hostile one, but these are the things that most women in Kenya meet. In the villages, women are strong. They're doing a lot of things that men are not doing. Maybe that's what men are afraid of, that women are strong.

Interestingly, three of the new groups have men as members; and, in a display of equity, Tototo supported one group made up entirely of men—fishermen who needed technical help.

The Tototo project is considered a success by both the Kenyan government and other agencies. A team of evaluators commented that, "although not without its share of problems, Tototo is arguably the best grass-roots development agency in Kenya."[13] Tototo started out with a clear focus on nonformal education, but by 1986, after considerable cost and painful lessons, the emphasis had turned to the development of small enterprises and, in 1987, a business adviser was added to the staff. Unlike most of Kenya's estimated 15,000 women's groups, Tototo members receive regular training, have access to loans, and get frequent assistance in accounting and business management practices. More than two-thirds of Tototo's groups were operating successful revolving loan funds in 1987; ten of the groups consistently made a profit and paid small but regular dividends to its members. To continue to be successful, two fundamental challenges must be met by Tototo—challenges that characterize similar undertakings by women whether in Bangladesh, Honduras, or Cameroon. As the project becomes more complex, more able to provide a permanent structure for income, both the village women and the staff need even more technical training than they now receive. A second and equally pervasive problem is the project's dependency on outside funding, frequently from foreign donors. It will be a long while before Tototo's programs can make it on their own.

Observers of Tototo cite the outstandingly high quality of the staff that Elvina has assembled. One observer said, "You don't build that kind of a staff overnight. Elvina must have gone through a lot of people before she got that group, and she was willing to go out to the villages and sit in the dirt and know what those jobs were about."[14] Elvina visits all the groups, no matter how remote. Her staff says with admiration and perhaps a touch of awe, "There is nothing she doesn't know" about what's going on.

Observing the changes for women since 1967, when she joined Tototo, Elvina takes satisfaction in the fact of their increased economic abilities and greater job opportunities. But she worries about the younger women in the villages. During the years in which they are still bearing children, they are more dependent on their husbands than they will be later. She notes that the young men are not sending money back to their families as regularly as the older men had done, and that more of the younger women have to fend for themselves. Educated women are more vulnerable too.

> The husbands often demand the whole packet of pay from the woman since it takes his permission for the woman to go out and work. If she resists, she can be beaten. Older, experienced women can be clever and say "no." In the villages you develop status when your children are grown up. Even if your husband leaves, you can stay in the village, and you don't have to get married again and go elsewhere.

For women in Kenya, Elvina believes, the UN Decade for Women Conference in Nairobi (1985) has had a positive impact—even if a national interest in women's problems does not yet exist. "It helped people to recognize what women's contribution really is. The NGOs are thought to be doing a wonderful job, and most NGOs are headed by women. Women are now really starting to take a stand. They're starting to know what is their position." One sign is that educated women in cities are finding more jobs in government offices and in business that have become available to them as the prejudice against women working in offices has abated. "Given the circumstances in which we found ourselves, women seem to have progressed more than men," says Elvina.

Elvina herself played an active role in the UN conference as an official delegate of the Kenyan government. It was an honor for her, but her heart was in the nongovernmental Forum in which she was a leader of several well-attended workshops. She found the Forum meeting exhilarating. Nairobi was turned over to the conference and thronged with women, thousands of whom had come from other African countries. She met dozens of women who work, as she does, in the villages. Many had heard about Tototo, which has increasingly been mentioned in Kenyan newspapers, on the radio, and in international journals. Immediately after the conference, Elvina took interested delegates down to Mombasa to visit the Tototo projects. But for all her worries that the projects might not appear as successful as they are, the evidence was clear: Tototo is considered the standard by which other women's programs are measured.

Elvina does not aspire to be an important figure in Kenya. She is rooted in the area where she lives and works—her farm, fifteen miles outside of Mombasa—and in the dispersed villages in which the Tototo groups are situated. The small, comfortable farm where Elvina lives with Benjamin (who is now retired) is planted with papaya and banana trees. It also features a model vegetable garden and a collection of small animals that seem to keep Elvina anxiously on the watch. Their children have done them credit; Janet and Albert are accountants; Myra is a doctor in the Kenyatta hospital; Edward is an auto mechanic; and Simon, who has a degree in economics, works for an agricultural financing firm. Elvina's interest and acumen in finance is clearly reflected in the career choices of her children. Her entrepreneurial flair has led her to invest in an antique and jewelry business in Mombasa as well as in a poultry business, which is thriving. She also keeps a sharp eye on the Tototo craft shop in the center of Mombasa that sells handicrafts from all the projects and some of the best tie-dyed fabrics and dresses in Kenya. The shop continues to make a profit.

Elvina has not lost her remarkable zest for what she does. "I keep having new ideas while I'm working. Several times I have been offered other jobs, but what I'm doing is a creation of my own, my own baby." Friends say that Elvina could easily have been a successful businesswoman in Mombasa but that she has a strong personal need to work for others. Her style has been described as a mixture of nurturance and control, although the control is barely apparent. She has become so nondirective, so imbued with the participatory approach, that a member of the Women's Business and Professional Club, of which she is founder and director, pointed out that she doesn't seem to be in command of the meetings she runs. Elvina admits she has had to adjust her style in such a setting.

Elvina Mutua remains a modest woman. Only recently, with the greater public recognition of her contributions, does she realize that she has something important to say to those who are interested in the advancement of women. She was invited by the Adult Literacy Organization of Zimbabwe to be a consultant on income-producing projects for women, and other invitations followed. Elvina has indeed been a key figure in promoting the expanding possibilities for women in Kenya and in evolving a way to work effectively with poor women based on their capacity to understand their own needs clearly and to take action when given the means. Through Tototo, she has created a network of inspired women on whose shoulders lay the best hope for positive change in community life.

NOTES

1. Mumbi Gakuo, "The Kenyan Women and Situation and Strategies For Improvement," *Women's Studies International Forum*, vol. 8, no. 4 (Oxford and New York: Pergamon Press, 1985), p. 374.

2. *UNICEF News*, Issue 110/1981/4 (New York: 1981), p. 7

3. Jeanne McCormack, Martin Walsh, and Candace Nelson, *Women's Group Enterprises: A Study of the Structure of Opportunity on the Kenya Coast* (Boston: World Education, prepared for U. S. Agency for International Development, Washington, D. C., 1986), p. 45.

4. Ibid., p. 265.

5. Margaret Strobel, "From Lelemama to Lobbying: Women's Associations in Mombasa, Kenya," in Nancy J. Hafkin and Edna G. Bay, eds., *Women in Africa: Studies in Social and Economic Change* (Stanford: Stanford University Press, 1976), pp. 199–200.

6. Noreen Clark and O. N. Gakuru, "The Effects on Health and Self-Confidence of Collaborative Learning Projects." *Hygiene: International Journal of Health Education,* vol. 1, no. 2 (1985), pp. 47–56.

7. McCormack et al., *Women's Group Enterprises,* p. 243.

8. "The Kenyan Women," p. 378.

9. McCormack et al., *Women's Group Enterprises,* p. 266.

10. "The Effects on Health," p. 53.

11. *The Weekly Review*, Nairobi, Kenya (February 21, 1986).

12. McCormack et al., *Women's Group Enterprises*, pp. 161–189.

13. Ibid., p. 54.

14. David Smith, Private Agencies Collaborating Together (PACT), New York, interviews by author (May 1986).

SUPPLEMENTARY READINGS

Boserup, Ester, *Woman's Role in Economic Development* (New York: St. Martin's Press, 1970).

Brekke, Toril, "The Family—Kenya," *Women: A World Report* (New York: Oxford University Press, a New Internationalist Book, 1985).

Clark, Mari H., "Woman-headed Households and Poverty: Insights from Kenya," *SIGNS: Journal of Women and Culture in Society,* vol. 10, no. 2 (Chicago: University of Chicago Press, Winter 1984).

Clark, Noreen, *Education for Development and the Rural Women* (Boston: World Education, 1981).

Etienne, Mona, and Leacock, Eleanor, eds., *Women and Colonization* (New York: Praeger Publishers, 1980).

Hay, Margaret Jean, and Stitcher, Sharon, eds., *African Women South of the Sahara* (New York: Longman, 1984).

Huston, Perdita, *Third World Women Speak Out* (New York: Praeger Publishers, in cooperation with the Overseas Development Council, 1979).

Leavitt, Ruby-Rohrlich, ed., *Women Cross-Culturally* (The Hague: Mouton, 1975).

O'Barr, Jean F., ed., *Perspectives on Power: Women in Africa, Asia and Latin America* (Durham, N.C.: Duke University Center for International Studies, 1982).

Obbo, Christine, *African Women: Their Struggle for Economic Independence* (London: Zed Press, 1980).

Pala, Achola, "A Preliminary Survey of the Avenues for and Constraints on Women in the Development Process in Kenya," Discussion Paper No. 218 (Nairobi: Institute for Development Studies, June 1975).

Strobel, Margaret, "African Women," *SIGNS: Journal of Women and Culture in Society,* vol. 8, no. 1 (Chicago: University of Chicago Press, Autumn 1982).

Strobel, Margaret, *Muslim Women in Mombasa* (New Haven: Yale University Press, 1979).

Swedish International Development Agency, *Women in Developing Countries* (Stockholm, 1974).

Morgan, Robin, *Sisterhood Is Global* (New York: Anchor Books, 1984).

REYNA DE MIRALDA
Organizing Peasant Women in Honduras

Reyna de Miralda married a man from her home city of Juticalpa in Honduras and raised seven children. It was a grindingly poor life, with little hope for anything better. Reyna's husband allowed her to take one course in nutrition offered by a local church group, but then he thought it better that she not leave home again. So she started a food cooperative in their home and became its manager. When her husband died, Reyna had to give up the house and the cooperative, and had no means of support. She found training as a health promoter, first as a volunteer and then as a paid worker, and went to the outlying villages to teach women child care and nutrition. This was the beginning of a remarkable struggle to organize the poorest of rural women and teach them the skills they needed to improve their lives. With the assistance of several other health promoters, Reyna formed the Federación Hondurena de Mujeres Campesinas or the Honduran Federation of Peasant Women (FEHMUC), now a national presence in Honduras.

Women's organizations are not often revolutionary. They tend to need and to seek the support of the government. When a country is politically polarized, women are faced with the dilemma of how to command a degree of political power without becoming subsumed by one of the opposing parties. Reyna de Miralda believes that women are best served by an organization that clearly represents their interests rather than those of the government or any political party. This decision has made FEHMUC's path a difficult and controversial one because critical issues are involved. In Honduras, a campaign for women's rights and access to land, for example, challenges both the male-dominated peasant unions and the government hierarchy.

Reyna de Miralda has chosen to skirt this controversy for the present and to continue to build up the strength of FEHMUC groups among the rural women of Honduras. In a setting of extreme factionalization, she has been able to pursue her single-minded goal of gaining influence and resources for *campesinas* (peasant women). Through personal

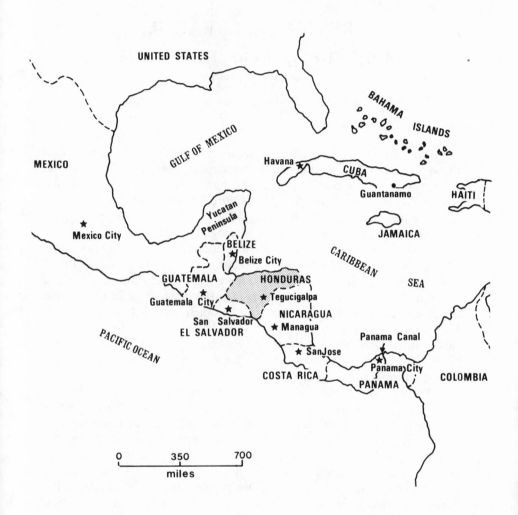

dynamism, she has succeeded in organizing peasant women—the most marginalized group in Honduras—with exhortations to "take destiny in your own hands." In Olancho province, where Reyna has organized the strongest and most numerous FEHMUC groups, the network of women provides a powerful source of support and reinforcement for each individual. It has also become an instrument that brings to the government's attention the long-neglected needs of peasant women.

1

Reyna Calix de Miralda knew a moment of vindication and pride when, at age fifteen, she was appointed a teacher in the local elementary school in the provincial city of Juticalpa, Honduras. For someone as poor as she was—of the lowest class, she thought—it was a great satisfaction to be accepted for such a job. The fact that she had completed sixth grade, unlike many of her friends, and had been an outstanding student qualified her to teach. This, of course, was not her first job. She had worked since she was seven, but now she would be earning a regular salary of 35 *lempiras*[1] a month at a job which she believed had real status.

Reyna was born in the achingly poor, dusty village of Empalizada, near Juticalpa, on January 26, 1938, and spent the first two and a half years of her life there. Her father, Jesus Enriquez Zapata, abandoned her mother six months after Reyna was born, leaving the two in the village. Reyna's mother, Antonia Calix, was also born in Empalizada to poor peasants, Izabel Calix and Salvador Banegas. Reyna remembers that her mother's parents, although they lived nearby, had little to do with her mother or herself for reasons that were never clear to her. As she was growing up, she heard her mother describe how strict and deeply religious her grandmother had been. Reyna's mother herself was a devout and demanding woman. Reyna's paternal grandparents, Jesus Enriquez and Ercilia Zapata, lived in Juticalpa, the chief city of the province of Olancho. Although they, too, were poor farmers, Reyna thought of them as better off and of higher standing than her mother's family and wondered if that was why her father had left her mother.

When Reyna was two and a half years old, her mother married Ceferino Vallecillo and they moved to Juticalpa, where they lived in one of the poorer parts of town, the barrio of La Joya. Shortly afterward, Reyna's first brother, Umberto, was born and the other children "came every two years." It was a struggle for her stepfather—a daily challenge just to provide enough food for his expanding family. He eked out what he could from his small plot of land and supplemented his meager earnings by opening a barber shop in their house. Reyna and her six brothers and two sisters had to find any job they could to add to the family income. Her stepfather, she says, "was very much a father to me." She has not forgotten his kindness, and his photograph is prominently displayed among the important memorabilia in her home.

At home, Reyna and her sisters performed the traditional female tasks: "We collected and carried wood to the house, brought water from the river half a kilometer away; we helped cook, clean house, wash and iron clothes, take care of the younger children, and put fresh soil and water on the floor of the house to keep the dust down." They felt lucky that even during the dry periods there was at least a trickle of water running in the river bed, so that they were never totally without water. The girls ground corn and beans every day and made tortillas each morning for the family. "We did everything that was necessary to be good cooks and good housekeepers." The boys did tasks "according to their age. As they got older they would accompany my stepfather to the fields and plant crops on a small piece of land we owned. Sometimes after school they would go there." It was a "parcel of land," she explained, "not really a farm," on which they grew the corn and beans that made up most of their diet. However, "we used very little of what was planted. Most of what we harvested was sold. The little we kept was not enough to last for long. The rest we bought in the store with my mother's earnings and ours. We would buy bread, oil, wood, beans, and sugar. Coffee we dried and ground ourselves." Since they owned a cow, they did have some milk. Reyna remembers that she and the other children often went to school after a meal of two tortillas and a glass of milk, which was their food for the entire day. "We suffered from not having enough to eat. . . . At the very beginning, when we were little, many times we would go hungry."

When Reyna started school, it was with the same sense of deprivation that seems to have haunted her childhood. She didn't know if she measured up to the other children. Fortunately, she had two teachers she

> loved very much who trusted me and understood my situation when there was a problem at home. Other teachers would nag, or insult or punish us. Children would have to kneel in a corner and pray for long periods of time as a punishment. Such teachers would say, "Your mother doesn't teach you good manners and your mother doesn't educate you or help with your homework." In school, when you are very poor, people put you apart . . . [and] teachers don't see you as very good.

Reyna was angered at any insult to her mother, who, although she had little education, checked each night to see that her children were doing their homework.

Reyna reports that she was always an excellent student and managed to avoid the petty and humiliating punishments that some of the teachers dispensed. She was a "good child," the kind that teachers reward with privileged tasks, and she was eager to win their favorable attention. When the class had dances or recitations, she was quick to volunteer as a leader. "Even though some people look down on the poor, I decided I didn't care. I wanted to do these things and I did." But the pride instilled by her mother and a defiance quite her own goaded her to prove herself. She says she wanted to be a teacher from her earliest days. After school she gathered together girls from her *barrio* and taught them what she had learned that day, emulating her favorite teachers.

After their move to Juticalpa, Reyna became reacquainted with her paternal grandmother, who took a particular interest in this bright, serious child. Reyna's recollection is that after her father deserted them, his mother offered to take Reyna into her home and to provide schooling. Reyna's mother, poor as she was, refused to give up her child. Because of that, Reyna has never lost her admiration for her mother. She also credits her mother with having given her the drive to make the most of herself. "She gave me pride in being a woman. She had no education but tried to give me all the good things she could." On the other hand, Reyna speculates that her life might have been easier if she had lived with her grandmother, whose family was better off. "I would have been free to do what I wanted." In addition, she would not have had to share with eight stepsisters and brothers the meager resources of the family; nor would she have had to work so hard to try to add to them.

Reyna did enjoy visiting her grandmother, whom she describes as an "eager and confident woman who liked business and knew something about it." She made candies and other sweets that she sold in Juticalpa. "When I was small—about seven—I used to go out with a basket of candies and cookies to sell in the streets after school. Later, I also sold various products for my mother."

As Reyna grew older, she started to do some trading and selling on her own after school, usually accompanied by her favorite brother, Umberto. "When I sold things for my mother, all the money had to go to my mother. When I sold things for others, I earned some money for myself." She would sell tomatoes grown locally and could buy such things as school supplies and "pins and thread" for sewing. She continued, however, to sell for both her mother and grandmother. She and her mother looked forward to the frequent town fairs at which they would set up a small stall to sell sweets. "I was in charge of selling at the table, and I was proud that everyone got to know me there."

Reyna might have been poorer than some of her friends in school, but few families had enough money or grew enough produce to meet their basic needs. Every family member had to help. Many of Reyna's friends went to school through the first three grades and then dropped out. Only a few fortunate children went on to secondary school. Reyna herself finished sixth grade before she had to stop. If there had been a night school, as there was three years later when her brother Umberto finished sixth grade, she believes she would have been able to attend. As she was fourteen years old, the oldest child in the family, and skilled at selling, she was expected to work. She found a job in a general store in town selling variety goods and was glad to be earning 15 *lempiras* a month. As her half brothers and sisters grew up, they all helped the family, and Reyna's stepfather was able to pay off some debts and buy a little more land to farm.

Reyna has few pleasant memories of her childhood. "As a child I wasn't that happy." The threat of poverty always hung over their heads. She did outstanding work at school and was proud of what she had learned, but she felt defensive about being poor. After school, there was hard work to do, and the misery and conflicts in the *barrio* were inescapable. "I was terrified by the men who got drunk at the neighborhood cantinas. They would spill out into the streets fighting. I saw two killings in such a fight. I have never forgotten it."

Other girls were allowed to play along the river nearby, but Reyna's mother would not take her there—perhaps, she thinks, because the other girls were "on a higher level" than she was. At least they had more time for play. "When I was older, I would sneak off to the river by myself to play in the water. The only place that my mother let us go was to church!" Her brothers, by comparison, had few restrictions.

After almost a year of selling in the general store, Reyna, at the age of fifteen, applied for a teaching position and was accepted at the local elementary school. It was the job she wanted most—a job she felt had importance and status, and one she knew she could do well. She set out to be the best teacher she could be. She signed up for courses in education to improve her skills, and for courses in mathematics to expand the range of subjects she could teach. Just as she has done all her life, she sought out any instruction or training that was available—as a passport out of poverty. As it was, by completing the sixth grade, she had earned the liberating opportunity to be a teacher.

Reyna met Filiberto Miralda when he came in from the countryside to find a job in Juticalpa, and they quickly realized that they loved one another. A few months older than she, he was a farmer from the nearby village of Pusunca. Their first child, Jose, was born in 1960, when Reyna was twenty-two. She continued to teach for the following year and even took another teacher-training course. Reyna says she generally found Filiberto an easygoing man, but as he objected strongly when she was away from home, she stopped her teaching and her courses. "I was very disappointed, but I realized that women had to stay at home."

As Filiberto could not support the family in Juticalpa after they were married, they moved back to his farm in Pusunca. After Jose was born they had children "about every two years. . . . I remember the day of the month but not the year." In succession, after Jose, came Dunia Alejandrina, German, Nolvia Janeth, Marlen Patricia, Diony Elizabeth, and Delmi Yaneli. The youngest was born in 1973. Although Reyna was busy rearing her increasing brood of children, she looked for ways to keep on with her teaching. She was able to set up an adult-education program in their house in Pusunca, teaching literacy and arithmetic, for which she charged each student a small sum. Enough pupils came, though irregularly, to allow her to continue the classes for eight years. The money was scant, but the teaching was the best solution she could find to answer her diverse needs—that is, to earn a few *lempiras*, to obey her husband's requirement that she stay at home, and to fulfill her resolution to continue teaching. Teaching, however few her pupils, preserved her sense of self-value. In her current biographical sketch, she marks the importance of that role by listing herself as a "rural teacher from 1953 to 1965."

Always on the lookout for new opportunities to earn money—which was always needed—Reyna persuaded her husband in 1968 to open a small cooperative store in their house in Pusunca. They had heard about the successful cooperative movement in the south of Honduras and believed it could work in Pusunca. The Miraldas organized a group of their neighbors to set up a cooperative, and Reyna herself was charged with getting information on how to organize it. She was also appointed its first manager. The Miraldas offered a room in their house to be used as the store, which the cooperative agreed to rent for 80 *lempiras* a month. This sum was meant to include Reyna's services as salesperson and manager.

Reyna was in charge of buying all the food, clothing and household goods the cooperative would sell. The Federation of Honduran Cooperatives helped her by providing a study of how to assess the needs of the community, how to stock the store, and how to build up the membership of the cooperative. The members of the cooperative discovered that what sold best were sugar, beans, coffee, cheese, butter, salt, machetes, work shirts, children's clothes, and towels.

For the first two years, Reyna was chief administrator, salesperson, buyer, and bookkeeper. She reports that the administrative committee for the cooperative, elected by all the members, paid scrupulous attention to the activities of the store. Regularly, every fifteen days, they looked over the books she kept and reviewed the plans for the store.

"The members felt like owners. . . . They checked everything, what the store needed, prices, invoices, daily sales, inventory. . . . They kept careful check of me."

Being manager of the cooperative was a useful experience for Reyna. She sharpened her skills in bookkeeping and merchandising, and learned important lessons about small-business management. Well organized and highly energetic, she was able to fit the duties into her household schedule. But even with the money they earned from the cooperative, the Miraldas were always on the edge; there was never quite enough. Filiberto farmed his small parcel of land, but produced barely enough to feed his family. There seemed to be no end to the struggle.

2

The poverty of most rural people was so acute that the government actively promoted programs to improve the skills of peasant men in agriculture and women in food preparation and nutrition. The Catholic Church also played an important role. In collaboration with the Ministries of Education and Welfare in 1971, it started to encourage Clubes de Amas de Casa, or Housewives' Clubs. The Church cited an encyclical of Pope John XXIII, himself a son of poor peasants, urging his followers to serve their communities as an act of devotion. The Housewives' Clubs were then designed to help peasant women improve their own standard of living and community conditions. Specifically, members of the Housewives' Clubs, who were often the wives, sisters, or daughters of the men in the peasant union, were taught basic health, sanitation, and nutrition, attended literacy classes, and were instructed in moral values and improvement of family relationships. Caritas, the social-action wing of the Roman Catholic Church, was the agency that promoted the Clubs and sought out women who showed promise as village leaders.

When Caritas decided to start a program in Pusunca in 1972, Reyna's friends suggested her as a candidate for training. Not only did she have the teaching experience, but she had shown her mettle as a leader in the village. Reyna was accepted for the job of volunteer community health worker and was then scheduled for the Caritas training course. She was enthusiastic about the training she would receive and the possible new paths such an assignment might open. What she did not take fully into account was her husband's reaction to this new interest. He did not like it at all. He disapproved of her involvement in the Caritas course, and he liked even less the possibility that she would be traveling around to neighboring villages as part of her job as a health worker.

Reyna talks about how keenly disappointed she was by his attitude, although it did not come as a total surprise. She was sure that part of her husband's objection to her taking further training was based on jealousy.

He was jealous because I was trying to improve myself and get more knowledge. He used to say that when women get more education it is no good for them. Sometimes they become more promiscuous. . . . They go out with different men, and he minded because of machismo. It was better for me to stay at home and work at home and not have any more education. The man, as head of the household, wants his wife to depend on him and wants her at home. . . . He doesn't want to be competing with her on the outside or to feel that if she gets a higher education he will become inferior to her. . . . Men don't want to see you talking to strangers, as your reputation is of most concern to them. Maybe they are right to fear that women, if they are away from home, might too easily go out with other men. Men believe they can do everything but women can only do limited tasks, below men's level. That's a sign of machismo. This is all part of our culture.

For Reyna, education was the only way to improve life for herself and her children. She would not accept her husband's restriction. Despite Filiberto's opposition, she accepted the Caritas assignment and participated in the training program. She was able to persuade him that the program would enable her to improve life for the whole family in many ways—including improving communication between them all.

Reyna recognizes that her husband had, in fact, a more positive attitude toward women than many men in the village. She says that she was fortunate he was not a heavy drinker—a problem that affected many men in the village and bedeviled so many of her friends. He cared as much as she that the children, both boys and girls, continue in school as far as they could. He too always urged them to make something of themselves. "He was jealous of me but not them." In their earliest days of marriage, he indeed kept her away from most activities outside her home; he feared her drive for self-improvement and determination to "make something of herself." But Reyna's obvious abilities, her restlessness, and her growing sense of authority could not be contained. By the time she was chosen for the Caritas training course, she had quite consciously decided to pursue her personal goals.

Reyna's role as a Caritas health promoter in the village was to demonstrate simple tenets of hygiene and sanitation, preventive health measures, the need for clean water, good basic nutrition, and child care. The role was made for her. She was learning and she was leading. She was still running the cooperative store and had recently had her seventh child, but the older children were well experienced in taking care of the younger. Moreover, as the small houses in Pusunca are close together, she was rarely far from home. Even so, her schedule was demanding—but Reyna liked being busy. As everyone who has known her is quick to point out, however, she has always taken on "too many things at once." She was stretching herself, testing her abilities in an environment that offered few challenges to an intelligent, ambitious woman.

The women of the village tended to gather together daily for the "glass of milk" children's program sponsored by CARE. This gathering eventually became the group that Reyna taught and led. CARE, an American-based relief organization, had feeding programs throughout Honduras. The presence in the rural areas of such nongovernmental agencies as CARE and Caritas, which focused on women and children as their primary concern, often gave women their first opportunity to receive training of any kind. By bringing women together in groups, such agencies often succeeded (if not always intentionally) in heightening women's awareness of their common problems. Because rural women tended to accept the cultural restraint that dictated that they stay at home, and as they were further isolated by illiteracy (which was as high as 43 percent in the countryside), these groups had the potential of making a real change in the lives of the women involved.

Whenever training was available, Reyna signed up for it. She was invited to take an intensive health-care course given by Caritas in 1973 and then attended three social-motivation courses sponsored by a voluntary development agency called Asesores para el Desarrollo, or Advisers in Development (ASEPADE). The next year she took two horticultural courses from the Instituto Nacional de Formacion Profesional (the National Training Institute) so that she could give advice on how to grow nutritious vegetables in kitchen gardens. Each course increased her information, her skills, and, most of all, her confidence. She discovered that she inspired trust in other women in the village, not only because she seemed to understand so clearly the subjects she talked about but also because she so obviously cared about their well-being. The special relationship that can exist between a leader and her supporters was slowly growing, and Reyna was savoring it.

Reyna's husband, meanwhile, had been troubled by a mysterious ailment. It became so debilitating that he had to stop farming. Reyna was forced to find odd jobs to earn the money to buy medicine and food. She had learned to do simple drawings for classroom use that a few of the teachers at school had commissioned her to do for them. "They were men who didn't like to—and couldn't—do that sort of thing." She also made and sold dress patterns and patterns for children's clothes. Poor as many of her neighbors were, they reached out to help her. When Filiberto's condition was finally diagnosed, it was too late. Nine months later, in early 1974, he died of a kidney disease, leaving Reyna with seven children and no prospect of support. Neither her mother nor her step-father could help her and her own father "really didn't care about me. When I was a child, he didn't do anything for me, and now that I'm a woman, I wouldn't go to him, first, because I get mad thinking about it. The other is, I'm ashamed of going and asking him." So she struggled to keep things going as best she could.

It was a critical and agonizing time. Reyna stayed in Pusunca for a year after her husband died, trying to keep the family together. She had learned to make bread during a Caritas course and was able to sell some of her loaves in the village. That kept the family from outright starvation, but the struggle to survive was almost overwhelming. Shortly after her husband's death, she had to resign as manager of the cooperative. She could no longer afford to live in their house, which was the site of the cooperative, but had to move to a smaller one. Part of what she and Filiberto had earned from the cooperative had come from renting out a room in their house for the store. With that income gone, Reyna had to find something more profitable than just managing the cooperative. "The other members of the cooperative liked me and trusted me and thought I was a very good administrator." They had succeeded in repaying their original loan of 3,000 *lempiras* and had earned an additional 8,000 *lempiras.* She was justly proud of her part in that accomplishment.

Reyna had always been an unusually resourceful and self-reliant woman, but there was little she could do to maintain herself and her children. Not only Pusunca, but the entire country of Honduras, was impoverished; thus, no government support services of any kind were available to her. In desperation, Reyna chose to move back to Juticalpa in early 1976 and live with her mother in her small, crowded house. She explored every path to earn money. "I had to put some of the children in houses to do housework." Five of them were in grade school at that time, except for Jose, the oldest, who was sixteen by then, and Delmi, who at the age of four was too young to work. The girls attended classes and then went off to their house-cleaning jobs after school. The boys ran errands or found other small jobs that would earn them a few coins. Somehow, they managed.

A turn in the family's fortunes came later that year, when Reyna was offered a job as a paid community health worker for Caritas. She had come to the agency's attention through her volunteer work in Pusunca. The job, one she knew she was suited for, paid 150 *lempiras* a month, more than she had ever earned before. However, the cost of living in Juticalpa was much higher than that in a village. Now she had to pay for electricity (Pusunca had none) and water, and more for food and schooling. Five of her children needed uniforms, books, and school materials. "It was always 'buy.'" The children had only one uniform each; one night a week the uniforms would be washed and ironed and worn again on the next day. They still had to work to help to support the family, but "at least not in other people's houses."

Despite the hardships at home, Reyna found pleasure in her new occupation. She supervised nine teams of volunteer health workers, who served their respective villages (as she had done in Pusunca). Each of the nine villages had Housewives' Clubs, formed by Caritas, and each Club had approximately fifteen women members. Reyna coordinated the health and family-welfare programs of the nine groups, provided the training, and arranged special meetings. She not only passed along skills and information but (and this was far more difficult) also had to motivate the women to practice what they learned. By all accounts, she was quite successful in her efforts. She reports that people from all over the region asked her to give courses or arrange conferences. She even organized a child-care center in her *barrio* of Juticalpa with the aid of Caritas.

In addition to building up a successful network of women's groups, Reyna developed a close camaraderie with other health coordinators working out of the Caritas office in Juticalpa. They would be the nucleus of her further organizing efforts.

3

Life in Pusunca had been sheltered from some of the crises that were battering Honduras during the 1970s. When Reyna arrived in Juticalpa in 1975 and began her job at Caritas, it was during a period of serious national turmoil. Her involvement with the cooperative movement had given her a taste of the broader social concerns of other Hondurans, as had her husband's connection with the rising National Union of Peasants. When Reyna joined Caritas, she became deeply involved in an organization with a national presence and scope. It was inevitable that her perspective would expand and that the critical problems facing Honduras would more directly impinge on her life.

Reyna had known poverty all her life, but now she was coming to understand it as a national problem. Honduras is the second poorest country in the Western Hemisphere (after Haiti), and as many as 65 percent of Honduran households have been assessed by UNICEF as living in absolute poverty. Whatever the statistics for the cities, the rural areas are manifestly worse off. A complicated set of social and economic conditions has caused an internal isolation within Honduras and a weak national identity. The fertile coastal lands, though developed, were owned by foreigners and a small number of Honduran families. In addition, companies such as United Fruit had inordinately high leverage with the government. Indeed, Honduras has been called a "banana republic," although the economy also depends on the sale of coffee, beef, lumber, and sugar.[2]

Unequal distribution of land, in terms of both quantity and quality, is a major cause of rural poverty in the country; estimates indicate that 47 percent of the rural population is made up of landless poor. Compounding the problems of poverty in the country is one of the highest population growth rates in Latin America, estimated at 3.25–3.6 percent a year.[3] The result is that out of 4.3 million Hondurans, almost half are below the age of fifteen, thus creating demands on social services, education, and health care that the government cannot meet.

As Reyna and her own family knew only too well, the majority of rural women live in common-law rather than legal marriages; most are not able to count on regular support from their men. Even when men do contribute regularly to the family, the income for landless males is so low that women must generate some cash by selling crops, eggs, and prepared foods, or by trading or sewing. In deference to the machismo of the society that Reyna speaks of with resignation and resentment, women are loath to admit that they earn income or that they work. The men are even more loath to admit it.[4]

It was in a context of widespread poverty, powerlessness, and deprivation for both women and men in the rural areas of Honduras that Reyna de Miralda developed her earliest values. She understood very clearly, however, that women bore the further disadvantages of a lower social status than men, a pervasive devaluation of their work and their accomplishments, a culturally limited set of options, and almost no role in the political world. After all, women were given the vote as late as 1955 in Honduras, the last country in Latin America to grant suffrage.

4

Several national events were of such magnitude during this period that their impact stretched to the dusty, isolated villages of Olancho. A hurricane that struck the north coast of Honduras in 1974 destroyed the country's export base, particularly its banana crops. The repercussions of this economic disaster exacerbated the growing conflicts among the competing peasant groups—one of which Filiberto Miralda had been a member—and between those groups and the conservative landowners backed by the government. Hurricane Fifi brought not only devastation in its wake but also a deluge of relief money from the international community, particularly from the United States. There was so much money, according to some international relief-agency workers, that a substantial amount was left over for development projects. Spearheading development efforts was a consortium of predominantly Catholic agencies that had been formed in 1971 with the participation of prominent members of the Christian Democratic party. At the time, the Christian Democrats were the opposition party, opposed to the military government.

The country had barely recovered from the hurricane, one of the worst natural disasters in years, when another shockwave hit. The chief of state, General Lopez Arellano, and other top Honduran government officials were implicated for accepting immense bribes from United Brands in return for special favors. The charges were grave enough to bring the government down. They also increased the natural suspicion with which the peasant groups had always viewed the government. Serious antagonisms already existed between the peasants and the government because of the deliberately slow progress of land reform. The Agrarian Reform Law, designed to distribute selected lands to peasant groups, had been passed in early 1975; but the government, torn by conflict, had delayed action until late in 1975, after the planting season was over. The delay enraged peasant groups, and some leaders of the movement considered land invasion (i.e., occupation of the disputed lands) as a tactic to force the government's hand.

The situation in Olancho was particularly tense. Olancho is one of the least populated, least developed, and most isolated regions of Honduras. It is a country of rugged forest-covered mountains and few roads, overwhelmingly agrarian and remote from any marketing center. Considered frontier country (the Wild West of Honduras), it has a reputation for lawlessness as well as a tradition of almost feudal power among its conservative ranchers and landowners. Because Olancho and its neighbor Gracia a Dios contain one-third of the territory of Honduras and most of the nation's state-owned lands, which were the focus of the land-distribution scheme, it inevitably became the center of the land-reform controversy. During the 1960s, many Olancho landowners began to enclose or appropriate state-owned lands, often through political influence, bribery, or outright illegal occupation. Many subsistence farmers were evicted by landowners from lands they had been using for years under squatters' rights. Thus the stage was set for the violent peasant protests that followed.[5]

Working with the peasant groups and encouraging their organization was Concorde, a consortium composed primarily of private agencies dedicated to rural development, including Caritas and other Catholic agencies. As the group became more politicized and more effective in organizing the peasant movement, it also became more controversial and stirred increasing government antagonism. Members of the Housewives' Clubs learned from the Caritas monthly newsletter about the inequities between social classes in Honduras and the economic and political injustices of the system. They were urged to think critically about their roles and to become involved in community affairs with the goal of seeking changes. While most members of the Housewives' Clubs continued to concentrate on learning domestic skills, others joined the organized peasant movements. When nongovernmental organizations urge social change, they run the risk of confrontation with governments that are not ready for—or actually oppose—such change. Even the once-docile Housewives' Clubs seemed to be threatening the social order.

In 1975, the National Union of Peasants (UNC) organized a march from Olancho to the Honduran capitol of Tegucigalpa to demand the implementation of the agrarian reform program and, more particularly, to protest evictions and the seizures of lands. They were met by government forces.

> In Olancho, the military, in coordination with the large landowners, massacred some peasant leaders, two priests and a social worker. These killings are known as "La Masacre do los Horcones." Some of the people killed were linked to the development process promoted by the Catholic Church at the time.[6]

Although Reyna was not one of them, dozens of Housewives' Club members were arrested during the peasant mobilizations.

According to some observers, the Church was appalled to find itself in the center of violent political and economic conflict. Furthermore, the military dictatorship then in control of Honduras had reacted with rough repression to the growth of the peasant movement. Several priests connected with the social-action programs of the Catholic Church were jailed in a government crackdown against dissidents. Other pressures were brought to bear on the Church to separate itself from the social-action programs. After the massacre, the Church removed its bishop from Olancho; some say he was expelled because of the activism of the lower clergy.

The effects of the political situation on Reyna's program were quick to follow. In 1975, Caritas informed its health promoters in Olancho, Reyna among them, that the Housewives' Club program was being canceled because of a lack of funds. Their recollection is that the Church was apparently frightened by the concept of an activist national organization it knew it would be unable to control.[7] Caritas stopped funding the Housewives' Clubs throughout Honduras, and all the workers in Olancho were let go. Reyna lost the best job she ever had.

Although the prospects were bleak, "four of us, each one in charge of a different region, chose to stay together and keep on being health workers. Different priests told us to stay together and to go to another institute to get help. We wanted to create our own organization." Women from the Housewives' Clubs in some of the villages begged Reyna and her colleagues to continue their visits and courses. Their reaction seemed a testimony to the encouragement and support that the Housewives' Clubs had provided them. Before the Clubs came into being, almost nothing in their lives had offered any promise of improvement. Reyna herself had found her greatest opportunity through the Clubs, after realizing that she was a talented leader with intelligence, courage, and drive. She would not let that opportunity slip away.

5

After Caritas left Olancho, several national organizations such as the National Union of Peasants and the Christian Democrats attempted to bring the women of the old Housewives' Clubs into their political orbit. Some Clubs did join with them, but another option opened—the newly formed and struggling Pre-Federation that was to become the Federación Hondurena de Mujeres Campesinas, known as FEHMUC. Reyna and her colleagues had been looking for a new affiliation to take the place of Caritas. One of the four health workers with whom Reyna had joined forces, Julia Saldeno, had become general secretary of the new organization.

The four women realized that FEHMUC could be more than an umbrella organization for the old Housewives' Clubs. It could also be a new power base for peasant women, who had no means of expressing their views and interests. Individual groups of women would have little effect on government actions but, together, women might become an effective force to win the attention of the government to their needs. Although FEHMUC would continue to require the support of the male political and peasants' groups, Reyna and her colleagues hoped to keep it as independent as possible. The dilemma—one they would have to face increasingly often—was how to steer a course between warring political factions, maintain FEHMUC as a nongovernmental organization, and yet share in government resources. The issue is a difficult one for women's organizations in most countries.

Although Julia Saldeno and Piedad Molina were the most prominent early members of FEHMUC, Reyna de Miralda is most often credited with being the organizing genius and driving force behind its growth. According to members of the FEHMUC Board of Directors,[8] the Olancho team at that time included fifteen women, coordinated by Reyna, who, along with the Western Region team led by Isabel Ochoa and

Rosadilia Rivera, were the key women in the organization's founding. Reyna's title at the time was coordinator of the Health Program for Olancho. In 1976, she became the first secretary of the group. This was her initiation to real political power, and she knew she had found her niche.

Although Reyna and her friends hoped to start a national movement for peasant women, their most crucial problems were local ones: how to keep their valuable program going, and how to earn a living from it. As health workers, the four women continued to visit the Housewives' Clubs in their old areas, but Reyna says that after the uprising in Olancho, the situation was tense and even dangerous. Although little was known of FEHMUC, it was under suspicion from the military government as part of the peasant movement, and the women feared political repression. They met with the Clubs at night and made little of their affiliation with the new organization, FEHMUC; they simply called it the Pre-Federation. Reyna tried to get assistance for the program from the National Bureau of Social Welfare, but couldn't even get an appointment. "We did not have contacts, so we got no help."

At an impasse, the women decided to ask their village clients to pay a small monthly fee for the training courses and demonstrations they provided. They had some early subscribers, but it was difficult to persuade women to continue after the first few months. Reyna points out that the Caritas program used to distribute clothes, medicine, and food (sometimes even meat) to participants in the program. "People had gotten used to constant gifts. When we could not give free things, people lost interest." Reyna also reports that other village people were resistant to working with what seemed an unaffiliated group. "People didn't know who we were connected with. They didn't trust us."

The four women worked for nine months without any outside funding, "but we kept on doing our activities." Reyna had to take out loans to support her family and sell the cows that she still had back in the village of Pusunca. "It was a hard life—a bad economic crisis—but we knew we had to stay together in order to have a chance." They raised money by selling food at small town fairs and holding raffles. And, slowly, more of the village women responded to their persistence and agreed to pay monthly stipends to belong to the groups. At first there were questions about the connection between the four women and FEHMUC, but the idea of being part of a national union of peasant women gradually took hold.

Nine groups of women, representing the vestiges of the old Housewives' Clubs in Olancho, became the nucleus of FEHMUC. Each group generally had about fifteen members. As the program grew and demonstrated that it could survive, and as the paranoia of the 1975 peasant protest died down, Reyna and her friends finally obtained help from the

Reyna de Miralda at a FEHMUC training session, Juticalpa, Honduras, 1985 (photo: de Miralda)

government. The Ministry of Public Health gave them a grant to run several two- and three-day training courses. The grant went to the Olancho division of FEHMUC, from which Reyna and the other promoters were paid.

Reyna helped to arrange children's centers in some of the villages. A children's center was often located in a covered area in someone's yard, where village women would take turns watching over the preschool children. Reyna persuaded CARE to provide milk and food supplements to the children in the villages where the health promoters worked. When no other transport was forthcoming, she even contracted for trucks to bring in the supplies. Receiving milk and food was a strong incentive to a mother to bring her children to the center.

Attracting valuable resources such as the CARE feeding program became one of the hallmarks of Reyna's success. She had successfully developed contacts that gave her access to agencies with funds, food, and training resources. Reyna was now sought after as an outstanding teacher and leader. She was dynamic and charismatic and inspired an awesome trust in the village women. "They treated her like a goddess!" said a woman who worked with her. She convinced the women not only to support her health training progams but also to be active members of FEHMUC. Olancho provided an ideal environment for the emerging organization; it was there that the strongest and largest network of Housewives' Clubs had been located, and there that the local leadership had proved to be outstandingly strong. Interestingly, the religious focus previously associated with the Housewives' Clubs (during their affiliation with the Catholic Church) had become more political. After the Church disassociated itself from the Clubs, they accepted financial support from the National Union of Peasants (UNC) and shared some of its political goals.

By 1977, Reyna had become an important force among peasant women in the Olancho region. That prominence demanded from her an incredible effort and exhausting hours of work because she still had a family and home to care for. Her lifelong penchant for taking on too many tasks and responsibilities was made more onerous by her inability to delegate authority. Few decisions could be made when she was not present. Political power—or community power—in Honduras is said to revolve around *personalismo*—that is, an acquaintance with someone who can apply pressure. Reyna was becoming that "someone." A few of the American development-agency personnel with whom she worked complained about what they saw as her ward-politics approach and her autocratic manner, a style far removed from the participatory approach of Hasina Khan in Bangladesh and Elvina Mutua in Kenya. But the realities of Honduran village life had led Reyna to choose a style that fit her own strong-minded dynamism and made success possible in a *personalismo* (or, in Reyna's case, *personalisma*) society.

That style was effective in the villages: The FEHMUC groups in Olancho were proliferating and most of them paid their monthly stipends. The very success of Reyna and her colleagues brought them into unwelcome competition with government agencies working in the villages. Reyna believes that a campaign was organized against them.

> The government had political reasons, but they claimed that *campesinas* women were not capable of training other women or being health promoters since we were without degrees. We worked hard to motivate women to go along with our ideas and suggestions. Then the government promoters would come to the same village and tell the people, "No, don't do it that way—don't follow those women. They're not doing anything for you." We spoke to the government promoters and said, "Please don't do that. Why don't you get together and join us? We could do more. You give the technical training and we'll do the motivational, organization training.

Actually, government agencies did provide technical training in such subjects as canning, household electronics, and animal husbandry, and FEHMUC members were able to participate in the training program.

It was true that many village women were torn between their loyalty to FEHMUC and the claims of the outreach workers sent in by the government. But FEHMUC held its own, and its groups continued to grow and generate strong loyalties to Reyna and the other leaders. They had perceived rightly that the women were seeking more than technical advice; they needed affirmation of their own individual value, and they wanted some small share of control over their own lives. As Reyna said, "When *campesinas* got together, they felt they were stronger and that they had rights."

The women even considered talking about their new hopes to their husbands,

> but their husbands really didn't give them any importance. Also they wanted to improve themselves so they could help their children and learn how to train them before they went to school. They wanted to get milk centers, to get better food, and [to] try to convince their husbands to join them and help them with their projects.

All these advantages would accrue to them, Reyna suggested, if their FEHMUC group worked well. Then they would begin to have some say in their families and in their communities.

As FEHMUC grew in Olancho and became firmly established, Reyna and her colleagues began to travel to other regions to find allies and to promote a nationwide peasant women's movement. They were aided in this effort by the men's National Union of Peasants (Filiberto's organization), from which they received support and funds. In her travels, Reyna was on the alert for important contacts with people who might provide future help.

Two people Reyna met would prove invaluable. One was Juan Ramon Martinez, of ASEPADE, a nonprofit technical and professional consultancy agency set up to assist the development of self-help groups in the Honduran countryside; the other was Vilma Pacheco of Escuela Radiofonica in Tegucigalpa. Both helped Reyna in drafting a proposal for funds relating to the health activities of FEHMUC. The proposal was sent to OXFAM, the British development agency. In early 1977, FEHMUC received from OXFAM a two-year grant for 20,000 *lempiras*. The grant supported the health workers of the Olancho and Occidente regions, with the lion's share going to Reyna's group. It was a great coup for Reyna. She was known to "take care of her own," in the best ward-politics style. Again, an international voluntary agency had made available to women's groups the resources that the government could not (or would not) assign to a volunteer women's association. The grant also demonstrated the willingness of a voluntary agency like OXFAM to take a risk. From Reyna's point of view, it was a better arrangement than any she had been able to effect with the government.

With the OXFAM grant, FEHMUC-Olancho was able to pay two health workers and one health coordinator, Reyna, to supervise and train them. Their first challenge was to establish systematic procedures and to elect officers for the groups that already existed. Second, they had to organize new groups so that the programs would reach the largest possible number of women. There were now thirty-eight women's clubs in Olancho affiliated with FEHMUC.

Reyna and her two assistants were to give courses to the village women in health, nutrition, canning, social motivation, administration, and food preparation to improve women's skills as homemakers. But the project had wider goals. OXFAM sent Reyna to Guatemala in September 1977 to look at successful productivity projects for women that the agency had initiated. Over the next two years, Reyna took training courses in food conservation, accounting and administration, adult education, and small-business enterprise. As always, she was able to draw people into her program. She enlisted the help of experts from the Ministry of Health and other ministries, and from advisers at the United Nations Food and Agriculture Organization (FAO). This was *personalisma* operating at its best.

FEHMUC was sufficiently organized nationally to hold its first Congress in 1978 in Valle de Angeles, a suburb outside the capital of Tegucigalpa. There, it formally changed its name from the Union of Peasant Women to the Federation of Honduran Peasant Women. It was a moment of exhilaration and hope for all of the women, and it marked an enormous accomplishment for the FEHMUC leaders—not least of all Reyna. The Olancho clubs were the strongest and most numerous in FEHMUC, and Reyna as the prime force in Olancho was a major power in the national movement.

The OXFAM funding formally ended in 1979, by which time the Olancho-FEHMUC clubs had become vastly strengthened and increased in number. Reyna says that after the OXFAM support stopped, the clubs were without money for staff, administrative, or program costs for almost a year. Some assistance came from the World Food and Food for Work Programs. Finally, they secured an important grant from the UN Voluntary Fund for Women in 1981. The Voluntary Fund worked out a program with FEHMUC to enlist fifty groups of village women who would be trained to produce selected crops, to set up stores to sell those crops, and to participate in the loan fund. The grant was for $35,400. Ten of the fifty women's groups were from Olancho. The grant provided some administrative support for Reyna and her colleagues, but women's groups that were not part of the Voluntary Fund program had to struggle along with neither staff help nor funds for project expenses. These lapses in funding, which were quite frequent, marked the negative side of receiving short-term support from international agencies, most of which seemed interested in awarding "start-up" grants for new projects.

Although Reyna had to spend many hours on national business related to FEHMUC then (as now), she knew a surprising amount about each project in each village. As she made her rounds, she asked careful and informed questions. She would unabashedly exhort the women to do better if she perceived a slackening of effort. She would tell them that they owed it to themselves, to all women, and to their country. She found ways to reward those leaders and groups that showed the greatest enthusiasm and willingness. A colleague reports that "the women try as hard as they can to live up to her expectations."

Ever in search of resources, Reyna made an important contact with a small nonprofit agency called Pueblo a Pueblo in Tegucigalpa. Through its co-director, Marijka Velzeboer, a highly innovative interchange project was set up as a connection between women's groups. Some of the women in Reyna's programs were to purchase grain locally, dry it, store it and then sell it—at a lower price than that of any other supplier—to the women in the Concordia Sewing Cooperative in a poor slum in Tegucigalpa. In turn, Concordia sent to Olancho a selection of clothes made by their cooperative that women there could buy at comparably low prices. Each group had small loan funds available for starting up their respective businesses. The project received funding from the U.S.-based Private Agencies Collaborating Together (PACT) in December 1981 through the efforts of Pueblo a Pueblo.

The Olancho groups were able to sell the grain far more cheaply than usual because the middleman—the "coyote"—was eliminated. The coyotes maintain a virtual monopoly on trucking and selling, and are right on hand when the poor peasants harvest their crops. As the peasants rarely have either the facilities for proper drying and storage of crops or the means to transport them, they must sell promptly. Usually such selling occurs when all the other peasants are harvesting their crops, the marketplace is flooded, and prices are at their lowest. Some coyotes are known to have two sets of scales, one for buying and one for selling—but both are rigged outrageously in their favor. By the time grain reaches Tegucigalpa, it may have quadrupled in price. Similarly, clothing costs as much as three times more in the rural areas than in the city. The reciprocal arrangement should have produced benefits for both groups of women. However, a surplus of cheap clothing in Olancho made it extremely difficult for the women of the Concordia Sewing Cooperative to compete at fair prices. The Olancho grain scheme, meanwhile, was hampered by a bumper harvest in 1983 that drove down the price of grain, filled the country's grain storage to capacity, and forced the FEHMUC women to sell at cost—all pitfalls that could never have been anticipated. The two groups of women had to call on all their courage and resources not to despair.

Small-business ventures with limited capital are always especially vulnerable to the vagaries of the market and the weather; the FEHMUC projects were no exception. But other problems symptomatic of women's small-business enterprises in every country, also came to the fore. The women lacked the skills to make the project work even under favorable conditions. Their knowledge of accounting, quality control, and marketing was minimal, and they had to learn to take advantage of the right moment to buy grain most advantageously—not several months after harvest when the prices are higher. Entrepreneurial skills beyond small-scale marketing were not part of their cultural experience.

The roadblocks that clutter the path taken by aspiring women's groups are simply part of the terrain, always unexpected but not really surprising. Another FEHMUC club was encouraged to start a solar-dried fruit-candy enterprise in the early 1980s. The women spent almost a year constructing a building for the project and installing a water pipe. Factions in town opposed to the project enlisted the support of the mayor,

Women in Olancho, Honduras, learning bee-keeping with a grant from the Voluntary Fund for Women, 1983 (UN photo 153311/John Isaac).

who instructed a team of men to rip out the water pipe and bury it in another part of the village. Only slightly daunted, the women found the pipe, dug it up, and relaid it next to their new building. Their gumption engendered enough community support to persuade the mayor to make peace. The donated solar dryer finally arrived, but only after it had been held up by the customs department for almost a year. After the dryer was installed, the women discovered that the local electric company was charging them a staggering amount to hook it up to the electricity because the project was "gringo backed." The project collapsed.

This series of setbacks destroyed the spirit of most of the members, and many left the group. For all their extraordinary efforts, they had still been defeated. Recriminations and conflicts were waged within the leadership, but a small core of women finally chose to press on—this time with a bakery. This was an enterprise with which they were more familiar.

The bread they produced became popular locally, but financial difficulties plagued the new bakery. Women sold the bread from their homes or paid their children to sell it because they considered street vending to be beneath them. That restricted their market drastically. More damaging was their tendency to sell the bread to neighbors and friends on credit, often not daring (or even wishing) to pressure them to pay. Very few of the women could keep accounts at all.

The project continues to this day, but on a smaller scale and a less regular basis. According to Pueblo a Pueblo, the consulting agency for the project, it takes time for women to make the transition from being full-time housewives and mothers to being responsible participants in a business venture. Such a transition not only requires a restructuring of their own activities and priorities, but it also requires a restructuring of their families. In spite of the many setbacks and conflicts, the women who remained in the group reported important improvements in their self-confidence and in their ability to make decisions and to work with others.

Reyna is keenly aware of the pitfalls she has faced. Her own projects have not escaped them, of course. One of her favorite enterprises is a bakery in Zopilotepe, Olancho, for which she helped secure a grant from FAO in 1983. The women's club that runs the bakery received a loan for an oven that it must repay. It is a large bakery, built with help from the community, and it has been set up with careful technical assistance. Recipes, printed in large characters and symbols for those who can't read, cover the walls as a reminder to the women to make all batches of bread in exactly the same way so the product will be standard. The teams of women employed there receive regular instruction and appear to work together harmoniously. A young American Peace

Corps volunteer worked with Reyna in supervising the project from 1983 to 1985.

The teams work terribly hard, sometimes for ten hours a day. Their bread is excellent; indeed, it is sought after in other villages too, although transport is difficult to arrange for. The women hired one man with a bicycle to deliver it; the bicycle broke down. They hired another man with a car; he is so unreliable that the bread is only intermittently delivered, and the women must pay him such a high fee that their own profits are greatly reduced. As they have had difficulties meeting the payments on the loan for the oven, they had to arrange an extension with FAO in 1986.

Some of the men whose women are involved are said to resent the whole project. And yet Reyna feels a special affection for this bakery, which is almost a monument to her ability to attract resources for her women. She visits it as often as she can. She has also taken the time from her overcrowded schedule to help the women bring fiscal reliability to the bakery's bookkeeping, as one step toward improved management. She is sure that if she can help the women find a better marketing arrangement, the project will be a great success. What does seem successful is the group itself and its spirit of confidence.

Reyna must spend much of her time overseeing the individual Olancho clubs, inasmuch as the national FEHMUC depends on the vigor of its grass roots. She is working against the reputation for failure and instability that plague other women's programs. Cecilia Callejas, in a study on women's groups in rural Honduras, reports that women told her, "We are killing ourselves for nothing. We work without hope." Some women leave their groups because of ill health or unsupportive husbands, she discovered, but the critical factors are the lack of good projects and too much conflict and infighting. If a given group provides women with a sense of solidarity, they will often remain with it, hoping that a good project may come along. But the unworthiness of so many of the projects and the friction that this problem has caused have made strong, stable groups with successful projects exceedingly difficult to maintain.[9]

Seen in that perspective, the Olancho groups that Reyna has led are even more impressive. Although their projects have had intermittent success, Reyna's respected—sometimes revered—leadership has apparently brought about a stability of membership and a sense of common purpose and unity among the women. They see themselves as a growing force, with influence on local agencies and affairs.

On the national level, FEHMUC in 1985 had 350 women's groups and a membership of approximately 5,800. Olancho, with 89 clubs, had by far the most at the local level.

Major strains and growing factionalism began to emerge within the organization, however. In June 1985, Reyna was due to step down as general secretary of the Olancho region because she could not be reelected for the same position. But she had carved out such an important role in FEHMUC for her Olancho group that she became fearful of the future without her leadership. She had been a genius at getting special funding for her projects and at ferreting out a whole range of special training for her *campesinas*. Some say that she has "cornered" funding for Olancho projects and, in true political style, has favored those loyal to her and isolated those who were not. Critics have also complained about her autocratic manner and the protective and secretive way in which she handles her Olancho groups.

More crucial in the struggle to control FEHMUC, according to observers, was the drive spearheaded by the Occidente clubs to politicize the movement. Reyna, determined to keep her clubs as separate as possible from political parties and philosophies, walked out of the FEHMUC Congress, taking her Olancho group and others with her. Women close to the situation point out that there was no single cause for the break but, rather, a series of tactical disagreements, personality conflicts, and clashing personal ambitions. The struggle between the groups continues with charges and countercharges that almost no observer wishes to try to untangle. The situation may be an example of what Cecilia Callejos identified as a major limitation for women's groups in Honduras—extreme factionalism.[10] Reyna has been accused of splitting the organization in two—the very organization that she had devoted herself to creating. But she would do nothing that jeopardized her financing from government and voluntary international agencies or that diverged from what she considered FEHMUC's primary focus—the direct improvement of the lives of peasant women.

6

Back in Reyna's office in Olancho, where one of her daughters acts as secretary, dozens of tasks are awaiting her. The funding is running out for several of her favorite projects. There are clubs with problems. She must arrange for one of her regular interviews on the radio. (She is proud that she has access to the radio to call meetings and make announcements of an event or a visitor.) On the office wall is a poster that quotes Berta Vargas:

> Por cada mujer que esta cansada de portarse como debil
> cuando se sabe que es fuerte,
> Hay un hombre que esta cansado de parecer fuerte
> cuando se siente vulnerable.

(For each woman who is tired of appearing weak
when she knows she is strong,
There is a man who is tired of seeming strong
when he feels vulnerable.)

The poster seems to express Reyna's own brand of feminism.

In her own life, Reyna demonstrates vividly the values she wishes to impart. Her home is a model of what the *campesina* woman could achieve with hard work. Her kitchen is scrupulously clean, and there is a water tap inside the house—a luxury. There is a fuel-efficient Lorena stove, made of local clay, but it does not yet have a chimney that would take the smoke out of the kitchen. There is, however, another and more typical cooking area in the garden. Several of Reyna's children still live with her, as does one of her grandchildren. Her financial situation is made more secure by the help of her children, but it is still marginal and precariously balanced. She is looking for a part-time job to help support the household. There is a CARE feeding program in her home, and neighborhood children congregate there daily, watched over by Reyna's daughters and other mothers. The children in the program are cleaner and seem more cheerful than those playing in the street just outside their door. Her own children have all received some education and have skilled jobs as secretary, mechanic, and carpenter. These are the traditional accomplishments by which to judge a woman; in her community, Reyna is a paragon of achievement.

Standing with a group of her women, she is an undisputed leader. When she is talking to them, she is said to know just when they're bored or restless, understanding instinctively what will inspire and unite them. According to other agency leaders, she has been able to organize one of the most marginalized groups in Honduras—peasant women. Her need for them to succeed gives her an evangelical power when she talks to them. People have questioned whether her expectations for women are not beyond their reach, but she's intent on proving the skeptics wrong.

NOTES

1. The official exchange rate is fixed at 2 *lempiras* per 1 U.S. dollar.

2. James A. Morris, *Honduras: Caudillo Politics and Military Rulers* (Boulder, Colo.: Westview Press, 1984), pp. 22–24.

3. United Nations, "World Population Prospects: Estimates and Projections as Assessed in 1984."

4. "Monografia de la Mujer en Honduras," from the report of Honduras to the 20th Assembly of the Inter-American Commission of Women (Santo Domingo, Dominican Republic: November 1980).

5. Morris, *Honduras*, pp. 77–83.

6. Celina Kawas Castillo, letters to the author (May 1985).

7. Marcella Peraza and Henry Maurer, *Honduras: Did the Church Start Something It Couldn't Stop?* (New York: *Ms.* Magazine, August 1977).

8. Castillo, letters to the author (May 1985).

9. Cecilia Callejos and Christina H. Gladwin, "The Examination of Factors Limiting the Organization of Rural Women in Honduras" (Gainesville, Fla.: University of Florida, 1983), p. 18.

10. Ibid., p. 19.

SUPPLEMENTARY READINGS

Beneria, Lourdes, *Women and Development: The Sexual Division of Labor in Rural Societies* (New York: Praeger Publishers, 1982).

Boneparth, Ellen, ed., *Women, Power and Policy* (New York: Pergamon Press, 1982).

Chaney, Elsa, *Supermadre: Women in Politics in Latin America* (Austin: University of Texas Press, for the Institute of Latin America, 1979).

Chaudhuri, Pinky, and Till, Naomi, *Participation of Women in Cooperatives and Productive Groups in Honduras* (Washington, D.C.: Economic Development Institute, World Bank, 1986).

Crandon, Libbet, *Women, Enterprise and Development* (Boston; Pathfinder Fund, 1984).

Gallup, Cynthia, "Observations on the Role of Women in the Agriculture Sector in Honduras" (Tegucigalpa, Honduras: U.S. Agency for International Development, 1982).

Nash, June, and Icken, Helen Safa, *Sex and Class in Latin America* (Brooklyn, N.Y.: J. F. Bergin Publishers, 1980).

Nash, June, and Icken, Helen Safa, *Women and Change in Latin America: New Directions in Sex and Class* (South Hadley, Mass.: Bergin & Garvey Publishers, 1985).

Pescatello, Ann, ed., *Female and Male in Latin America: Essays* (Pittsburgh: University of Pittsburgh Press, 1973).

Safilios-Rothschild, Constantina, "Women and Agrarian Reform in Honduras," *Land Reform, Land Settlement and Cooperatives* (Rome, Italy: Food and Agriculture Organization, 1983).

Staudt, Kathleen A., and Jacquette, Jane, eds., *Women in Developing Countries: A Policy Focus* (New York: Haworth Press, 1983).

ELIZABETH O'KELLY
Technology for Women and the Corn Mill Societies of Cameroon

Elizabeth O'Kelly began her international career by teaching basic literacy and homemaking skills to wives of plantation workers in British Cameroon. She moved on to the British Colonial Service as an education officer working with the women of Bamenda province. Because women spent most of their waking hours farming, collecting water and fuel, cooking, cleaning, caring for the family and, most arduously, grinding corn for the daily meals, they had little time for such niceties as literacy. Elizabeth searched out a hand-propelled corn mill and helped the women organize corn mill societies. The mills saved the women hours of work every day and allowed time not only for literacy classes but for other important learning as well. That was the first of Elizabeth O'Kelly's attempts to find appropriate ways to lessen women's labors.

Rural women are too often engaged in underproductive and energy-consuming labor. The International Labor Organization has called attention to their high expenditure of energy on agriculture, food processing, and water and fuel collection. Technology related to such activities has not been a high priority for governments. When in the face of widespread famine the fact emerged that up to 80 percent of agricultural work in Sub-Saharan Africa is done by women, the need to upgrade women's skills and tools was dramatically illustrated.[1]

Elizabeth O'Kelly understood this need three decades before such appraisals were made. Her approach was two-pronged. She wished to lighten the onerous workload of rural women so as to free them for other activities, and she hoped to make their labors more efficient and productive. The medium through which she worked in Cameroon was the organized women's group known as the Corn Mill Societies; later, in Sarawak, she worked through the Women's Institutes, which she founded. She was also keenly aware of the impact that new technology, introduced with high hopes by developing countries, was having on women. Paradoxically, it often had the effect of destroying their only

source of income, just as the rice-hulling machine took away the liveli-
hood of countless poor women in Bangladesh.

As Elizabeth O'Kelly wisely counseled, "It is important that a saving
of unnecessary arduous labour should not be confused with a saving of
manpower. . . . That is not usually desirable in developing countries. We
do not need to use a sledgehammer to crack nuts, but we do need to
find better ways of cracking them than with our bare hands."[2]

Elizabeth's unique interest launched her into undeveloped territory
in the 1950s. She is best known for the extraordinary success of the
Corn Mill Societies and the Women's Institutes of Sarawak, both of
which she initiated; but her true legacy may well be the attention she
directed to the nature of rural women's work.

1

"I was a little afraid of going up into Bamenda. I would have been caught
up again, you know. I couldn't have gone up and not seen all the
women. . . . It would have been a very emotional time," says Elizabeth
O'Kelly, speaking of some of the thousands of women who belonged to
the Corn Mill Societies. She was describing her first return to the Cameroon Republic since she had left, unwillingly, twenty years earlier. In
1961, she had been warned by the government that she would be in a
difficult and dangerous position during the plebiscite that was to decide
whether British Cameroon would join Nigeria or unite with newly independent French Cameroon to form a republic. Her influence with the
members of the Corn Mill Societies, numbering almost 30,000 women,
was greatly feared by politicians who supported the union with French
Cameroon. The plebiscite did favor joining the French, and Elizabeth
was allowed to return for about ten months to set in order, for a promised successor, the remarkable project she had initiated. When she left,
it was with great sadness and only a partial awareness of the forces she
had set in motion.

From the day in October 1950 on which she arrived at the port of
Victoria in British Cameroon until she left Sarawak in 1965, she wrote
regular letters to friends in England, carefully chronicling her daily life
and work. Her letters reflect the delight she felt in living and working in
the villages of Africa and later in Asia, her growing awareness of the particular hardships that women faced, and her struggles to relieve some of
the daily burdens that impeded women's advancement. She hoped to
have the letters published in order to "try to show something of the
working life and problems of that now almost extinct and often misun-
derstood breed, the colonial officer." In a world where the concept of

colonialism is viewed with almost universal bitterness and disdain, such a goal may seem wistful, if not quixotic. But Elizabeth O'Kelly's lifetime work, as a British colonial officer and then as a consultant to many newly independent Third World countries, demonstrates the far-reaching impact that one highly talented, compassionate woman can make on the welfare of women. She had chosen to work as a government agent but carved out for herself a surprisingly autonomous sphere within the bureaucracy. To do that required strength of purpose, courage, and continual negotiation with peers and superiors, especially as she came to perceive women's welfare in increasingly broader terms.

Elizabeth O'Kelly was born in Didsbury, then a rural outskirt of Manchester, England, on May 19, 1915. Her father, Alfred Percival O'Kelly, of Irish descent but born in Britain, was an agent in the clothing trade. Her mother, Nina Stevens O'Kelly, came from Somerset. Elizabeth, an only child, first attended a local preparatory school known as Miss Cooke's; she then went on to Withington Girls School. She and her parents lived a quiet and private life. There were few relatives other than a maternal aunt and her family. Elizabeth remembers her early childhood as uneventful. She enjoyed active games, developed a keen interest in sports, and loved to sing. Her father had suffered lung damage as a result of being gassed during World War I and experienced intermittent bouts of illness. Unemployment was a constant threat during the economic depression of the 1930s, and he changed jobs with distressing frequency.

My father's health deteriorated to the extent that, when I was fourteen, we left Manchester to live in the country near Poynton so that I had to leave Withington Girls School without matriculating. . . . I did nothing for the two or three years we remained there except run wild and develop my abiding love for country things. I was always a keen reader. . . . You might say that from the age of fourteen I was largely self-educated.

Her years in Poynton were lonely and isolated. Her father was now bedridden much of the time, a victim of tuberculosis.

The family returned to Withington when she was seventeen, where Elizabeth did part-time clerical work and babysitting for a year or so. She found a job at Withington Girls School supervising the domestic staff as well as the various electricians, plumbers, and carpenters who worked at the school. Although such a job might have been viewed with some condescension by her friends, Elizabeth had few choices. She had neither a formal education nor family connections, and it was necessary for her to work. "Money was always a worry."

Elizabeth enjoyed singing and had a "quite good, if small" singing voice. She had often been encouraged to pursue a musical career. When she became convinced that her job at Withington held no future, she decided to approach the nearby Royal Manchester College of Music. Lacking the requisite secondary-school degree, she had to study on her own to reach the standard for admission. It took great effort and the strictest self-discipline to master the subjects she needed for admission, but she was accepted into the college in 1937 at the age of twenty-two. By living at home and working at whatever jobs she could find, she managed to earn the modest fees required. She remained at the college through the beginning of World War II, working as a full-time ambulance driver for Civil Defense and fitting her college lectures and music training into a frenetic schedule. "It was an exhausting process. . . . In the end, I made myself ill trying to do too much so that my course took four years instead of the usual three." In 1940, her father died and her mother went to live in Wales for the duration of the war. Elizabeth received her teacher's diploma in music in 1941 but did not even consider starting a career in that field. World War II was consuming England, and she had already been drawn into the war effort. With no family ties to keep her at home, she joined the Women's Royal Navy Service (WRNS).

Elizabeth's promotions led her to the rank of officer, and she was placed in charge of the WRNS Welfare and Quarters at several posts.

> This was undoubtedly the most formative period of my life; even now I can detect the Navy's influence in something I may do. As an only child I had not mixed much with other people. In the civil defense and later in the WRNS, I met all types of people and had to learn to get on with them. The life accustomed me to authority, to both giving and receiving orders, to long and irregular hours of work, to considerable responsibility as a young officer in charge of a large number of women, and to not losing my head in a crisis.

In 1945, at the end of the war in Europe but before the Japanese had surrendered, Elizabeth was sent to Trincomalee in Sri Lanka (then called Ceylon). It was her first experience living abroad, although life on a British naval base gave her little opportunity to savor it. She was demobilized there in 1946 and had to reconsider what she would do with her life.

Elizabeth's hope for making a career of singing was considerably diminished by her five-year hiatus while in the service. "In any case," she says, "I found I had more of a bent for working with people, so I went to Primrose Hill College in Birmingham, which was then starting one of the first courses for community development workers—the object being to train us to work in the neighborhood centers in the new towns and in the poorer districts of the big cities." It was a one-year nondiploma course, which she completed in 1947—just at the time that her mother died. Although they had seen little of one another for almost seven years, Elizabeth and her mother had planned to set up housekeeping together again. Now she had no family ties and no particular place she considered home. She had never seriously considered marriage; at least, she had never met a man for whom she would give up what she hoped would be a rewarding career. If she had not already accepted a job as assistant secretary to the Yorkshire Rural Community Council, she says now, she might have applied right then for the Colonial Service.

Her work was to advise villages on building community halls and playing fields, to help women's groups arrange for vocational classes, and "generally [to] try to increase the amenities in the village to stop the drift to the towns. . . . It was work which I liked immensely, but it was very much a male-oriented world." Women had little prospect for promotion, and she had grown accustomed to far greater authority in the WRNS than she was likely to have again. She was restless in this confined society and knew that she sorely needed greater challenges. Three years later she applied and was accepted for an assignment as education officer in Africa—not with the Colonial Service but with the Cameroons Development Corporation (CDC). The CDC was a quasi-government department (under the authority of the Nigerian government) which had an administrative responsibility for British Cameroon (as it was commonly called) through a UN Trusteeship arrangement. The CDC had taken over the German-owned plantations of Cameroon after World War II and had run them as a commercial concern. By the terms of an agreement between the government and the United Nations, the profits from the plantations were to be used for the benefit of the local people. The rich soil produced such profitable crops of cocoa, bananas, rubber, and palm oil that the Nigerian government, under British rule, was prodded into undertaking more extensive community projects. Foremost among them was a well-funded literacy program directed to the corporation's 20,000 employees and their children, for which Elizabeth was hired.

In October 1950, Elizabeth set sail for the United Kingdom Trusteeship Territory of Cameroon, where she was to live at the corporation's station in Buea. British Cameroon, a narrow strip of land some 700 miles long and 50 miles wide, had a population of slightly less than 1 million people. In 1950 it was one of the least developed countries in Africa. It had no railroad (except for one on the plantations along the coast), no trunk road that penetrated the interior, no electricity or telephones north of the coastal area, no newspaper or periodical, and only 125 miles of paved road. In the rainy season, from July to December, the coast was cut off from the rest of the country for long periods. But Elizabeth's first view of Cameroon captivated her. As she wrote in a letter,

> I began to wonder if I had been altogether wise to commit myself to this for the next two years, but all such doubts vanished when Ambas Bay hove into sight, with Mount Cameroon (more than 13,000 feet high) acting as a gigantic backdrop to the small port of Victoria where we landed. . . . The prospect was magnificent.[3]

Elizabeth lived in a pleasant house provided by the Cameroons Development Corporation and had a retinue of servants. "This last week has been one continuous round of dinner parties, and even the missionaries change for dinner here," she wrote. She was launched on what appeared to be a singularly comfortable adventure, well supplied with the amenities of colonial life. But in recalling those days, she says quickly of Cameroon, "It wasn't the sort of country you went to if you were worried about your health or liked an easy life. As a result, there were no settlers to cause the problems that arose in East Africa." Three men traveling with her on the boat from England died of tropical diseases within months of their arrival in Cameroon. The coastal areas in particular were considered unhealthy.

Elizabeth quickly became engrossed in her work and set off to visit all the corporation's camps that dotted the plantations. She planned the literacy classes, hired and trained the adult-education officers, and employed the teachers. She was elated about the funds given her for the program. The educational plan that she drew up, involving the corporation in an expenditure of almost a quarter-million pounds, was accepted in ten minutes. She spent many an evening in the camps where the classes were held, and was struck by the great value that people of all ages placed on education. One small boy of nine, she recalls, walked more than a hundred miles to inquire of her whether he had won a scholarship to a corporation school.

By May 15, 1951, 2000 students were enrolled in the literacy classes. Within months, Elizabeth began to question whether the education the students were receiving had much to do with their needs. She argued that although "we are aiming to make the adults as well as the school children literate, we do not yet provide anything for them when they have achieved this." Never content to let a program slide along in a comfortable rut if there was a better way to do it, she initiated follow-up classes in African history, geography, arithmetic, hygiene, and diet.

Elizabeth became increasingly interested in learning more about local customs and practices. She visited the villages around Buea and examined firsthand the activities of the local Bakweri women. Like most

African women, they did not own land but depended on the use of tribal lands for their farming. The most fertile lands belonged to the plantations, and the next best and most accessible lands were used by the Bakweri men for their cash crops. Because women often had to walk several hours to reach their farms, they planted the crops that grew most easily—coco yams and cassava—even though they did not provide an especially nutritious diet.

While traveling through the villages, Elizabeth noted the heavy labors of the African women and what she considered to be idleness on the part of the men. The degree to which her Western assumptions had influenced her impressions was not apparent to her then; nor did she believe at the time that a Western view of women had shaped colonial policy, as indeed it had. In retrospect, she realizes that agriculture on the plantations was organized along gender lines that were not natural to African culture; rather, they reflected the English division of labor, which was considered a superior arrangement. Agricultural agents, for example, gave instruction to the men but not to the women; they did not understand that women were the traditional farmers, and they hoped to overcome the "laziness" of men. It is true that the agents, as men, would have had difficulty making direct contact with the women, but they overlooked the fact that women provided the food for the family and achieved most of their status from that activity.

Although Elizabeth could see that solid accomplishments were accruing from her work, a conflict with the CDC command began to fester. A new director had arrived who seemed to have no understanding of either her program or the Cameroonian culture, and she could foresee only a steadily worsening of relations with him. The tension she felt in the face of his directives and his attitude caused her to be edgy and easily provoked. She realized that she was issuing impossible orders. She recounts the time that her driver, just as they were about to set off on a long drive, asked (to her annoyance) whether he might bring his young brother along. Noticing the small boy's hacking cough, she grudgingly gave permission on the condition that he not cough during the journey. "I sat in the front in angry state until, glancing round, I saw the poor child sitting there with a rag stuffed into his mouth and came to my senses." There was only one solution possible. She resigned.

2

Elizabeth's fascination with Africa and with the job she could see herself doing led her to find another assignment in Cameroon. She got the job she wanted. In October 1952, she became a woman education officer in

Her Majesty's Overseas Civil Service (the Colonial Service), which was attached to the Nigerian government, and was assigned to work in Southern Cameroon, then still part of Nigeria. She was to be stationed at Nsaw in Bamenda Province—the high plateau Grassland area—about 260 miles and some two or three days' journey from the coast. The trip up to Bamenda by truck was as difficult as she had heard it would be. "The road was appalling, deep ruts up to and above one's knees and deep sticky mud everywhere. It took us six and a half hours to cover two miles, dragging, pushing, and digging all the way."

Until the mid-1950s, the road (such as it was), stopped at Bamenda Station, the administrative headquarters for the province. All journeys past that point had to be made by foot or on horseback. During the six-month rainy season, Bamenda Station was almost inaccessible by road from the coastal area; whatever had to be transported, such as mail, was head-carried by runners. As there was scant communication between the tribes living in Bamenda, of which the Nsaw was by far the largest, each developed its own vernacular. Cameroon, as a whole, has one of the most diverse populations in Africa, and English (or its pidgin form) was the only common language.

Upon her arrival in Bamenda, Elizabeth learned that she was to take over the duties of the provincial education officer who had just been transferred. He was part of a team of British civil servants stationed in Bamenda that included a doctor, veterinarian, engineer, police officer, agricultural agent—and, often, their wives. Elizabeth was to live in a town variously called Nsaw or Kumbo, 65 miles past Bamenda Station with a population of about 4,000, a school, and a hospital. Elizabeth loved the remoteness and the great beauty of the area. She made friends with some of the hospital staff, but most of her time was taken up with work and traveling. She walked everywhere, trekking miles to villages that were connected only by paths, facing physical challenges and occasional danger.

One of her first obligations was to call on the Fon (chief)—of Nsaw, the most important chief in Bamenda province. The Fon was an old man who had ruled many years in Nsaw, and his word was law within the tribe. Elizabeth needed his support if any project was to succeed. "He was an example of the last of the old feudal chiefs, with considerable power, but he fit uneasily into the new Africa." Elizabeth's meetings with him went well; the Fon gave his approval for the work she would be doing, recognizing that his wives would benefit from it as well. Next, she won the support of his wives, (called Ya, or Queen Mothers), who wielded great influence in the villages.

The women in Bamenda province, like those in coastal Bakweri, were engaged in subsistence farming, providing just enough food for their families from their small, scattered three to four-acre farms. In one village, some women had as many as fourteen different plots, the nearest of which were located about twenty minutes from the village and the farthest requiring overnight stays in the little huts built for periods of planting or harvesting. The women's farms were often situated on the sides of hills in the hope that they would be safer from the destruction of grazing cattle.

The women grew maize, finger millet, yams, and a variety of fresh vegetables including cabbages, carrots, and potatoes. The staple diet was maize, laboriously hand-ground by the women into a flour and made into a dish called *foo foo*. Combined with vegetables, this diet was better than that of the coastal people, but it lacked protein other than the occasional chicken and eggs that people ate.

The men in Bamenda province grew coffee and kola nuts, which they could sell for cash; they also traded in palm oil and often looked after the banana and plantain crops. In addition they performed most wage labor and were responsible for providing money for items that had to be purchased for cash, such as salt, palm oil, and cloth. Because they received money for their labors and women generally did not, women's farming was considered less valuable. Before cash became the measure of value, women's and men's labors were more complementary and thought to be equally necessary.

Elizabeth noted that,

> in 1952, the life of the people, both men and women, was a hard one, especially that of women. They worked in the fields during the hours of daylight (which, so near the equator, extended from roughly six o'clock in the morning to six at night) and then, when they returned home, had to prepare the evening meal for their families, often stopping on their way back to gather up large heavy bundles of firewood or to carry water.

The women also contributed their labor to their husband's fields.

The villages of Nsaw, unlike the plantations, were not developed along Western models; nor had the people been exposed to Western ideas. Elizabeth took pains to learn what she could about the people of Nsaw in order to be effective in setting up literacy classes. An unexpected source of advice and information was Phyllis Kaberry, an English anthropologist who had carefully documented the customs of Nsaw, especially as they affected women—customs such as the division of labor in the family, property and custody rights, marriage and divorce, land use, and inheritance. Dr. Kaberry was in Bamenda both before and during Elizabeth's stay there. Elizabeth found her work to be of inestimable value and felt that it helped her to avoid many mistakes.

On one occasion, Dr. Kaberry asked two longtime missionaries in Bamenda what they thought about women's status among the Nsaw people. The first said, "Women have achieved a remarkable degree of freedom and independence." The second replied, "The status of women is alarmingly low." The women then added, "Woman is an important thing, a thing of God, a thing of earth. . . . A woman is a very God. Men are not at all. What are men?" They pointed out that people mourn three days for the death of a man and four days for the death of a woman. Dr. Kaberry decided that any effort to determine whether "a woman's position is high or low, good or bad is, in my opinion, likely to prove profitless."[4]

Dr. Kaberry did, however, make a careful study of women's access to land, a primary determinant of their status. Although women were not allowed to own land (the land was usually controlled by the head of the extended family), they were generally given undisputed farming rights for parcels of land. The use of those lands could be passed along from mother to daughter. The Nsaw people would say "Men own the land; women own the crops." Dr. Kaberry observed that women tackled their work "with interest, zest, and pride." But some tasks, such as grinding corn, were considered onerous,—the more so during the hungry period (between crops) when the women did not have enough to eat or when they were sick. In rainy, cold weather, she noted, "women drag themselves out to the fields while men stay in the compounds around a fire and drink palm wine." Men were grudging about sharing their palm wine with the women, in the apparent belief that the women would not work properly if they drank wine.[5]

Dr. Kaberry found that although the Nsaw women hoped for husbands who would provide salt, oil, and extra food when it was needed, they held in contempt any woman who depended on her husband's earnings to buy food. Women were expected to ask their husbands' permission to engage in trade and to turn over the profits they received. But because the profits tended to be small and the women usually bought needed household utensils, tools, or seeds with those profits, men generally did not intervene. As women increased both their trading and their profits, however, the issue of who controlled the profits became more pointed. The men felt that they were entitled to all cash but worried that the women were witholding some of it. They did not believe that the women knew how to handle money, but they also feared that with a little more cash, women who were so nearly independent already might leave them.

3

Elizabeth was not at all sorry to hear that a new provincial education officer would be arriving in June, thereby releasing her from her extra administrative duties. In April 1953, she learned that she would be given complete control of the literacy classes. When the literacy plan was announced, many potential students came forward. The men and women were almost equal in proportion, in contrast to the mission schools, where the students were predominantly male because parents were loathe to spend money on school fees to educate girls.

The literacy lessons were illustrated with drawings or photographs that Elizabeth discovered to be more confusing than helpful. When students looked at a drawing of a hand, for example, some did not recognize it as such. Others found it bewildering because they wondered what had happened to the rest of the body. Elizabeth was reminded of the time when she had shown a film about malaria to the local staff in her barracks in Ceylon in order to encourage them to use mosquito netting. The film showed close-ups of mosquitoes, greatly enlarged. After the filming, one of the men came up to her and said that he realized why she was making such a fuss about mosquitoes, but that she needn't worry. "They may be the size of horses in your country, like the picture showed us, but it is different here. Our mosquitoes are only tiny." Elizabeth's story, which has been repeated often, drove home her point about the need for an outsider to understand the culture.

Elizabeth had the greatest respect for Phyllis Kaberry's understanding of Bamenda society. When Dr. Kaberry suggested that women needed some sort of hand-grinding mill for corn, Elizabeth's interest was sparked. She, too, had noticed that women were sometimes so tired from their task of grinding corn that they would prepare only enough for their families—even if they had to go hungry themselves. She seized on Dr. Kaberry's idea and asked her department for money to undertake an experiment with corn mills. She located a mill of English manufacture from a time when mills were not power-driven and ordered two of them. As she was allowed a great amount of autonomy in her work, Elizabeth was able to map out a plan to form societies of women in two villages to operate the mills on a cooperative basis.

> It won't be easy. . . . They are intensely conservative, but I think I already have the confidence of one village near my house where there is an excellent African teacher [Boniface] who I am sure would help me with the women. One-half of the battle is over already in that the Fon has approved of the idea in a big way and has agreed to let the senior Queen Mother (a person of enormous prestige) be president. The idea

is that the village women will pay for their mill over a certain period of time, probably a year.

Boniface was to be the first paid corn mill organizer and his village of Kimar, the site of the first corn mill. He had actually seen the mills at work in Nigeria and knew how much they could lighten the workload of women. This first mill had to be presented as a gift because the women had no idea of its use and were deeply suspicious of anything unknown. It took all of Boniface's eloquence and persistence to persuade the women. "Eventually, however, a very elderly woman much respected in the village came down in its favour and the women reluctantly agreed to a demonstration." Two women, expressing serious misgivings, agreed to turn the mill handles when the maize was poured down the funnel. To Elizabeth's chagrin, nothing happened. She had not understood that unless the new corn was dried over a fire, it would stick between the grinding plates. In addition, the women were not able to turn the handles of the heavy machine in unison. They announced that it was too difficult. The demonstration was a failure, and the corn mill sat unused for several days. But the bolder spirits tried it again and, having learned from the first experiments, dried the corn first and found the proper rhythm for turning the handles. The mill was soon in almost constant use.

The success of the corn mill at Kimar and the women's keen pleasure in its usefulness were much talked about around Nsaw. People stopped by to see it in action, and requests began to come for help in starting corn mill associations. The concept of women's groups was natural to the Cameroonians in as much as the women had long had savings and social assistance groups as well as traditional secret societies. Elizabeth had worked out careful rules for the Corn Mill Societies, regarding the use of a corn mill, how its cost would be repaid, how many members ought to be in a society, and what their responsibilities should be. The women agreed to pay back the mill's cost (the equivalent of approximately US $56 in 1953) within a year. At first they were charged a few pennies each time they used the mill, but the accounts grew to unmanageable proportions. They then decided on a fixed sum to be repaid by each person every month; this worked much better.

As she gained experience with the new Corn Mill Societies, Elizabeth learned that the number of women involved in any group was critical to its success. With too few participants, the mill was not economically feasible; but more than a hundred put too great a demand on the mill and caused quarrels over whose turn it was to use it. Seventy or eighty members seemed to be optimal.

A basic principle of the societies, as envisioned by Elizabeth, was that they must be open to any woman in a village who wished to join, regardless of her social, religious, or political affiliation. The only exception applied to the Fon's wives, who received a mill for their own use because they did not customarily mix with the other village women. (It was said that when the Fon's palace burned down, shortly after his wives received their corn mill, several of them risked their lives to save the mill; it was the only object from the compound that survived the fire.) Elizabeth cherished the hope that the societies could break down some of the tribal barriers. She encouraged women to wear their society badges when they traveled to other villages, for if they met women wearing the same badge, they would know they were among friends.

Requests for help in setting up new Corn Mill Societies began to pour in, and more men had to be hired to help Boniface. Strange as it might seem for a women's organization to have only male organizers, Elizabeth believed that such an arrangement was necessary. The job entailed traveling on foot or by bicycle from village to village, carrying mill payments, and sometimes spending the night in a strange village. Being away overnight was especially difficult for women who worried about being harassed or attacked. But Boniface and his co-workers did a creditable job and were believed to have the women's best interests in mind.

Elizabeth O'Kelly before she left Cameroon, Nsaw, Bamenda, 1961

Having received initial funding for ten mills from the director of education, Elizabeth set up the first one in July 1954. By October, eight Corn Mill Societies were flourishing. Contrary to her apprehensions, the machines withstood the hard wear they had received. They did, however, need to be protected from rain, from small children, and from unauthorized use. Around them, women built huts that could be locked with the keys kept by the head women chosen by each society. These head women were also responsible for the financial accounts. Though often illiterate, they knew accurately who had or had not paid her share for the mill. When all ten mills had been distributed, no more could be issued until those had been paid for by each society. The women paid their monthly contributions with scrupulous care; they seemed to have had little trouble in raising the money now that they had extra corn flour to sell in the market. They also had more food available for their families.

The Corn Mill Societies were successful far beyond Elizabeth's expectations. She was encouraged by their success, but, as she often remarked, the mills were really a bait to attract women to the societies and to classes that might help them in other ways. Now that the women had more time, freed as they were from their most time-consuming task, they did begin to consider other activities. They enjoyed the sociability of gathering around the corn mill and many societies initiated regular meetings. Some women decided that they wished to learn more about cooking and making soap. Because soap was costly and women had to ask their husbands for the money to pay for it, soap-making became popular in many of the societies and had the wholehearted support of the men. Sewing classes tended to attract those women who did not do the heaviest farm work. "Some women farmer's hands were too work-roughened to hold a needle easily," says Elizabeth.

Elizabeth was a constant visitor to the villages and a sensitive observer of women's daily lives. She realized how troubled the women were about the incursion of cattle onto their farms and how acutely they needed to learn better farming methods. Like most subsistence farmers, the Nsaw women were reluctant to try new crops and seeds because if they failed, they had no other food supply. Although their farming was not as productive as it could have been, Elizabeth was in total disagreement with the Agricultural Department, which preferred to replace farming women with men. "Our schools do nothing to help either. When Rural Science is on the timetable, the girls, who are the ones who will be putting its teaching into practice later, are marched off to Domestic Science." She struggled to find an answer but she was hampered in two ways: There were few teachers available to go to the societies, and the British agricultural agents were not willing to teach women. Ironically, the societies had expanded in the meantime and now offered a great potential to reach many women.

Just coping with her own living situation spurred Elizabeth's interest in useful, simple technologies. She knew how to mix cement in the proper proportions and could supervise the making of bricks. She oversaw the building of two water tanks for storing rainwater at her house. Each could hold about 4000 gallons which would see her through the dry season. She could perform most minor and even some major repairs on her car. In fact, she once walked ten miles from her disabled car to borrow plasticine from a mission school, walked back, and packed the plasticine around a cork to mend a hole in her gas tank.

Encouraged by the women's acceptance of the corn mill, Elizabeth looked for other devices that might make their work less burdensome. As gathering scarce firewood for cooking was a major demand on the time and energy of both women and children, a stove that used less wood could have major benefits. Elizabeth discovered the Hurl smokeless stove, developed in India, which not only used less fuel but also eliminated the smoke that often filled the small huts during cooking. The huts had traditional thatched roofs through which the smoke escaped, but more and more families were using zinc roofs because they were fireproof and did not require constant repair. The zinc did, however, trap smoke in the huts, causing the eyes to smart and respiratory troubles to develop. Despite her enthusiasm, Elizabeth found that most of the women were not interested in her new smokeless stove. They had always cooked on wood fires on the floors of their huts and did not wish to change.

The reader will recall that the advantages of the corn mills had been quickly apparent. "Women realized that in half an hour's time they could grind enough corn to feed their family for a week. Once the women's confidence had been gained and they had seen that their work did not necessarily have to be so hard, it became comparatively easy to introduce fresh ideas." But Elizabeth failed to persuade them to try the new stoves, which would have to have been purchased individually and whose benefits could not easily be seen. Only when it became sufficiently difficult to find firewood would most women consider another kind of stove.

Watching women working on their farms, Elizabeth also realized that their agricultural tools needed to be improved. The tools, made by local blacksmiths, had insufficiently sharp edges, so she arranged training for the blacksmiths to improve their honing skills. In addition the women were accustomed to cutting sticks out of hedges to use as handles, not realizing that the wrong length or thickness would make their work harder. Elizabeth found examples of properly balanced tool handles that the women themselves could copy. The improved tools cost the women no more than their old ones and had demonstrable advantages; most of the women were happy to adopt them.

4

Elizabeth welcomed some changes, but she resisted others that were altering the tempo of life in Bamenda. In late 1953, a 200-mile ring road was completed, making a circle from Bamenda through Nsaw and beyond, and then back to Bamenda. Elizabeth could now use her car to visit the more distant Corn Mill Societies regularly. She had become used to day-long walks and week-long camping trips as she made her rounds. The ring road also allowed access to trucks transporting local produce to new markets, thus opening up economic opportunities for the province. The same trucks brought back refrigerators and portable electric plants, glass for windows, and stone and cement for building. These new technologies added to the amenities of the government officers and tribal chiefs who could afford them, but they also widened the gulf between these higher-ups and the villagers. The similarly traditional community they had lived in was now being ruptured by the intrusion of modernization. "The chiefs, too, had cars and would drive quickly through their tribal lands, no longer spending time with their people."

The peacefulness of Bamenda was shaken as well by the growing forces of nationalism. Guerrilla warfare was widespread in French Cameroon, fostered by nationalists who were demanding independence and union with British Cameroon. On October 1, 1954, the new constitution of British Cameroon came into effect, making it a "region" within the Federation of Nigeria though not yet a self-governing one. As the colonial order was being threatened throughout Africa, Elizabeth anticipated the changes and deplored the shortness of her time in Cameroon. As she wrote in May 1955,

> I've been celebrating—though that is, perhaps, hardly the word—the most depressing landmark, my fortieth birthday. Even so, I might at one time have hoped for a further fifteen years in which to get this work finished (retiring age here is 55). But not now; I fear the way things are shaping politically. It is this knowledge that there is so very much to do and so little time in which to do it which weighs heavily on us all.

5

An explosive issue that Elizabeth wished to address in her remaining time was the controversy between the Fulani herdsmen and the women farmers. Although the Fulani had been invited to the Grassfields by the government some thirty years earlier, their numbers—as well as the size of their herds—had increased. So, too, had the population of Bamenda. The Fulani were required by government regulation to limit their herds, but they were known to drive their cattle over the French border for a few days whenever the tax officer came to do an annual count. The increase in cattle corresponded directly to the damage done to the women's farms. But another development had exacerbated the problem. With the introduction of coffee farming, a cash crop, the men had taken over the land nearest the villages. As a result, the women were pushed out toward the no-man's land between the village farms and the Fulani grazing area.

"During the dry season," notes Elizabeth, "when good grazing gets scarce, Fulani have been known deliberately to drive their cattle onto a farm. If a woman can prove whose cattle have done the damage (in itself difficult), she can take the Fulani to the tribal court; but the cattle owners are wealthy, and money, I am afraid, talks." The women rarely won their cases for they were poor witnesses. They tended to exaggerate ("a thousand cattle came!"), to ramble, and to make the truth almost impossible to determine. The Fulani were far more persuasive. Elizabeth took to coaching the women before they appeared in court and encouraged them to present their complaints collectively. Her strategy paid off and more Fulani were fined for damage to the women's farms; but this outcome was only a token. Many women were driven to planting on the slopes, which were safer from cattle but made farming difficult and inefficient. As the women did not employ contour farming but instead planted vertically, their practices caused serious land erosion, which was so wasteful that the government decreed that the women plant in contours or be fined. But the women did not understand this new technique and fiercely resisted.

Fencing was the only answer, Elizabeth decided—but the challenges were formidable. The idea of enclosing land was viewed with great suspicion, as a potential plot to take the land away from its traditional owners. She hoped to experiment in the village of Tabenken, about thirty miles from Nsaw. As the village had a Corn Mill Society and a literacy class, Elizabeth anticipated an outpouring of confidence and support. Also present was a large tract of farm land that could easily be fenced in to protect it from destruction by either Fulani cattle or village sheep and goats. But the project ran into immediate resistance. The administration was afraid that she would stir up land disputes, and the Agriculture Department thought she was interfering in its work. Using all her persuasiveness, Elizabeth finally won clearance to proceed.

After months of delay, the special sheep-wire fencing she had ordered from England arrived. Against Elizabeth's strong recommendation, the fencing was presented as a gift to the people, paid for with government community-development funds. She was convinced that the people should pay for it themselves. "I would not give the corn mills to the women if I could. Even the women who are my loyal supporters are suspicious. They argue, not unrealistically, that no one gives something for nothing." Although the women did accept the wire as a gift, it sat unused in the fields. For one thing, the cutting of fencing poles was considered men's work, and the men were not eager to do it. Hearing of this, Elizabeth decided to visit Tabenken, knowing that her visit would stir up some activity. When she arrived, she found the men cutting and carrying the fencing poles and the women digging holes for them and nailing on the wire. Some women told her that they had refused to prepare food for their husbands until the poles were cut. The fence, several miles in area, was completed during her stay.

6

Not all relationships with the women's groups were peaceable and productive, however. A war of sorts was brewing with the women of the Kom tribe in Bamenda. They had a long tradition of secret societies that put social pressure on anyone believed to have treated any one of them unfairly or cruelly. The offenses to which they reacted in particular were serious mistreatment of a wife, beating or insulting a parent or a pregnant woman, incest, and abusing an old woman. The women had effective ways of punishing the offender.

> The women of the quarter and sometimes the neighboring quarters then were enlisted. On a set day they dressed in leafy vines [and] articles of men's clothing, and paraded to the culprit's compound around five o'clock in the morning. There, they danced, sang mocking and usually obscene songs composed for the occasion, and defiled the compound by defecation or by urinating in the water storage-vessels. If the culprit was seen, he could be pelted with stones or a type of wild fruit called "garden eggs."[6]

The culprit usually tried to make amends quickly.

At the height of their power, the Kom women's societies regulated an extraordinary range of women's activities. They controlled the markets. They could prevent from farming any women who did not follow their leadership and regulations. They ruled that any woman who sent her children to school or used the hospital, churches, or courts, would be exiled. They were known to beat a woman or to destroy her crops if she refused to join their group. As they grew more powerful they actually ran many of the Kom villages, and as they became more organized they acted together when the cause was important enough. Not surprisingly the politicians came to perceive their usefulness. In Kom, two men tried to incite the women to unseat their political rivals by persuading them that the government was going to sell their farming land to the hated Ibo tribe. Elizabeth reported that an Ibo agricultural agent who happened to be teaching the women contour farming was accused by the politicians of trying to get the women's lands. He was killed, and an investigating agent was poisoned. Four of the women leaders were summoned for questioning by the government.

Stirred to rebellion by the two politicians, 2,000 women marched the 38 miles to the government station at Bamenda in November 1958. The Kom women were also outraged about the regulation that they had to replace their traditional vertical patterns with contour farming on the slopes. That seemed proof enough that their land was going to be sold. As several women had in fact been fined for that offense, their belief was reinforced; for years thereafter, women associated contour farming with loss of their lands. They also continued to express anger over the damage done to their crops by Fulani herds. In the Nsaw area, some women killed a number of Fulani cattle in revenge and were subsequently sent to jail.

The rebellion against the government persisted in Bamenda for more than a year, eventually involving close to 7,000 women. Finally, the authorities met with the women, reassuring them that their land was not being sold, that the contour farming regulation would not be enforced, and that fines for violation of the regulation would be reimbursed. In exchange, the women would have to stop their harassment of those who did not want to join them. The women seemed satisfied; although their societies continued, there were no more large demonstrations.

Elizabeth's reputation was so substantial by this time that she was asked by the government to attempt to bring Corn Mill Societies into the area as a means of pacifying the women. She could foresee difficulties however. On December 29, 1958, she wrote:

> Things, I'm afraid, go from bad to worse in the Kom area. A detachment of police and some army men are there now; one headmaster has mysteriously died, [and] so has a senior police officer. The schools are still boycotted and the women's secret society, which has started all this, continues to terrorize the other women.

She postponed the assignment because she thought the timing was wrong. She also refused to make her first entry into the Kom villages escorted by heavily armed soldiers, as the government had intended. When she went, she had to go alone; and she would do so on her return from leave.

When Elizabeth returned to Bamenda, she began negotiations with the Kom women. She believed that the situation there had become less fractious, although resentments were still close to the surface. Her strategy was to expand the Corn Mill Societies in ever-widening circles around the Kom area. She counted on the popularity of the literacy classes to help her gain a foothold and, indeed, found little opposition in eight of the villages. About a year passed before the leaders of the secret society in Kom realized that competing societies were growing up around them and that some of the Kom women were drifting off to the corn mill groups. The head woman was infuriated. She visited the surrounding villages, forbidding women to use corn mills and threatening to destroy any she found. But the Corn Mill Society women had been using the mills for several months by this time and found them far too useful to give up. Now almost 500 strong, they were not afraid to stand up to the head woman of Kom.

Elizabeth was not surprised to be summoned to a meeting in Kom with the local authorities and the secret society leaders. Her anxiety was heightened on the road to Kom as she passed groups of women wearing tufts of grass and leaves, a sure sign of trouble. "I was scared stiff that day!" She did not bring an interpreter with her. It would have been unfair to involve any of her staff in what might have proved to be, literally, a bloody business. The head woman accused Elizabeth of giving corn mills only to those women who were members of the opposition party. Elizabeth replied that so long as secret societies were boycotting the corn mill groups, such a distribution was inevitable. The secret societies might, however, have the mills any time they wanted them. The head woman demanded that the mills be removed from all the villages; if not, the secret societies would attack. Elizabeth refused. She pointed out that there were now 500 members of the corn mill groups, as compared with the 400 secret society supporters. At that point in the standoff, Elizabeth left, with no further resolution in sight. A year later, when she visited the area, none of the corn mill groups had been attacked and their mills were still functioning.

In January 1958, Elizabeth was able to report the existence of 69 active Corn Mill Societies as well as other groups, already formed, that were waiting for mills. She was now able to address an issue that had long challenged her: how to increase the training programs available to women. She suggested that the societies form into regional groups.

Each group will be encouraged to build a meeting house in a central village which they can all reach easily. We shall then hold monthly meetings in these halls to which each member society will be able to send members. In this way one teacher will be able to cast her net over almost a dozen villages.

Each society within walking distance was invited to send two members to the first course. The corn mills had made such a difference in the women's daily workload that many women were able to attend, especially now that they could bring their children. The women learned the usual domestic-science subjects: cooking and nutrition, soap- and bread-making, and simple sewing. During meals, the women watched as their teachers ate eggs. "After a few days, they [did] so also (they believe that European babies are born bald . . . because of our passion for eggs). When they saw that Boniface was not taken ill after drinking milk, they [were] willing to risk it themselves." The courses were well received and the women were enthusiastic. Elizabeth observed that illiterate people often had "phenomenal memories," and she hoped that the women "will then return to their villages and repeat what they have learned here."

Soon there were six regional groups, each representing fifteen to twenty societies. "They are all busy building their meeting halls. The

Elizabeth O'Kelly and Boniface meeting with Corn Mill Society members, Bamenda, Cameroon, 1958 (photographer: Phyllis Kaberry)

women are making the bricks, wherever possible on the site, and carrying in the grass for the roofs." With the new centers as focal points, Elizabeth arranged for a much-expanded program of instruction.

7

Elizabeth was to be granted an unexpected honor. The Fon of Nsaw chose to make her a Ya, or Queen Mother, of the tribe. Known as "Bunning the Fon," the ceremony is somewhat akin to the process of being presented at the British Court and receiving a title. It was a complex ritual. A necessary part of the event involved the gifts offered to the Fon by the family of the person being honored. The women of the Corn Mill Societies announced that they were Elizabeth's family. On the day of the ceremony, more than 1,000 women came to the Fon's palace, each bearing a six-foot length of firewood, the traditional gift to the Fon. Some had come from villages that were three days' walking distance from Nsaw, and even Corn Mill Society members outside the Fon's tribe asked to attend.

Elizabeth wrote, "They are as proud of the honour as I am, but perhaps the thing that pleases me most is my title—'Ya O Ngalim, Queen of the women who work.'" The women of the town had made all the arrangements, including the housing and feeding of more than 1,000 women.

After years of agitating, Elizabeth finally persuaded the Agricultural Department to lend her program an agricultural assistant. She wanted him to help the women of Tabenkin to contour their land and improve their farming. For all the resistance, contour farming was far more productive than their downhill method. That fact, however, had yet to be demonstrated.

> The policy of the Agricultural Department, for a number of years, had been to actively discourage women from farming at all and to try to persuade the men to take their place—with a conspicuous lack of success. As the influence of the societies gradually made itself felt, however, the department began to appreciate that the women were far more open to new ideas than the men and far harder working.[7]

In time, agricultural assistants were appointed to work in the dozen or more villages that belonged to each of the regional groups, and some of the women actually began to do contour farming.

Cooperative farms were proving to be profitable ventures for some Corn Mill Societies. The chief advantage of the farms, in Elizabeth's view, was that women were willing to experiment with new crops because a failure on land other than their own would not force them to go hungry. Several agreed to try a new high-yield maize that the Agricultural Department was eager to introduce, but before they would agree to grow it, they had to taste a sample and then test it for grinding in the mill.

At Kimar, the women decided to raise poultry; for feed, they would use the bran that was left over after the maize was ground. Other societies were starting up fuel plantations. The government supplied the eucalyptus seedlings, and the women provided the labor and the land. The hope was that by planting seedlings every year for seven years, there would be a steady supply of firewood after the trees matured. "Altogether we are making immense strides forward now!"

A cooperative store became another sought-after project. The head women of all the societies joined forces and opened the first cooperative in Kumbo in 1960, somewhat short of stock but with 4,000 women shareholders. The shop was stocked with enamel basins, cutlery, hoes and spades, rope, barbed wire and chicken wire, notebooks and pencils for school, caustic soda for making soap, "and, of course, corn mills!" It did not carry merchandise that women could easily buy from local traders, especially cloth, so as to avoid incurring the antagonism of these traders. At the opening of the Kumbo shop, Elizabeth wondered if all 4,000 shareholders had turned up. Customers thronged the store, and almost everything for sale in the shop was bought. "As the novelty wore off, the sales became less spectacular and settled down to a steady but not dramatic weekly income." The women did have difficulty managing the cooperative stores and keeping accurate records. They hired a retired male schoolteacher, to do these tasks, "but the women took every opportunity of reminding him that they were in charge."

Elizabeth found it difficult to keep track of the actual number of Corn Mill Societies in existence because they were multiplying so rapidly. By the end of 1959, she estimated, there were more than 200 societies and at least 20,000 members. After years of "pushing up hill," she felt that she had finally come to the top. Her success was officially acknowledged when she was made a Member of the Order of the British Empire by the Queen in 1959.

8

Elizabeth's fascination with small-scale technological improvements was strongly shaped by the overmechanization she observed in development projects. She speaks despairingly about the introduction of tractors for

farming in Cameroon. Highly touted by agricultural officers and beneficial in some circumstances, they were generally nevertheless inappropriate for much of the shallow soil. They were also impractical in the
mountainous terrain of Bamenda, where there were few facilities for
repair and maintenance. In Elizabeth's view, farmers were worse off as a
result of the well-intentioned but misguided aid programs that had
diverted their energies. Elizabeth hoped to draw important lessons from
the failures and successes of the new technologies so as to encourage
more rational development. Such observations led her to wonder why
no one had published a book of simple drawings and plans for such
things as water connections, community halls, market stalls, and cattle
grids or fencing, as such materials could be used by village people and
community agents alike. It was an idea that, given sufficient time, she
would undertake.

In the progressive village of Kimar, Elizabeth discovered a way to
bring water to the center of the village. Women and children had to walk
a significant distance to the mountain streams for water. She located a
light-weight piping that could be used easily by the villagers and had a
stone tank built that would fill up during the night. The town of Tabenken wanted water too. The men there were particularly helpful, pre-
sumably because they were the ones who washed the clothes. Although
she had heard that men in some villages did the washing, she had not
observed it herself. "When I commented on this to Boniface, he was
surprised that I should think there was anything odd about it. As he said,
only too truly, 'the women have enough work to do already.'" When the
water projects were finished in Kimar and Tabenken, they were opened
with great rejoicing.

Always at issue was the determination of whether a particular new
technology was useful enough to people that they would protect or
maintain it. A year after the opening of the Tabenken water point, a great
cloudburst washed away the small dam that held back the water for the
tank. Many of the pipes as well were either washed away or shattered by
the force of the current. The men and women of the town quickly
started to build a stone breakwater to prevent the banks from collapsing
further. The men worked up to their waists in the swift-flowing icy
water, and the women carried the stone and the sand. The village water
supply had become important to them all, including the men, and they
had learned how to repair and maintain the technology underlying it.
The project itself stood in contrast to many a broken, abandoned well
in other rural areas.

9

On February 13, 1961, the people of the southern region of British Cameroon voted to become part of the new Republic of Cameroon. The northern region voted to remain with Nigeria. Elizabeth wrote, "I have nine months to round off work here when I had hoped for nine years." Elizabeth had been at great pains to appear totally impartial about the plebiscite, but she was naturally suspected of "using influence." The women of the Corn Mill Societies were jokingly described as her army. The sheer numbers of the societies' women were tantalizing to politicians.

> Both political parties are after them, as is only to be expected, as the most intelligent and progressive women in a village could easily turn out the vote. . . . Everywhere I go, the women ask me which way they should vote (and so do the men), and I have to reply that I cannot help them.

In Elizabeth's view, the Bamenda people did not favor union with Nigeria, partly because of their antagonism toward the neighboring Nigerian Ibo and partly because of the appeal implicit in the politicians' promise of "one Cameroon." Some women from the Corn Mill Societies came to Elizabeth after the plebiscite to say that they had voted for joining the French territory because they had been told that if they did, she would be able to stay.

After the plebiscite, the country was in a turmoil, breaking down again into tribal entities. "Politicians would not be politicians if they did not practice 'divide and rule.' There is an even broader split between the Grasslanders and the forest dwellers of the south." Old grudges were being paid off. Boniface's life had been threatened twice, Elizabeth believed, by the Fulani herdsmen he had testified against.

For Elizabeth, the next months became a race to get things in order. There was a possibility that she would be invited by the new government to work in the Community Development division that she had helped to organize. Her other options were to apply for a comparable post with the government in Nigeria, where others would have prior claims for advancement, or to retire. She decided on the latter course.

It was a difficult decision. She had hoped to end her career in Cameroon and to see her work firmly planted there. She tried but failed to find an African woman to replace her. Kate Steane, an education officer, was highly qualified but she already had an important post in Buea. Other women were not willing to take a job that might require them to travel alone or were fearful of remaining in Bamenda if they were from the coastal area. Elizabeth could only hope that the Corn Mill Societies were sufficiently established that they could continue on their own. "They have their agricultural assistants working with them now, land utilisation is being looked into, corn mills are readily obtainable, and they know how to put up fences and water points. I fear, however, that the educational programme will slip back." She consoled herself with the recollection that UNESCO had sent in two community development workers to take over some of her activities in Buea, and that the Dutch Peace Corps had sent two volunteers to continue her work on appropriate technology. But she was not happy to hear that the volunteers had built "beautiful and elaborate hen houses. The hens were housed better than the people! When the volunteers left, the hens died. Since the building was too grand for anyone in the village to live in, they decided to make it a school."

Elizabeth left Cameroon at the end of September 1961. Under instructions from the government, she was not to tell the Corn Mill Society women that she was leaving the country, for fear that her leaving might cause demonstrations; she was also told, upon her departure, that she could not have a visa to return. The women believed that she was going to Buea to work in the Community Development Bureau, where she could continue to help them. She did not return for a visit to Cameroon until 1982, and even then she chose not to go up to Bamenda because she feared that the event might still be too emotional. "The importance of being made a Ya [Queen Mother] still had force." She did learn that a lack of government attention and resources had undermined some of the societies. Many others, however, had been integrated into the National Women's Organization of Cameroon, providing a strong backbone for that organization. Still others, according to community development workers, had become the hub of the cooperative movement in Bamenda. The cooperatives started by Elizabeth and the societies had indeed taken hold.

Elizabeth also discovered that when the Premier of Cameroon visited Nsaw, about a year after her departure, "several thousand women gathered to see him and demanded to know why nothing had been done for them since I left. . . . Boniface is to work with them again. I am told that the Premier was quite intimidated." Dr. Hilda Platzer, who had worked at the Catholic mission in Nsaw and was a close friend of Elizabeth, said that she had heard in 1983 that old hand-powered corn mills still existed in the smaller villages. In the larger towns at present, new mills are diesel powered and are run by men, with the result that some of the old Corn Mill Societies have become oil societies. The women rent trucks to bring oil up from the coast to Bamenda and make good profits selling it. Moreover, some of the old groups have developed into savings societies, now that women have cash income. Vincent Ngo, whose mother had attended one of Elizabeth's literacy classes, was a student at the London School of Economics, and visited Elizabeth occasionally to bring her news of Bamenda. Vincent asserts that it was his mother's participation in the literacy class that laid the groundwork for his own education. Elizabeth cherishes those connections, especially insofar as they reinforce her hope that the work of the societies continues to expand the lives of the Bamenda women.

Elizabeth's success in Cameroon was shaped, in part, by her profound respect for women's capacity to act in their own best interests—even when the reasons for their behavior were not apparent to outsiders. The moment had been ripe for her work in Bamenda. The old structures were changing, women were ready for new opportunities, the resources were available, and Elizabeth was the inspired catalyst.

10

Elizabeth's work in Cameroon had led her into a totally unexpected area, one that was to win her world recognition—the development of intermediate technologies to make women's work more productive and less burdensome. More immediately known was her success in helping women to establish their powerful Corn Mill Societies. The two accomplishments are intertwined. As she explains, "intermediate technology is really the best approach for rural development programs." Her successes were written about in foreign service journals and other publications. The Department of Technical Cooperation in England naturally seized upon her rare experience and talents and asked her to go to Sarawak, in Borneo, to organize women's groups. She happily accepted a three-year assignment there.

Sarawak, with its 1 million inhabitants, occupies part of the island of Borneo, sharing it with Indonesia to the south and Brunei and Sabah to the east. It had been ruled by an English-born rajah and his descendants from 1839 until 1946, when it was ceded to the British Crown. One year later, in 1947, Sarawak became an independent state—specifically part of the Malaysian Federation.

The British government hoped that Elizabeth's success in organizing women's groups in Cameroon could be duplicated in Sarawak. As Britain relinquished its colonial holdings, some departments attempted to leave behind social-welfare structures, and an organization of women was thought to be capable of contributing to such an end. When in March 1962 Elizabeth arrived in Kuching, the capital city, her reputation had preceded her, "which made my work much easier." In addition to government funds, her program received a special grant from the American Asia Society, which supported a range of development programs in the Far East. Elizabeth did not know much about this part of the world, except through reading, but she knew enough to listen and ask questions. Her first question about her assignment to start a women's organization in Sarawak was, "Do women want one?"

She asked this question of the women she met as she went through the villages. With a rucksack on her back, Elizabeth traveled the waterways of Sarawak. The country is marked by dense jungle, heavy and frequent rainfall, a vast network of rivers that provide the main routes of transport, and a primarily agricultural population. Elizabeth spent nights in the traditional longhouse dwellings of the Dayaks, sharing many a meal. Her digestion was less hardy than in the past, but she dared not refuse the dishes that women had gone to so much trouble to prepare. She invented a skirt with pockets lined in plastic into which she would surreptitiously slip food she considered inedible. The only problem, she confided, was that "after supper as I walked through the village center, every dog within range would follow and bark after me."

The Land Dayak women Elizabeth met with, though Muslim, did not observe *purdah*. They were actively engaged in farming, but because men carried the major responsibility for the crops, the women of this region had more free time than those of Cameroon. Unlike many of the women of Africa, however, they did not have a history of local clubs and groups. Elizabeth missed the scholarly insights about women's lives that Phyllis Kaberry's studies had provided in Cameroon, but she had her own sensitive perceptions based on experience. She was careful to inquire about the social customs and legal provisions affecting women and, in fact, discovered a society of relative equity. The women generally enjoyed equal rights with men in such matters as inheritance, divorce, and ownership and management of property. Polygamy was rare, and the husband and wife relationship was for the most part viewed as a union of equals. Traditional women, especially the Malays, were expected to remain close to home, however. Elizabeth realized that a rural organization would have to be flexible in order to meet the needs of such diverse groups as the Malay, Chinese, and Dayak women she met. Drawing on her experience in Cameroon, Elizabeth hoped to find a labor-saving device that would again act as a bait to capture the women's interest. Noting that women spent hours every day hulling paddy to provide the daily allotment of rice, she decided that a paddy huller was the answer.

Five months after she arrived in Sarawak, and many boat trips, longhouse visits, and jungle treks later, Elizabeth submitted a proposal for the organization known as Women's Institutes (W.I.s). She had discovered among the women a wellspring of interest in participating in training courses and groups, thus answering her question, "Do they want one?" She was fortunate to have the support of James Cook, Sarawak's director of agriculture, for her women's program, as many of her colleagues considered the prospect of organizing women to be a ridiculous waste of resources. Without the specially designated funding for a women's program from the Asia Society, a nongovernmental organization, she might have been more vulnerable to these attacks. As it was, she said, "my colleagues often remained obstructive to what were, to them, unorthodox ideas."

In the Land Dayak longhouses near Tarat, Elizabeth had organized six Women's Institutes by January 1963 with the help of a retired schoolteacher. The rice-hulling machines had not proved to be successful "bait," but they also "weren't a failure." The institutes that had received them "realized someone was trying to help them." The rice hullers had proved difficult for the women to use and were prone to break down. Any woman who could afford to took her rice to the large hullers on the traders' boats that plied the rivers.

One year after her arrival in Sarawak, Elizabeth transferred to the capital city of Kuching, where she could direct a network of Women's Institutes. Arriving at the department headquarters, she was shown to the room that would be her office. "After one look at its air-conditioned glory, with a guard at the door and glossy paint everywhere, it was obvious to me that no W.I. member from the rural areas was ever going to get near me, if, indeed, she found the courage to approach the building at all." Elizabeth refused to move in, thereby precipitating a bureaucratic brouhaha. She believed that her critics in the department were wondering more than ever why she had been hired—"why Cook had ever done it." She chose instead to rent a small wooden house in a neighborhood that was simple and pleasant and far more conducive to visits from the women. Informed by her office that it was illegal for a European to rent a house in a Malay quarter she was urged to shut it down. In response, she persuaded one of the Malaysian institute members to take over the lease, although she continued to pay the rent from her own pocket. She remained in her own headquarters resolutely and withstood the criticisms leveled at her.

The Women's Institutes were spreading rapidly. In Kuching itself, a half-dozen groups had started up. (Elizabeth discovered one reason why: The Malay women were encouraged by their husbands not to leave their homes except for organized meetings, but the institutes provided legitimate opportunities to socialize.) There were 2,000 members by August 1963. Many were already able to meet the costs of running their groups through sales of crafts and food. Some groups even sent small sums of money to the headquarters. But they were far too poor to support a national movement, and Elizabeth knew that outside funding still remained an absolute necessity. The pattern tended to repeat itself. It was almost impossible to start up and sustain such a movement while relying only on the resources that the women could provide. Women first had to develop the capacity to generate their own resources. This factor became increasingly important in Elizabeth's plans.

Despite limited funds, the institutes made astonishing progress. Several groups, with the help of men, were building their own meeting places. Word of the institutes' activities was now being broadcast by Radio Sarawak over transistor radio sets made available by the station. Institute members prepared a half-hour weekly radio program, which was translated into Chinese, Iban, Land Dayak, Malay, and Melenau. It was heard by women all over Sarawak, reaching into remote regions long isolated by difficult terrain. Women were going beyond a home-economics agenda, and were asking questions about probate wills, how to put out fires, how to give first aid, and so on.

As in Cameroon, the situation was ripe for the explosion of interest in women's groups, and Elizabeth was the dynamic instigator. By the end of 1965, 100 Women's Institutes had been established. The programs were going so well and the membership had increased so significantly that Elizabeth suggested they apply for membership in the Associated Country Women of the World (ACWW), the coordinating body for rural women's organizations. They did apply, were accepted, and went so far as to suggest to ACWW that its next regional conference be held in Sarawak. The conference actually did take place in Kuching in September 1964. It was the largest gathering of women that Sarawak had ever seen. More than 1,000 women attended. Some from the distant regions flew to Kuching, but most walked through the jungle, sometimes for two or three days, to a place where they could be picked up by bus or river boat.

Elizabeth wrote:

> The women are increasingly showing their independence, which pleases me greatly. Recently the Limbang members decided that they would like to visit the oilfields at Miri, something I would never have dreamed of suggesting since they are 150 miles away. However, they wrote to Shell and suggested that Shell lay on a boat for them and then a bus and also provide them with accommodation for the two nights they would be there, and Shell has meekly agreed to do all this! And these are women who have never been away from home before! *And* their husbands are letting them go!

Shortly after the conference, Elizabeth learned that she was to be awarded the Order of the Star of Sarawak.

It is doubtless immodest of me . . . but it pleases me greatly because it sets the seal of approval on the W.I.s and because, too, it is a decoration originally created by the rajahs and now revived with Independence, so that I feel that it can be regarded as coming from the Sarawakians themselves, not just a routine "gong" handed out by the Colonial Office.

As one of the first foreigners to receive the award after Independence, she deeply appreciated the honor. In later years she considered it one of the greatest accolades of her career—a fitting end to her assignment in Sarawak.

To Elizabeth's great satisfaction, her well-trained deputy director, Datin Hajjah Rugayah Majid, took over the leadership of the institutes as planned. Rugayah speaks with warm affection of Elizabeth, crediting the present status of the institutes as the largest and most active women's organization in all Malaysia to the "strong, sound foundation" laid by Elizabeth. By 1984, there were 12,000 members and the movement was "entrenched in every village."

11

When Elizabeth left Sarawak at the end of 1964, she hoped to stay in England for a time.

After some sixteen years in the tropics, working at full pitch most of the time, I am beginning to feel rather like a squeezed orange. . . . I [would] like a quiet unadventurous job at home, preferably in a rural area. . . . This sort of work, when things go well, is immensely rewarding and I shall look back on my time here with much happiness, but it is also a tremendous drain upon one's energies and even emotions. One comes to a country and gradually builds up a relationship with the people there, and then one leaves and has to start all over again somewhere else. One rarely sees the end result of one's labours or meets one's friends again. . . . Mine are scattered all over the world. . . . I want to work somewhere where I can put down some roots. Not that I envy those who have never left home, [as] my life has been infinitely richer; but I think it is time to call a halt, if only to enable me to get my breath back.

Elizabeth returned to England in 1965. She was fifty years old, interested in working for a charitable agency, and eager to try the rural life of her own country. Eventually she took a job in the north as a regional officer for the Spastics Society. However, when she was asked two years later to go to South Vietnam for eighteen months to work with the Asian Christian Service, she accepted. The agency was part of the South East

Asian Conference of Churches, and its goal was to unite the efforts of refugee relief groups, "believing, quite erroneously, that the war was drawing to an end."

She left for Vietnam in September 1967 and was stationed in Saigon. She was the only European woman at the headquarters, although some Australian nurses were employed in the field. For all, it was a period of extreme stress and agonizing experiences. Elizabeth later became the director of the program.

> I have no letters from this period. There was very little time to write them. As you can imagine, it is not a time that I like to think back to very often. . . . We came across so many tragedies. . . . There was so much suffering and so little one could do about it, and I hated Saigon, with its corruption, bars, noise, heat, and gigantic traffic jams that could last for hours. The slums were appalling, huge rubbish dumps every-where. . . . I certainly never saw such extreme misery.

Elizabeth remained in Saigon for almost twenty months, was there during the Tet offensive, and visited field stations when travel was possible.

When she returned to England in May 1969, she accepted the post of general secretary of the Associated Country Women of the World, an association she had been part of since her Cameroon days. Elizabeth organized the group's Triennial Conference in Oslo in 1971, but she

> resigned in 1972 as I felt I wanted to go back to field work. . . . The general secretary of ACWW spends her time in committees. . . . I decided therefore to become a free-lance consultant in rural-development programs for the Third World, with particular reference to their effect on women and the use of simple technologies to help them; but, to keep the wolf from the door whilst I got established, I also worked as the senior associations officer for the National Associa-tion of Mental Health in London.

She was able to retire from the Mental Health association in 1975 to become a consultant to governments and voluntary agencies, including UNICEF and the FAO. Her rich experience in helping women to form strong community organizations has been drawn on by major develop-ment agencies all over the world. In addition, her pioneering experi-ments in what she chose to call intermediate technology laid the groundwork for other development experts. UNICEF invited her to visit Bangladesh over an extended period to examine its programs for women and children. The result was a widely copied series of booklets on sim-ple labor-saving technologies for women, as well as detailed suggestions for small-scale enterprises. UNICEF made wide use of the booklets and engaged her to do similar booklets for Indonesia.

Elizabeth lives in rural England now. She is busy writing about technology and development theory, continues to accept consultancies in Third World countries, and lectures at international conferences. In her more recent writings, she has placed a greater emphasis on income-producing projects for women. This emphasis accurately reflects the changes that have occurred in attitudes toward women's needs—and ambitions—relative to those of earlier days, when household skills were considered the paramount concern of women. Elizabeth was one of the first to recognize that poor women in poor societies primarily want to know how to add to family resources. Only by reducing the time they spend on household tasks, a responsibility most women can never escape, can they truly become free to pursue economic or educational goals. Elizabeth was also one of the first to recognize that where women are the mainstay of agriculture, as in Cameroon, the food supply of the nation ultimately depends on them and their skills.

A friend who was in Yaounde in 1984 wrote, "Every Grassfielder I met asked after Yaa Woo Lim."[8] Elizabeth had written it "Ya O Ngalim," but whatever the spelling, the translation was the same—Queen of the Women Who Work. Indeed, it was for thousands and thousands of "women who work" that Elizabeth O'Kelly changed the daily landscape and made it a more fruitful field on which to plant and grow.

NOTES

1. "Women, Technology, and the Development Process," an International Labor Organization contribution to the African Regional Meeting of the United Nations Conference on Science and Technology for Development, Cairo (July 1978).

2. Elizabeth O'Kelly, *Rural Women: Their Integration in Development Programmes and How Simple Intermediate Technologies Can Help Them* (London: Privately printed, 1978), p. 3.

3. Elizabeth O'Kelly, "Letters of a Woman Colonial Officer in Africa, 1950–1961" (unpublished, 1965–1966).

4. Phyllis Kaberry, *Women of the Grassfields: A Study of the Economic Position of Women in Bamenda, British Cameroons* (London: Her Majesty's Stationery Office, 1952), Introduction, pp. vii.

5. Ibid., pp. 69–71, 85.

6. Robert E. Ritzenthaler, "Anlu—A Women's Uprising in the British Cameroons," *African Studies,* vol. 19, no. 3 (1960), pp. 151–156.

7. Elizabeth O'Kelly, *Aid and Self Help: A General Guide to Overseas Aid* (London: Charles Knight & Co., 1973), p. 118.

8. Hilda Platzer, letter to the author (December 3, 1983).

SUPPLEMENTARY READINGS

Ahmed, Iftikhar, ed., *Technology and Rural Women: Conceptual and Empirical Issues* (London: a study of the International Labor Organization, published by Allen & Unwin, 1985).

Boserup, Ester, *Woman's Role in Economic Development* (New York: St. Martin's Press).

Carr, Marilyn, *Appropriate Technology for African Women* (Addis Ababa, Ethiopia: UN Economic Commission for Africa, 1978).

Charlton, Sue Ellen M., *Women in Third World Development* (Boulder, Colo., and London: Westview Press, 1984).

Dauber, Roslyn, and Cain, Melinda, eds., *Women and Technological Change in Developing Countries* (Boulder, Colo.: Westview Press, 1981).

Etienne, Mona, and Leacock, Eleanor, eds., *Women and Colonization* (New York: Praeger Publishers, 1980).

Hay, Margaret Jean, and Stichter, Sharon, eds., *African Women South of the Sahara* (New York: Longman, 1984).

Le Vine, Victor T., *Cameroons from Mandate to Independence* (Westport, Ct.: Greenwood Press, 1977).

O'Barr, Jean F., ed., *Perspectives on Power: Women in Africa, Asia and Latin America* (Durham, N.C.: Duke University Center for International Studies, 1982).

Strobel, Margaret, "African Women," *Signs: Journal of Women and Culture in Society,* vol. 8, no. 1 (Chicago: University of Chicago Press, Autumn 1982).

Swedish International Development Agency, *Women in Developing Countries* (Stockholm, 1974).

Wellesley Editorial Committee, *Women and National Development: The Complexities of Change* (Chicago: University of Chicago Press, 1977).

CEUTA
MELILLA
Tunis
Algiers
TUNISIA
Rabat
MOROCCO
Tripoli
Benghazi

ALGERIA
El-Ayoun
**WESTERN
SAHARA**
LIBYA
Cairo
EGYPT

**CAPE
VERDE
IS.**
Praia
MAURITANIA
Nouakchott
MALI
NIGER
CHAD
Khartoum
SUDAN

SENEGAL
Dakar
Bamako
Niamey
DJIBOUTI
Djibouti

**THE
GAMBIA**
Banjul
BURKINA FASO
Ouagadougou
Ndjamena

GUINEA-BISSAU
Bissau
GUINEA
Conakry
BENIN
Porto Novo
ETHIOPIA
Addis Ababa

SIERRA LEONE
Monrovia
**IVORY
COAST**
Abidjan
GHANA
Accra
NIGERIA
Lagos
**CENTRAL AFRICAN
REPUBLIC**
SOMALIA

LIBERIA
TOGO
Lome
CAMEROON
Bangui
Mogadishu

EQUATORIAL GUINEA
Malabo
Yaounde
UGANDA
Kampala
KENYA
Nairobi

**SAO TOME E
PRINCIPE**
Libreville
GABON
RWANDA
Kigali

CONGO
Brazzaville
Kinshasa
BURUNDI
Bujumbura
ZANZIBAR
Dar es Salaam

ZAIRE
TANZANIA

Luanda

ANGOLA
ZAMBIA
Lusaka
Lilongwe
MALAWI

Harare
MOZAMBIQUE

NAMIBIA
ZIMBABWE

Windhoek
BOTSWANA
Gaborone
Pretoria
Maputo

**SOUTH
AFRICA**
SWAZILAND
Mbabane

LESOTHO
Maseru

154

AZIZA HUSSEIN
Family Law and Family Planning in Egypt

Aziza Hussein grew up in a privileged family in Egypt and married a man who became the minister of Social Affairs. As a young matron, she was drawn into his work in community development and it transformed her life. At his invitation she went to one of the small villages to help women improve their embroidery to make it more salable. She developed such an understanding of their needs and such empathy with them that she returned to Cairo a committed and eloquent spokesperson for the advancement of women. She spoke out not only for rural women, so many of whom were miserably poor, but for all women struggling for the protection of a more enlightened family law.

It was thus fitting that she be appointed the first Egyptian delegate to the UN Status of Women Commission. After stepping down from that post, she spearheaded the drive in Egypt for amendments to existing family law so as to provide women with greater legal protection.

Aziza had learned in the villages how much women feared closely spaced pregnancies, which exhausted them and often undermined their health. But counterbalancing that was the fear that they would lose their husbands if they didn't continue to bear children and that without children they would have no security for their old age. Most women preferred to space their pregnancies, but birth control was a subject to be approached with the greatest care because it touches on one of the most culturally sensitive topics, female sexuality.

Aziza understood that despite the taboos, fertility control is critical for the improvement of women's lives. As president of the International Planned Parenthood Federation, she learned that most of the young women who had been interviewed as part of international fertility surveys wanted fewer children than their mothers had had.[1] Because a fundamental factor in limiting child bearing is the availability and use of contraceptives, Aziza pioneered the effort to ensure both. She became the kinetic force behind the family planning movement in Egypt; in fact, "she *was* family planning in Egypt," as one of her early colleagues remarked.

Aziza's arena was the elite world of Cairo and the corridors of influence of the international agencies. Through all her life, she has remained a confirmed volunteer. In her view, volunteer work was the only way she could keep her own voice and her independence. A woman of powerful family connections, she has consistently used her privileges and power in tireless pursuit of greater equality for all women.

1

When Aziza Hussein first faced an audience of American women on a lecture tour in 1952, nothing in her life in Egypt had prepared her for it. Like many novices, she was not only panic-stricken but also felt like a woman out of context. "But," she recalls, "I told myself that if people think I can do it, perhaps I can do it." She was also buoyed up by the recollection of Huda Shaarawi, who had electrified Egyptian society almost thirty years before by throwing her veil into the sea in a gesture of feminine protest and pride. Aziza made three speeches on that first day of her tour, attended a reception in the evening, and was interviewed on a radio program the next morning. She knew that at the very least she could keep up a brave front.

Aziza Shoukry Hussein was born in 1919 in the village of Zifta, Gharbiya, Egypt, the eldest of five children of a doctor, Sayed Shoukry. The family lived on one side of the Nile, and the children's school was on the other. "It was very exciting," she says, "to cross the river by boat each morning. The house had beautiful gardens with flowers and fruits— grapes, oranges, mangoes, papaya—and even a small zoo where my father kept gazelles, peacocks, and little monkeys. It was a wonderful setting. It was a happy, happy life until I went to boarding school."

Dr. Shoukry, according to his daughter, was "a man very far in advance of his times." He was born in Mit-Yaish of a family of respectable and prosperous farmers. He had been educated in Dublin, studied in Paris, and returned to Egypt to practice medicine. His mind was free ranging, thoughtful, and open to new ideas. He married Hekmat Aref, a daughter of Mahmoud Aref, whose Turkish ancestors had been military rulers and large landowners in Egypt during the Ottoman Empire.

Aziza, the firstborn, had two brothers and two sisters. One brother, a deaf mute, died at the age of twenty-one; the other, Mohammed, became a doctor himself. The three sisters, Aziza, Esmat, and Laila, benefited from their father's interest in education for girls. While growing up, all the children felt a conflict between the "Turkish" ideas of their young aunts and uncles who had the "values of opulence" and their father's energetic idealism.

Aziza and Esmat were sent to the French Pensionnat de la Mère de Dieu, considered the best school for girls in the vicinity. But Aziza disliked it intensely. She recalls vividly the sense of shame about one's body that she learned there, and an asceticism that was barely tolerable to such a robust girl. The school was run with a rigorous discipline that Aziza could value only in retrospect. At home her mother, who was frequently ill and depressed, was going through a particularly difficult period. The strain that the whole family felt added to Aziza's unhappiness.

It was with relief and anticipation that Aziza entered the American College for Girls in Cairo (actually a high school and junior college). By contrast to the convent, life at the college was bursting with energy and openness. Aziza's ebullience and gregariousness found a happier setting. The combination of sports and academic work was "wonderful. I joined everything . . . . I was a varsity baseball player. There was a wonderful relationship between students and teachers that gave you a sense of respecting yourself. I also had the chance to catch up on written and classical Arabic, which I didn't have at the convent."

Aziza went on to the American University in Cairo and majored in social sciences, one of the few courses of study other than journalism and teaching that women were encouraged to pursue. Opportunities had expanded slightly since the first class of women entered Cairo University in 1927, when career openings were limited to teaching and midwifery. Most women at American University were not planning for a career; they took courses that gave them personal satisfaction. For Aziza, a budding activist, the social sciences allowed her to "think and do at the same time."

Aziza had grown into a tall, young woman with a wonderful smile and great animation. American University had an international atmosphere with large numbers of foreign students, and she went to school with young men for the first time. Her father, by allowing her to attend the university, had given his approval for this, but Aziza felt that she had to be scrupulously careful in order not to embarrass him. Most of the daughters of the Shoukry family's friends would not have been allowed to go to the university: Aziza and her sisters considered themselves pioneers.

At graduation in 1942, Aziza had no job and couldn't travel because of the war. "If you really needed the money, you would take some jobs," but it was not the sort of thing that a woman from her kind of family did. Aziza stayed at home and turned her prodigious energies to practicing the piano, attending volunteer society meetings, and heartily disliking the lack of direction in her life. She was offered an escape when a friend, leaving a job at the American Office of War Information, asked Aziza if she would take it over. The propriety of such a job was questioned by most of her family, particularly as she might "fall in love with a Christian." Her father, however, understood her boredom and restlessness and encouraged her to take the position. His response to the family was that he had done his best with his daughters to give them the right values, to make them feel respect. "I gave them all the confidence to do that. If after all I have done Aziza comes to tell me 'I have to marry a Christian,' then I will go with her to church."

It was a challenging and adventuresome move for Aziza, bringing her into a different world with new demands and disciplines. "Some people were antagonistic [about the fact] that I worked for Americans. It was considered an odd thing to be doing, especially in war time . . . . It was a very big risk, but it was impossible for me to stay at home." She had not anticipated the rigors of working eight hours a day, especially in an American-run office. "A long time! Terrible!" However, for Aziza the job was preferable to the vacuum she had lived in after leaving the university. She did translating, researching, and was "loaded with correspondence . . . too much work and routine."

When Aziza began to be courted by Ahmed Hussein, a highly regarded social scientist, she was ready for a change. He had received a Ph.D. in agricultural economics from the Higher Agricultural University in Berlin in 1927. They had met several times at social gatherings, and Ahmed had heard favorable reports about Aziza. He was known as a brilliant, practical man, deeply engrossed in work related to community development and peasant cooperatives. Though more conservative than Dr. Shoukry and Aziza, he considered their somewhat advanced social beliefs to be acceptable. According to Aziza's description, Ahmed was a man who was "ambivalent about things. . . . He wanted an educated girl, but I'm sure he did not consider the details of what that meant, what kind of person might have done that."

Aziza knew about his interest in her, although it took him several years to express it directly. Ahmed finally "came around and decided he was going to marry me—a strange way of marrying, but anyway. I had a wonderful network of friends and family members and all that, which sort of linked me with my husband. It isn't as if we 'fell in love' with each other. There wouldn't have been an opportunity anyway." Aziza was twenty-five years old and still working at the Office of War Information when she became engaged to Ahmed, then forty-two, and, with some relief she quit her job.

After Aziza and Ahmed were married in 1945, they lived for several years with Ahmed's family, both because it was expected of them and because housing was difficult to find. Ahmed Hussein may not have anticipated the extent to which his marriage to Aziza would affect his closely knit family, but Aziza had forebodings. Much like Hasina Khan in Bangladesh, she had enjoyed relative social freedom at home and had been encouraged to make her own decisions. The Husseins held the view that a wife was subservient to her in-laws; in addition, they were "very possessive and always wanting me and my husband around. They were always advising and wanted to know everything . . . . But they were also very nice and very decent, which made it more difficult to cope with the in-law problem. I had to get away from that." Aziza believed that they did not approve of the kind of life that she or her family led, and she had to work at not antagonizing them. Although she chafed under their restraints, Aziza felt free enough to continue her activities outside their home. She had the experience of being employed, which gave her confidence, and the precedence that had been set by other women of her class.

Aziza chose to become an active member of the Cairo Women's Club (CWC) and to keep her close ties with the American College for Girls through the Alumnae Association. The tradition of Egyptian clubs for elite women had started with the Feminist Union, founded in 1923 by the same Huda Shaarawi who had thrown her veil in the sea after returning from an international women's conference. During Egypt's struggle against the British for independence in 1919, women had organized protests and strikes and had disrupted communications. After their active part in the revolution, many were not willing to return to seclusion, and they were supported in their rebellion by Egyptian nationalists. Nor did they generally choose to wear the veil in public, although there were class distinctions with respect to veiling. Women working in fields and factories had rarely worn veils; rather, it was the well-to-do women who did so.[2]

Active women turned to the social services, where they began to supervise philanthropic organizations as they never had before. Because they were not in competition with men, the government supported their efforts. Women became the "unpaid public servants."[3] In the 1940s, Aziza and her friends joined the network of volunteers who worked in clinics, child-care centers, and schools under the auspices of the Cairo Women's Club.

The Cairo Women's Club had been started by American women and was part of the American-based General Federation of Women's Clubs. The club gradually became Egyptianized; when it adopted Arabic as its official language in the 1950s, the foreign community dropped out. However, it had its roots in a Western view of women, as had Huda Shaarawi's Feminist Union, started after her exposure to women of different cultures at an international conference in 1923. Aziza's attendance at the American College for Girls and the American University, as well as her membership in the Cairo Women's Club, had brought her into an orbit of Western influences, which were in conflict with more traditional Egyptian values. Aziza and her sisters may have felt like pioneers in attending a coed university, but they were not alone among upper-class women in Cairo in experiencing that conflict.

Ahmed Hussein's work took him to the rural areas of Egypt, where he designed community development projects that would be forerunners for many others worldwide. By 1947, he had become undersecretary of the Ministry of Social Affairs and was appointed minister in 1950. Aziza was fascinated by his work in rural communities and learned as much as she could about it. At her urging, Ahmed came to speak to the Cairo Women's Club about his community development projects. Impressed by the seriousness of the club members, he invited them to visit the villages and to help women style and market their embroidery. This he did not do without a certain anxiety, however. "Don't give the women new ideas!" he told Aziza. "Don't you come and spoil our work and tell the villagers all kinds of things. We have to be careful and respect tradition."

There was no question in the minds of Aziza and the others that village women needed far more than help with their embroidery. Their poverty was crippling. The club decided to start its own program in the village of Sandyoun, thereby complementing Ahmed's community development efforts. The program would begin by teaching cooking and sewing, the traditional social-service agenda for women. First, the club women had to inform the village men of their plans and gain their approval. "Men were very particular about keeping women under control." They systematically visited each of the village's most influential families to win the support of both men and women. Although the village women themselves did not have clubs, and although they were not accustomed to attending classes, the initial sewing and cooking lessons were well received.

Aziza noticed with distress the condition of the children in the village. "I hadn't had any children and I felt an obligation to help. . . . I would have loved to adopt children, but my husband couldn't accept that." She suggested a children's center whose modest aims were to give children a safe place to play, provide them with a small amount of nutritious food, and clean them up. She described the attitudes of the mothers toward child care:

Cleanliness, for example, was a superfluous bother, and quite unrelated to health; dirt had no association in their minds with disease. Children were ill on account of the evil eye; children died by preordained divine will. Remedies for illness ran from primitive concoctions to magical prescriptions for warding off the evil eye—one of which was never washing a child. The maternal and child health centers set up by the government for their benefit were hardly frequented by them. They preferred the advice of the village midwife.

Children used the dirty canals as swimming pools, and thus caught the bilharzia disease early in life. Flies settled comfortably on the young faces who made no effort to drive them away, as their skins had become insensitive to their bites. Trachoma, the dreaded eye disease, was a common occurrence. The mother had no sanitary facilities at home, did not wash her children, and had too many children to have time to supervise them.[4]

The members of the Cairo Women's Club were persuaded by Aziza's eloquent presentation of the need for a children's center. They were afraid, however, that the mothers in the village would not trust their children to the care of other women. But the club women had become well accepted by the village families, and the children's center opened. Girls from the village, who would normally never have been allowed to take jobs, had agreed to be trained as nursery teachers. The nursery school "gave the entire village a feeling of optimism and rising expectation for the future of their children which made every effort worth exerting," wrote Aziza.[5] "We invited all the women to a big function. Many had not left their homes in [the] daytime before. But they came—their husbands permitted them to attend. I think the event affected their behavior." The Cairo Women's Club was not seen as trying to organize the village women; it was too soon for that, but "women had been moved ahead."

The Sandyoun center became extremely popular in the village, as did many of the other centers in the Egyptian countryside organized by the Bureau of Social Affairs under Ahmed. Their reputation for excellence brought UN teams and international visitors. The ensuing competition within the Egyptian government to share credit for the rural centers was intense. Unfortunately, during one of Ahmed's trips abroad, the government Wafdist party, of which he was not a member, placed its own people in the Ministry of Social Affairs—without his knowledge or consent. Instead of carefully trained field-workers, a new breed of government employees took over who were more interested in buildings than in community development. Hussein threatened to resign, and the government, after much stormy infighting, agreed to replace the new appointees. Hussein resigned anyway, embittered by events and by what he considered to be widespread corruption throughout the government.

Six months later, in July 1952, the government of King Farouk was overthrown in a revolt led by Gamal Abdel Nasser. The new government

immediately passed an agrarian reform law that ultimately had important consequences for all segments of society. Ahmed Hussein took heart
and devoted himself to forming the Fellah (Peasant) Society, which was
committed to national land reform in tune with the new government.

2

Aziza had become sufficiently well known for her leadership in developing the Sandyoun project that she was invited in 1953 to make a lecture tour of the United States. The sponsor was the American Friends of
the Middle East, a nonprofit organization founded in an effort to foster
American understanding of the Middle East. Again, as with Reyna de
Miralda and Hasina Khan, a nongovernmental agency was providing a
timely opportunity for a woman leader to gain experiences that would
open her future options. Aziza was asked to speak about the Sandyoun
project, demonstrating how a women's club could be an important part
of the social reform movement. Other topics included Egypt: People and
Problems, The Muslim Woman, and The Palestine Question. Aziza was
proud to say, "I never had anyone help me write speeches. I used my
own approach to things."

The idea of making a tour filled her with misgivings. "I had no idea
of what a lecture tour meant, but Ahmed encouraged me and so I
accepted." According to her close friend Margaret Pennar, who had been
a classmate at the American College and was then working in the United
States for the Voice of America, Aziza was feeling so panicky that Margaret had to accompany her for the first three or four days of her tour.
Aziza, recalling how terribly crowded her schedule was, said, "At least
they didn't give me time to sit and worry and cry! but . . . I was frightened all the time." An extemporaneous speech in a Sunday School room
left her literally wordless; she lost all her ideas and had to stop. From
then on she was careful to follow a written text.

Aziza traveled at night by train to reach her next lecture site, according to a schedule calling for visits to thirty states and speeches to twenty
colleges, universities, and organizations during the seven-week tour. She
spoke in Pittsburgh, Philadelphia, Chicago, Portland, San Francisco, Los
Angeles, New Orleans, Washington, New York, and other cities. She was
exhausted much of the time. Hoping for a respite, she went to Ithaca to
visit her sister Laila who was studying at Cornell University. To her
despair, she discovered that Laila had booked her for yet another speech.
The strain also affected her physically. She had numerous pains, wasn't
eating or sleeping well, and couldn't relax. A doctor prescribed six
phenobarbitol a day. In typical self-deprecation, she said, "I had become

a great lecturer but never on my own. . . . I had to take these pills! . . . I had never suffered so much in my life." But she didn't stay on the pills, and she became an accomplished speaker. "My God, how she changed," said Margaret Pennar. For Aziza, it was an experience that "prepared me for a role I've been playing ever since."

Aziza's travels through the United States gave her a sense of expansion beyond the national and cultural boundaries that she had known. It was her first international experience, other than visiting the Caribbean with Ahmed on a United Nations assignment, and it showed her "something in common between me and other human beings, even though they're so different." She responded warmly to the "openness, friendliness, and hospitality" of the people she met and the women's groups she addressed. Although they knew little indeed about the Middle East and Islam, Aziza could give them a vivid picture of Egyptian women's lives from urban Cairo to the village of Sandyoun. Nor had they heard the Middle Eastern point of view regarding either Palestine or the conflicts with the Israelis. Aziza's focus, of course, was directed not to the politics of the region but to the human aspects of issues that she hoped would generate understanding and sympathy from an American audience. She saw American women and men as equal, and was not conscious of the grievances of the feminist movement as they were subsequently expressed.

Shortly after Aziza's return to Cairo from her speaking trip in 1953, Ahmed was appointed ambassador to the United States by the Nasser government. After the Husseins' move to Washington, Aziza found herself on the lecture circuit again, responding to a range of requests: to address the annual meeting of the American Foreign Policy Conference, to lecture at the University of Chicago on the status of women in the Muslim world, and so on.

In 1954, the head of Egypt's permanent delegation to the United Nations, Mahmoud Azmy, asked Aziza to address the Third Committee of the General Assembly. She thus became the first woman member of the Egyptian delegation. In honor of her outstanding services, she received the Kamal Medal from the government of Egypt in 1955.

The Husseins were at the embassy in Washington for almost five years. But it was a difficult period to be representing Egypt in the United States—a period filled with suspicions, misunderstandings, and cross-purposes. The last year was particularly distressing because of the deteriorating relationship between the United States and Egypt. The Suez Canal dispute had erupted, the Aswan Dam negotiations had collapsed, and the United States was highly critical of Egypt's socialist tilt. A tug of war for influence in Egypt was being won by the Soviets. And U.S.-Egyptian tensions were clearly reflected in the world that the Husseins inhabited. "Every half-hour I remember hearing something antagonistic about Egypt. I was no longer a human being but a representative of my country. It became so vicious in the end!" As the Husseins were enduring the criticism of the U.S. community, they were seen as pro-American by the Nasser government. When the United States used its power in the World Bank to cancel the loan to Egypt for the Aswan Dam, the antagonism reached its highest point.

Ahmed had asked on several occasions to be relieved of his post as ambassador (Aziza thought he was "never meant to be a diplomat. . . . He didn't have that personality"). When, in 1958, he was finally ordered to return to Egypt, his abrupt recall seemed to be a dishonor. He was so embittered by the experience that he determined never again to accept a government post; Aziza's subsequent strong espousal of volunteer rather than government service also reflected a disillusionment with bureaucratic power and politics.

3

Back home, in spite of her prominence and recognized talents, Aziza felt she had lost her sense of identity. "I don't belong," she told close friends. It was a time of personal stress for both Husseins. Ahmed retreated to his home and left it so rarely that he was rumored to be under house arrest (he did, in fact, appear regularly at the Gazira Sporting Club for lunch). Aziza, in her turn, had lost her natural ebullience. She had been exhausted and drained by her last years in Washington, and there was an ambiguity about the Husseins' status with the government.

Choosing to become active again in the Cairo Women's Club, Aziza began to revive her old networks. "After 1958, I decided to work with nongovernmental organizations. I enjoyed the freedom of it." By the time she was elected president of the Cairo Women's Club in 1959, her natural expansiveness and enthusiasm were returning. "It was a very new, important experience having to get things organized." Aziza led the club to an affiliation with the Associated Country Women of the World, the same international group that Elizabeth O'Kelly had joined with her Corn Mill Societies.

Aziza renewed her visits to Sandyoun, eager to observe what changes had occurred during the years of her absence. She says that she regards visits to Sandyoun as a personal renewal for her—as "a tonic whenever I have been discouraged." Some of her favorite projects continued (and still do): including a chicken-raising project for women, a pioneering day-care center, and a training program for local girls who want to be day-school teachers. As Aziza talked with the village women, she was struck by their complaints about having too many pregnancies and about the physical problems they caused. This was a new development. The women had been hearing of birth control and surreptitiously asked questions about this still-taboo subject. Contraceptives were intermittently available in the region, but most women did not have access to them. This was a problem that Aziza intended to address when she could.

Aziza's successful speaking appearances in the United States in behalf of the Middle East, as well as her prominence at home, made her a candidate for the distinguished honor of serving Egypt on the UN Status of Women Commission. In 1962, President Nasser appointed her to the post, and she attended her first Commission meeting at UN headquarters in New York later that year. This meeting was her initiation into the issues of current Western feminism. Writing about it later she said,

> I inadvertently raised a hot debate on account of my reference to the "natural duties" of women. The subject under discussion was nursery schools and their place in the life of the working woman. In my inexperience I had warned the Commission against encouraging women to be relieved of their maternal duties in order to pursue their public avocations.[6]

Blasts came from members of the Commission who were committed feminists and from psychologists who disputed her assertions.

Aziza presented to members of the Commission the history of women in Egypt, depicting them as having been subservient to men in the past, and able to achieve status by bearing many children. But, Aziza asserted, the end of foreign domination and the publication of the National Charter of 1962 marked the evolution of Egyptian women from subservience and the segregation of harem life to the freedom of full political citizenship. It was true that Egyptian women had received the vote in 1956; but because they were not required to vote (as men were), women's suffrage seemed less important than that for men. It was a mark of Aziza's skill that she presented the truth in its best possible light. She struggled with the issue of whether she was simply a spokesperson for the government, delivering propaganda, or whether she could be an "agent to create change." In the process, she was moved to consider in more careful detail the actual rights of women in Egypt. The very fact of having its policies in public view had encouraged the Egyptian government to consider its own stance on women's rights, as was true of many of the countries represented at the United Nations. The lack of information about "women's work" was striking. But for Aziza, the interchange she experienced with so many knowledgeable and articulate women was a crucial factor in her intellectual development.

4

Two very different aspects of the population equation intrigued Aziza: the women who wished to limit or space their pregnancies for important family or personal reasons, and the governments concerned about the "population explosion" that had followed the drop in mortality after World War II. During her participation at the 1962 UN conference in New York City, Aziza visited the Margaret Sanger Center, well known for its international family planning training programs. It was her first contact with the organized family planning movement, and she realized how wholeheartedly she shared its goals. She also met the heads of the International Planned Parenthood Federation (IPPF), who were attempting to develop affiliates in countries that needed family planning; Egypt was a prime candidate. Aziza's skills at bringing people and groups together to work effectively had been amply demonstrated at UN meetings attended by IPPF leaders. Moreover, her description of the Sandyoun project provoked great interest as an example of how to reach the vast majority of women who live in rural areas. IPPF recognized Aziza as a "pivotal person" and invited her to attend its meeting in Singapore in 1963 to speak about community development and the means of introducing new ideas in rural areas.

Birth control was still controversial in Egypt, even though the National Charter of 1962 had approved it in principle. As a result, serious studies about people's knowledge, attitudes, and practice of contraception—considered crucial to family planning strategies—did not exist. Ahmed Hussein suggested that Aziza do a survey in the village of Sandyoun on the attitudes of women toward family planning, in support of her comments at the Singapore conference. Assisted by a demographer, Aziza and her team interviewed 120 women in Sandyoun and found that more than half would use family planning for health reasons and to space their children further apart. After the Singapore meeting, IPPF asked Aziza's assistance in initiating a family planning program in Egypt, particularly inasmuch as the government had not yet developed the capacity or will to provide more than token services. She agreed but knew there was preparatory work to be done, attitudes to be changed, and support to be marshaled before any such step could be taken.

Her new understanding of population problems convinced her to include family planning in an address she gave at the UN Status of Women Commission three weeks later. When Aziza said that controlling unwanted births was an essential human right of women, the statement "exploded like a bomb" at the Commission meeting. Until then, she explained, "nobody had mentioned family planning or birth control. Even the word *pregnancy* was treated as taboo. People didn't think that there was any relationship between family planning and the status of women!" The feminist beliefs of many Commission members did not extend to family planning. Delegates told her later that she was "very courageous." The Colombian delegate confided that if she had mentioned birth control, she could not return to her country.

While Aziza was preparing the official report of the meeting on the last day, some delegates asked her to delete any mention in her speech of family planning; she refused. Although many delegates agreed with her, they did so privately.

The relationship between fertility control and women's rights and status was a subject that Aziza persuasively brought to national and international attention over the years. Yet, in 1963, the subject was still considered inappropriate at a meeting on women's issues. The fact that delegates to the Status of Women Commission were government representatives surely constrained individual women from speaking out on a subject their governments did not support. Aziza's reputation as a gentle, warm, consensus-seeking mediator made her the fitting person to take up the gauntlet for this divisive topic.

Upon her return to Cairo, Aziza made family planning her chief concern and set about making the subject a priority for the country. The National Charter of 1962 had included a comprehensive population policy for the first time, but that policy still had to be translated into action. It was too late, she argued, for "timidity and taboos." The previously held "idyllic notion of the political value of a large population" had become a luxury that the country could no longer afford.[7] The government became increasingly alarmed at the influx of people into Cairo, where the lack of housing and food posed the threat of civil strife. It could not afford to subsidize food for urban residents; as only 4 percent of the land in Egypt was cultivated, the annual loss of thousands of acres to urban spread was critical.

Aziza was eager to dramatize the impact on Egypt of an unsupportably high population growth rate, but her real worry was about the women themselves. Although infant and child mortality had decreased, especially in the 1950s and 1960s (thus contributing to the population increase), it was still unacceptably high. The spacing of pregnancies to more than two years apart not only tended to reduce the total number of children borne by women; it also improved the survival chances of those born and was less threatening to the health of the women themselves. An effort to change the old patterns could not wait on the government's initiatives. Aziza led the Cairo Women's Club to form a Joint Committee of Family Planning in 1963. With support from the Pathfinder Fund, an NGO working in the field of population, the committee sponsored a six-week training course for volunteers, doctors, and demographers on how to organize and run a family planning program.

Aziza recalls that "we began with as much fanfare as we could." The press reported the new venture, and public discussions involving prominent Egyptians were arranged on the subject. Aziza excelled in her ability to attract and motivate supporters, for the cause was surrounded by controversy. Although the government half-heartedly favored family planning, most doctors and public leaders avoided any public identification with the movement. The subject was too new and the culture too traditional to take such a risk. Aziza herself was risking her reputation on a radical and unpopular issue.

After weeks of persuasion, several prominent members of the medical community joined the committee, and women members of Parliament added their support. Next came the religious and community leaders, followed by a few brave politicians. The Cairo Women's Club organized a forum at which religious scholars testified that they could find nothing in Islam that was opposed to birth control. Aziza was described as invaluable in this process because she knew and had access to leaders from every field; indeed, she herself was highly respected.

For all the flurry of attention and acceptance given it in Cairo, the family planning movement had to prove itself in the villages, where for centuries traditions had rested on contrary values—that children are a blessing of God and will come when they come; that they add to family strength, prestige, wealth; that God will take care of his people. Aziza was sure that the village of Sandyoun would be the place to start, and that the day-care center and its group of mothers would provide the nucleus. But they had to move carefully, "step by step, avoiding the wrong approach which would have brought resistance from the men. . . . We called meetings and got doctors and religious leaders to talk to the men and answer their questions. . . . Once they realized what we were suggesting was not sterilization, nor abortion, and, hence, not against religion, they decided it made sense." In Sandyoun, the successful community development program that had been in place for years gave the villagers a positive sense of change. Even the local sheik and teachers spoke in favor of family planning to the village men.

A clinic was created in the day-care center, where women naturally congregated, and teachers and local midwives were trained to act as family planning promoters, introducing the idea to women in the community. Aziza was right on hand through it all.

The program would never have succeeded, however, if the women's committee with whom we had worked on the development of the day-care centres had not supported us, visiting the people in their homes, tracking down rumours, telling us about the failures in the use of contraceptives, and even suggesting new channels of communication. "If you want to reach all these people," they told us, "use the village crier." This proved excellent advice. In fact, the village crier, as subsequent research proved, became the main source of information about family planning for most people in the village.[8]

Aziza was surprised to find the village response so favorable. The clinic really caught on (even more so when a woman doctor was assigned to it), for the village women then came not only for information on birth control but also for other gynecological care, including infertility services. As Aziza expected, many women who used contraception wanted to ensure longer intervals between childbirth, rather than to limit the size of their families. A woman feared that if she didn't produce children regularly, her husband might divorce her or take another wife. A popular Egyptian film of the 1960s, "The Bride's Mother," is cited by the writer Naila Milai as an illustration of the dilemma. The film

dramatizes a housewife's reluctance to give up her role as victim. Overwhelmed by the pandemonium that his numerous children unavoidably raise in a small house, a man begs his wife to be excused from fathering more. "I'm yours forever. I'll never leave you and our children," he pleads. When the youngest baby wants to crawl into her parents' bed at night, he eagerly welcomes her to avoid sex. But the wife has her way in the end and does not give up proving her "youth and usefulness" even as she begins to nag her newly married daughter to have a child. "That's the only way to keep a man," the mother tells her.[9]

Contraceptive use was slow to take hold. As the pill was considered far too expensive at that time, the clinic offered foam tablets and V-shaped intrauterine devices (IUDs), which unfortunately caused some women pain and had harmful side-effects for others. The concept of family planning was quite clearly more acceptable than the technology. Aziza, who was in charge of the clinic, needed government approval to import the Lippes loop which had a markedly higher success rate than other IUDs and caused fewer side-effects. "I was allowed to do it, I'm sure, because the minister of Social Affairs was a woman."

In Cairo, Aziza worked tirelessly to coordinate the agencies that were setting up clinics. It seemed that "almost anyone or any organization that had a room could request approval to start up a family planning clinic." Aziza was able to bring the groups together for training on family planning methods and clinic administration. As ad hoc as the effort appeared to be, the separate organizations did actually manage to collaborate. Within two years they were operating twenty-two clinics and had formed the nucleus of the future Egyptian Family Planning Association. "It was a wonderful expansion. We enjoyed it immensely."

Prodded by the advocacy efforts of the Joint Committee on Family Planning, the government finally announced an official population program in 1966. The voluntary clinics had not only set a high standard of quality but had also proved public acceptance of birth control. Aziza claimed that without the pressure and preparation of the volunteer effort, the government family planning program might have been delayed ten years. "People do not analyze the factors that go into change. They talk of official decisions as being the starting point."

The Egyptian family planning program was the first in the Middle East. Aziza and her associates rejoiced. But during a public announcement of the new program, they were stunned and infuriated to hear no mention of the voluntary agencies' pioneering clinic programs. They had started the movement and had prodded the government for years to follow, but "it was as if we had never existed!" They were also shocked to learn that the government was about to blanket the country with contraceptive pills, which were to be distributed by 2,400 doctors stationed in public-health centers. The government considered the pill to be the panacea for Egypt's population problem. Aziza thought the approach distressingly simplistic because it disregarded all the cultural and psychological factors that made family planning such a sensitive issue.

Aziza and her allies had lobbied for years for government responsibility over family planning programs. Finally, in 1967, the Joint Committee was subsumed by the newly established Egyptian Family Planning Association, under the aegis of the Ministry of Social Affairs. Aziza had been a leader in the founding of that association; but now that it was sponsored by a government ministry, its nature had changed. She did, however, stay on as president of the Cairo Family Planning Association. In fact, by soliciting private funds for it, she managed to preserve the semi-autonomous nature of the agency. Aziza could only regret that "the cohesive little program began to break up—the program which had given us so much joy."

5

After the UN Status of Women Commission meeting in Teheran in 1965, Aziza came home with a reinforced determination to establish a Commission for the Status of Women within the Egyptian government. It did not seem possible to her that significant changes in women's rights could occur without a government commitment to pursue those changes. Although she realized that a powerful commission within the government could advance that cause, she also understood all too well the bureaucratic resistance to change; accordingly, she started a Commission for Women within the Federation of Cairo Social Welfare Agencies, a highly regarded nongovernmental organization. Its mission was to study the actual condition of Egyptian women. "I had to find my way to start something that would be really effective."

Under the Nasser government, laws relating to the employment and education of women were considered the most advanced in the Middle East. However, family law, which had the most basic impact on women's lives, had changed very little; hence Aziza and her colleagues concentrated their efforts on family law, speaking to women's clubs, social-welfare groups, and government officials—anyone who might have some influence. Family law was "the unaddressed question—a real social grievance—and that little committee stimulated public interest in that issue."

Reviewing the status of women and family law at a UN seminar in 1964, Aziza reported that "a source of pride for a Muslim woman is her independent legal status, not affected by marriage." She can keep her family name after marriage and own property independent from her husband. She has also been protected by the traditional responsibility of her father to maintain her if she is unmarried, divorced, or widowed, no matter what her age. However, women had many grievances about existing family laws—primarily about the right of a man to divorce his wife by repudiation, the most common form of divorce. A man need only say three times, "I divorce you," allowing appropriate intervals of time to elapse between the pronouncements, in order for a divorce to become irrevocable.

Aziza pointed out that

> a Moslem woman can marry only one man at a time. A Moslem man can marry up to four wives with the injunction that he must be just to all wives. As a deterrent to polygamy, family identity cards are now required for the registration of a marriage contract. Such cards indicate the marital status of the bridegroom, and by this means a plural marriage based on deception at least is avoided.[10]

Another rankling grievance for Egyptian women was the right of a man to refuse to grant his wife a divorce while taking another wife himself. In Aziza's view, the first wife was "held a prisoner—terrible!" Furthermore, a husband did not have to support his wife if she insisted on pursuing a career against his will. Women were also incensed about the fact that their testimony in court was, by tradition, valued at half that of men.

One of the most heartbreaking issues for women centered on maternal rights. If a woman was caught in an intolerable marriage and wished to leave her husband, she would almost certainly lose custody of their children after they had reached a certain age. According to existing law, the children of separated parents remained with the mother until a boy reached the age of seven and a girl the age of nine, unless the courts extended that period by two years. After that, the children were placed in the custody of their father, their "natural guardian."

The Nasser government had instituted a set of revolutionary changes that brought about new social, economic, and political patterns in Egypt. The socialist policy pursued by the government for more than twenty years had taken some power away from the rural, conservative landowners and the wealthy elite, thereby loosening the grip of traditional customs. In 1956, women were given new opportunities and received

Aziza Hussein addressing the Arab World Regional Council, Tunis, 1981 (photographer: Jeremy Hammand/IPPF)

the right to vote and to run for political office. Under the Nasser government, there was also a marked increase in education for girls and greater access to government jobs, which provided women additional opportunities for skilled and professional employment. In such an environment, women challenged the discriminatory family laws more openly.

No significant women's rights movement existed in Egypt to organize a challenge, however. Aziza's group chose to collect data, hoping to demonstrate the connection between women's status and social problems, rather than confronting men or religious authorities about rights.

> For example, we are trying to prove to our legislators that the present insecurity of the women in the family, because of easy divorce, is contributing to the overpopulation problem. Clipping a husband's wings to burden him with any number of children has been a standard procedure of wives to keep their husbands from flying away to another woman.[11]

Aziza brought together leading Egyptian lawyers to develop amendments to the existing family laws that would offer greater protection to women. They were joined by an important nucleus of men who believed that Egypt had to correct some of the worst inequalities suffered by women.

After two years of concentrated effort and lobbying by the group, the government finally took up the issue of family law. Amendments submitted by the group were apparently considered during the time in which the government was drawing up its own amendments. The traditionalists and the religious "fanatics" (in Aziza's eyes, that is, those people who did not take a positive view toward new laws to protect women)—were arrayed against many of the amendments. When the government's draft was issued, Aziza noted disappointing omissions in it, but she gave it her support because she believed it addressed some basic problems without creating undue friction and confrontation. In spite of the opposition, the first Family Law Amendments in fifty years were passed by Parliament in the summer of 1979. Aziza credits President Anwar Sadat for their passage; her work over more than a decade helped set the stage for that success.

Yet the amendments, as finally passed, did not address the two major grievances of most women. A husband retained his unilateral right to divorce his wife without recourse to the courts, and he could still marry more than one wife. Nonetheless, certain restrictions were placed on a man's freedom to divorce: He had to register his divorce or be fined, and his first wife was entitled to a court divorce within a year of her knowledge of her husband's marriage to another woman. As for maternal rights, a mother could now keep custody of a boy until he reached the age of ten and a girl until twelve, subject to extension by the court. A wife could also petition for a divorce; if the court failed to reconcile her with her husband after nine months of mediation, she was to be granted the divorce. This amendment was considered by Aziza and her colleagues as having resolved somewhat more equitably one of the "burning issues" for women. The religious fundamentalists continue to this day to oppose the codification of laws, prefering to leave such issues to the Muslim code, or Shari'a.

To the despair of Aziza and her colleagues, the 1979 Personal Status Law, of which the amendments were a part, was declared unconstitutional in May 1985—a direct reflection of the growing power of the fundamentalists and the conservatives. In June, however, the Egyptian Parliament—responding to intense pressure from adherents of the amendments—passed a law giving Egyptian women the right to divorce a husband who takes a second wife. If there are children involved, the husband is obliged to see that the family is properly housed. The seesaw battle continues for codified legal protection for women, although in actual practice the amendments of 1979 are often ignored.

6

Aziza was elected to the Governing Body of the International Planned Parenthood Federation in 1966, and by 1973 she was vice-chairman. As the agency's representative to the first Conference for the UN Decade for Women in Mexico City in 1975, she was able to present the issue of a woman's right to control her fertility to this important gathering of women. It was also in 1975 that Aziza was portrayed on the Ceres Medal, designed by the UN Food and Agriculture Organization to honor distinguished contemporary women.

Aziza also considered it an honor to be named president of IPPF in 1977. The position demanded high public visibility. She found a welcome platform from which to speak out about her own ideas, including the fact that family planning was most successful when seen in the context of other community needs, and when based on a true understanding of women's motivations. Under her leadership, IPPF launched its innovative Women in Development projects, which supported a wide spectrum of development activities in an effort to enhance the status of women.

IPPF underwent a rapid expansion of country programs, total budget expenditures, and worldwide influence. After Aziza's initial reaction of pleasure and pride about her new assignment, she found herself swamped with correspondence, functions, interviews, visits, and bureaucratic demands. It was both an exciting and a difficult period. As mediator, catalyst, motivator, and integrator, she was at her best. She was known to be a scrupulously fair and firm leader, eager to keep discussions separate from personal attacks and directed toward policy issues. She used all her skills to effect compromises and reconciliations, and suffered when she witnessed signs of conflict. Aziza says that, without meditation, she would not have been able to survive those conflicts. Indeed, the practice of meditation became an increasingly necessary part of her life, tempering the intensity and fervor that she invested in all that she did.

It was not an easy life, for she was away from Cairo and her husband more than she wanted to be. Ahmed had come to depend on her as his contact with the outside world, and although he encouraged her trips, he seemed to mind keenly when she was not around. Aziza had the highest respect for his intelligence (he had "such a brilliant mind," she says) and was deeply distressed that he had shut himself away, particularly because she herself would not have responded to adversity in that way. Her IPPF peers believed that she often felt guilty staying away from home for any length of time, and that she was under great pressure to return quickly.

7

Brewing for a long time in the back of Aziza's mind had been the highly sensitive and controversial issue of female circumcision, or genital mutilation of girls. It had emerged as a worldwide issue among feminists at the 1975 UN Decade for Women Conference in Mexico City. Female circumcision, as it is euphemistically called, describes a range of procedures practiced on girls before puberty, from a slight cut of the clitoris, to its excision, to the removal of all the external female genitalia and a sewing up of the vagina. It is a custom practiced in parts of the Middle East and Africa, most radically in the Sudan and very commonly in Egypt. When reports of that widespread custom surfaced at the Mexico City conference, many women and men were astonished and appalled. It had been a well-kept secret; even educated Arab women knew little about it. Aziza was one. "I had at that time been under the impression that this practice had been discontinued in Egypt by law. . . . Upon investigation, we discovered that we did not have a law—but only administrative measures to prohibit the practice in public hospitals." Aziza gathered evidence from Egyptian doctors about the prevalence and seriousness of the procedures. She discovered that 80 percent of the women coming to the family planning clinics had been circumcised and said they intended to circumcise their daughters.

The subject aroused international indignation. Aziza warned that world opinion considered female circumcision a serious mark of backwardness and a poor reflection on Islam. She seemed stung by her own ignorance of the practice and by the universal condemnation of it outside the Arab world. She persuaded her colleagues at the Cairo Family Planning Association to launch an investigation of circumcision and then negotiated funding for it from IPPF. The investigation revealed the customs that kept circumcision thriving. It was commonly believed that if a girl was not circumcised, and was thereby unlimited in her sexual responsiveness, she would have no sexual restraint. "She would run off to the men." The implication was that no man would marry an uncircumcised girl—that she would be too much like a man.

The custom persisted with the strong support of the women of the family, who celebrated the event with elaborate ritual. The young girls involved, commonly eight to ten years old, often enjoyed the preparation for the ceremony. Dressed in new clothes and decorated with henna, they would join in the ritual songs and dances. There would be special foods and gifts—especially money. These girls accepted the circumcision operation because they had grown up learning to submit to custom and tradition. The procedure was often performed by a village midwife, a barber, or an old aunt—far less frequently by a nurse or doctor. The conditions for the procedure were often unsanitary, and the incidence of septic infection and hemorrhaging were high. Some girls did in fact die; others suffered later complications in childbirth and difficulty in sexual relations. The psychological damage of "this betrayal perpetrated on her in the midst of ceremonies" was thought by some psychologists to be the most destructive element.[12]

Instead of executing a quiet and scholarly investigation of female circumcision, the Cairo Family Planning Association, under Aziza's direction, chose to bring the issue to public attention. In October 1979, the Association arranged a seminar on "Bodily Mutilation of Young Females," which was attended by representatives from government agencies, universities, voluntary agencies, the press, the Arab League, UNICEF, the World Health Organization, and the medical and scientific communities. The seminar received the broadest press and public attention. It was

> a course in sex education for the public at large, the likes of which had never been experienced before. The question dealt basically with the way taboos can perpetuate ignorance and violate the female child's

body in the name of chastity and hygiene. . . . We also saw in it the sexual oppression of women in the attempt to deny them sexual expression.

The audience reacted with great seriousness, respect, and appreciation, reported Aziza. "Some participants even claimed that the seminar had been the most important contribution that I had personally made to Egyptian women's welfare and social welfare in general in my thirty years of work as a volunteer."[13]

The press continued to keep the subject in the public consciousness. The adverse effects of circumcision were made known in nurses' training courses and to women who attended family-planning clinics. One population funding agency let it be known that no doctor who performed circumcisions could be employed in its clinics. Aziza points out that the seminar had continuing impact: More scholars undertook research on circumcision, and schools and women's groups began to ask for information about it.

Aziza's friends suggest that both her image and her usual careful marshaling of forces had helped to legitimize this difficult subject. Aziza believes that the seminar was accepted because the time was right and it had a scientific orientation. At no point was circumcision discussed in terms of women's sexuality, an explosive subject; rather, it was treated as a health and psychological hazard. "People have to be sensitized slowly. Any direct or confrontational attack is doomed." African women expressed this opinion vehemently at the UN Conference for Women in Copenhagen in 1980 and again at Nairobi in 1985, arguing that the issue of female circumcision must be approached by Africans within the context of each society. Western feminist diatribes were viewed as an insult to the culture.

With the family-law issue seemingly settled, Aziza turned her full energies to the promotion of family planning in Egypt and helped to form an organization called Family of the Future (FOF). It set out to attract major new segments of the population by means of a citywide campaign to market contraceptives, street rallies, posters throughout Cairo with "messages" supporting contraception, and television advertising. Startled audiences watched an aggressive television promotion of spermicides. Criticism of the organization was acute, and Aziza admits that "the campaign didn't work and it gave a wrong impression. A bad business!" It did, however, pave the way for the subsequent acceptance of ads for condoms, which resulted in dramatically increased sales.

Family of the Future is now attempting to answer some formidable questions for the family planning movement. What kind of health risks are faced by women who buy their contraceptives from pharmacists?

Egyptian women listening to a description of contraceptive methods at a family planning clinic (photo by Bernard Wolff courtesy of the United Nations Fund for Population Activities)

This question is a critical one, given that women tend to prefer pharmacies over clinics because they can acquire contraceptives more anonymously there. Why is there such a high dropout rate among contraceptive users? How can the society deal with teen-age pregnancy when suggesting that young girls be given the pill "would mean the end of family planning in many countries?" The agency attempts to keep separate in the public consciousness the use of contraception and the preservation of chastity—an essential distinction in a culture where the purity of women is of paramount value.

Assessing the current state of family planning, Aziza sees the lack of ideal contraceptive technologies as the Achilles' heel of the movement. If better methods existed, both unwanted pregnancies and abortions (legal and illegal) would diminish in number. She takes heart that President Hosni Mubarak, in describing Egypt's overpopulation as "the problem of problems," has pledged strong action to expand and improve the national family planning program. The magnitude of Egypt's challenge to gain control of its population growth lends an urgency to the work of Family of the Future, whose achievements are clearly getting to the heart of the struggle.

Musing over her years as a volunteer, Aziza says,

I'm never discouraged because I'm realistic about things. . . . I know it's going to take a longer time than [I] think. I don't oversimplify the problems ever. That makes one more discouraged. I started in 1962, but only in 1983 has Egypt signed the UN Declaration on the Elimination of Discrimination Against Women. It takes a long time. It has taken me a lifetime. When everything is blocked, you have to rethink your approach and find other ways.

Aziza is a role model for young women from many countries who have met and worked with her. She is known for never having lost sight of her goal, for having always been willing to wait until the moment was absolutely correct, and for never lacking the courage to act. She has almost always been available when a project near to her heart could benefit from her experienced advice, her extensive social contacts, or just encouragement. Speaking of the women of her generation, she mourns the "many wonderful, broken women who could not continue to the end. . . . It is so difficult for women to achieve." Aziza refers to women for whom the pressures from family and peers to lead a traditional life are too great to withstand; in her eyes, they are "hidden suicides." Such women are often educated and aspire toward careers or active volunteer lives but, after marriage, are essentially "put away" by their husbands.

Aziza developed cancer in 1984 and underwent a mastectomy. After a surprisingly brief period of recuperation, she was back at work; but the illness frightened her. She suffered another severe blow just months later, when Ahmed, who had been ailing since 1980, died of a stroke on November 30, 1984. Aziza was by his side. Her illness and Ahmed's death seemed to increase her interest in meditation. As she has tended all her life to be dynamic, restless, and intense, the meditation is her safety valve.

The Hussein apartment in Cairo, which overlooks the Nile, is huge, old-fashioned, high-ceilinged, and decorated in muted tones. Grey though the decor may be, "what happens inside that apartment," said a friend, "is wonderful and warm, comfortable, generous. Everyone from the international world stops by out of a high regard and affection for Aziza. They want her friendship, her perspective, her advice—she has started many a novice on the right path. . . . She is a true hero."

NOTES

1. *Population Today*, vol. 15, no. 5 (Washington, D.C.: Population Reference Bureau, May 1987), p. 5.

2. Nawal el Saadawi, *The Hidden Face of Eve: Women in the Arab World* (London: Zed Press, 1980), p. 174.

3. Afaf Lutfi-al Sayyid Marsot, "The Revolutionary Gentlewomen in Egypt," in Lois Beck and Nikki Keddie, eds., *Women in the Muslim World* (Cambridge, Mass.: Harvard University Press, 1978), p. 270.

4. Aziza Hussein, "Changing Conditions of Women and Its Effect on Children," Address to the UN Commission on the Status of Women as Representative of the United Arab Republic, New York (1965).

5. Ibid.

6. Aziza Hussein, "Voluntary Efforts: Family Planning in Egypt," Paper given at the Conference of the Friendship Organization of Egyptian Scientists Abroad, Cairo (December 28–31, 1974).

7. Ibid.

8. Aziza Hussein, "Emancipation Comes to the Village," *UNESCO Features*, no. 676/677/678 (Paris, 1975).

9. Naila Minai, *Women in Islam* (New York: Seaview Books, 1981), p. 169.

10. Aziza Hussein, "The Status of Women in Family Law in the United Arab Republic," Paper given at the UN Seminar on the Status of Women and Family Law as Representative of the United Arab Republic, Lome, Togo (August 18–31, 1964), with technical legal aspects approved by Mr. Hussein Awad El Boreigi, Legal Adviser of the UAR.

11. Ibid.

12. Camilia Abdul Fattah, "Address to the Seminar on Bodily Mutilation of Young Females," Cairo, Egypt, Cairo Family Planning Association (October 14–15, 1979).

13. Aziza Hussein, "*Dispelling Controversies: A Task of N.G.O.s,*" Keynote Address at the National Council for International Health Conference, Arlington, Virginia (June 11–13, 1984).

SUPPLEMENTARY READINGS

Ahmed, Leila, "Women and the Advent of Islam," *Signs: Journal of Women and Culture in Society,* vol. 2, no. 4 (Chicago: University of Chicago Press, Summer 1986).

Beck, Lois, and Keddie, Nikki, eds., *Women in the Muslim World* (Cambridge, Mass: Harvard University Press, 1978).

Fernea, Elizabeth Warnock, ed., *Women and the Family in the Middle East* (Austin: University of Texas Press, 1985).

Hussain, Freda, ed., *Muslim Women* (New York: St. Martin's Press, 1984).

Huston, Perdita, *Message from the Village* (New York: Epoch B Foundation, 1978).

Huston, Perdita, *Third World Women Speak Out* (New York: Praeger Publishers, 1979).

Jayawardena, Kumari, *Feminism and Nationalism in the Third World* (London: Zed Books, 1986).

Shaarawi, Huda, *Harem Years: The Memoirs of an Egyptian Feminist* (New York: Feminist Press, 1987).

Sullivan, Earl L., *Women in Egyptian Public Life* (Syracuse, N.Y.: Syracuse University Press, 1986).

Youssef, Nadia Haggag, *Women and Work in Developing Societies* (Berkeley, Calif.: University of California, 1974).

ABOUT THE BOOK AND THE AUTHORS

This collection of biographies of five women leaders from the developing world describes some of the social and economic changes that are rocking that world, changes that often make the lives of poor women even poorer and more precarious. Each of the five women has set out to redress the balance for women in her own community or country. Each story gives a face and a voice to issues that confront many poor, rural women around the world.

Elvina Mutua of Kenya concentrates on income-producing programs for poor farm women; Hasina Khan of Bangladesh works in nonformal educational and integrated rural development; Aziza Hussein of Egypt is in the forefront of the family planning movement and the effort to win greater protection for women under law; Elizabeth O'Kelly, a former British colonial officer, pioneered in appropriate technology as it relates to women's work and started the successful Corn Mill Societies of Cameroon; Reyna de Miralda of Honduras helped to form a national organization of peasant women, bringing them into the political process for the first time. Their fields of expertise and endeavor fairly outline the issues that are of primary concern to most rural women.

Marion Fennelly Levy served as the women's program director for Save the Children Federation, an international community development and child assistance agency, for six years. She has also taught about women in the developing world at Hunter College in New York. Ms. Levy has visited many of the women's projects described in the book and taped interviews with the five principals so that they could tell in their own words about the successes and failures of the non-governmental programs they helped initiate. Sue Ellen Charlton, professor and chair of the Department of Political Science at Colorado State University, is author of *Women in Third World Development*.